THE ANALECTS OF CONFUCIUS

DISCOURSES AND DIALOGUES OF K'UNG FÛ-TSZE

COMPILED BY HIS DISCIPLES

BASED UPON THE 1893 TRANSLATION OF JAMES LEGGE

THE ANALECTS OF CONFUCIUS

DISCOURSES AND DIALOGUES OF K'UNG FÛ-TSZE

COMPILED BY HIS DISCIPLES

BASED UPON THE 1893 TRANSLATION OF JAMES LEGGE

Interpreted and Illustrated by

Holly Harlayne Roberts, D.O., PhD

Holly Roberts

ANJELI PRESS

THE ANALECTS OF CONFUCIUS

DISCOURSES AND DIALOGUES OF K'UNG FÛ-TSZE

COMPILED BY HIS DISCIPLES

BASED UPON THE 1893 TRANSLATION OF JAMES LEGGE

Interpreted and Illustrated
by Holly Harlayne Roberts, D.O., Ph.D.

Calligraphy by Mr. Yi Jiu Chen

Published by Anjeli Press
www.Anjelipress.com

ISBN 0-9754844-8-6

Printed in the United States of America
by Lightning Source
Distributed by Ingram Distributors

In memory of my father

Nathan Fallick

A prophet in his own time.

For giving me guidance and love,
and for teaching me that although others
may take from you all you own,
they can never take
your knowledge, your integrity, and your wisdom.

ACKNOWLEDGEMENTS

I offer my appreciation to James Legge and Professor Yi Wu from whom I learned the meaningful and noble philosophy of K'ung Fû-tsze.

James Legge, D.D., LL.D. (1815-1897) left England in 1839, to serve as a young Christian missionary to China. As he began to teach his Western wisdom and values to the people of this distant land, he recognized the highly evolved wisdom and values of theirs. He studied both the Chinese language and the sacred texts that had laid the foundation of Chinese philosophical thought. Then he translated these works. By 1861, through the help of benefactors, he was able to publish 1,200 copies of his English translation of the *Confucian Analects*. He went on to translate the thirteen sacred classical texts of Chinese philosophy. Without his years of dedication analyzing the meaning of Chinese characters as they were used in 500 BCE, the wisdom of K'ung Fû-tsze might have been lost to the Western world.

Yi Wu, PhD, a dedicated professor of Asian Religion and Philosophy, taught me to recognize K'ung Fû-tsze's wisdom, respect for others, integrity, humanitarian values, and compassion. Without Professor Wu's insight, I might not have fully appreciated the timeless wisdom of K'ung Fû-tsze's teachings. Because of Professor Wu's subtle, insightful guidance, I have been led to recognize how K'ung Fû-tsze's teachings, if followed in present day society, have the potential to lay the groundwork for world peace.

CONTENTS

THE ANALECTS

BACKGROUND

INTRODUCTION

One cannot help but wonder what inspired the quiet, humble sage known throughout the Western world only as "Confucius" to spend a lifetime wandering and spreading his subtle words of wisdom and guidance amongst all whom he met. What deep-rooted emotional passion or need lay deep within the heart of this man, so focused, that he took it upon himself to try to correct the ills of the entire world, a world not ready to listen?

Confucius was not just a legend. He was a real individual. He was K'ung Fû-tsze of Lû, a state in eastern China. He was a man, a husband, a father, a Minister of Justice, a devoted teacher, and a loyal friend. He was a man who spoke up to the monarchy, who fled from enemies, who left the security of official rank, who sought tenderness for the elderly and the orphans, who amassed a huge number of devoted followers, and who, at times, also cried.

His life's mission was not merely to disseminate brief aphorism or pithy phrases. It was to teach others how to gradually, carefully, and solidly develop their character. He taught others to uphold that character at all times and during all situations and to strengthen their own committment to what was right.

He strove to assist others in cultivating the inner fortitude to live as honorable, devoted, respectful, sincere, honest, knowledgeable, humble, careful, intelligent, concerned, compassionate, fair, and wise human beings, at all times and in all situations.

He sought to awaken human consciousness to recognize that the ability to enact change and to make ours a more just and kind world lay not within an external deity, but within the will of each human being. K'ung Fû-tsze strove to inspire both the leaders and the populace that all members of society must live a lifetime of sincerity, concern, and respect for one another for that society to sustain itself.

K'ung Fû-tsze did not consider himself to be one born with exceptional abilities. Rather, he viewed himself as one who sought out, studied, and applied the wisdom of the past. It was by studying the pattern of events that had occurred throughout China's ancient history and the teachings of China's ancient sages, that K'ung Fû-tsze formulated his philosophy.

His was a philosophy based not merely upon lofty ideals, but on solid observations of how, over thousands of years, specific actions led to specific outcomes. It is this philosophy that has come to us in the form of the *Confucian Analects*.

At first glance, K'ung Fû-tsze's words may seem simple. But nothing could be further from the truth. They are brief, direct, pure, sometimes blunt, and always truthful. But they are not simple. To live up to them by weaving them into one's life, demands an extremely high level of committment.

I appreciate having had the opportunity to study K'ung Fû-tsze's teachings. By writing this version of the *Confucian Analects* in a form that English speaking people of the twenty-first century can easily read, I hope that you, my readers, will benefit from the wisdom in its teachings. While reading the *Analects* please fully immerse yourself in K'ung Fû-tsze's life and thoughts. Reading them in their entirety, you will realize that K'ung Fû-tsze does not merely teach rules, he teaches a way of life.

One seeking to understand K'ung Fû-tsze's wisdom, will not be able to do so merely by reading a random collection of his aphorisms. For, to gain full insight into the essence of his teachings, one must seek to understand the level of character that K'ung Fû-tsze was seeking to instill within each of his followers. K'ung Fû-tsze was not just advising others on how to act during specific situations. He was advising them on how to act during every situation.

K'ung Fû-tsze observed that when people are guided by idealistic, honest goals, their actions lead to honorable outcomes. He observed that when they strive to do what is sincere, kind, respectful, and fair, at all times and in all situations, the best possible outcomes occur for themselves, for their cummunity, and for all humanity. He taught people to commit themselves fully to follow the highest levels of integrity in every aspect of life. He taught that one must fully absorb such values into one's character. It is K'ung Fû-tsze's constant commitment to ethical, honorable, and meaningful values that one gains by reading the *Confucian Analects* in its entirety.

My hope is that you gain as much from K'ung Fû-tsze's pure, honorable truths as I have.

Because visual images are such a powerful tool through which to convey beliefs, I have sought to convey the philosophy of K'ung Fû-tsze not only through narrative, but also through illustrations. Actually, since the earliest beginnings of humankind, civilizations have sought to express that which they consider sacred through art. Certainly, the Chinese civilization has been no exception.

By looking into the choices of people, places, and scenes China's artists have chosen as their subjects, as well as the mode through which they seek to present these, one can recognize that which has been considered sacred throughout China's ancient, highly evolved civilization.

Chinese society is founded upon the 2,500 year old philosophies of two of its great sages, Lao Tzu and K'ung Fû-tsze. The philosophy of Lao Tzu is expressed in the *Tao Te Ching*, and the philosophy of K'ung Fû-tsze in the *Confucian Analects*. Both of these philosophical works convey the wisdom that humankind must act humbly, sincerely, carefully, respectfully, and meaningfully, in all situations and at all times, for humanity to have any hope of sustaining its existence on this planet.

China's concept of sacredness, based upon these philosophies, has not been a belief system founded upon the concept of a deity. It has been a belief system based upon the realization that humankind holds the key to creating its own sustainable, responsible, and compassionate existence.

Throughout the many centuries the Chinse have been expressing this belief system through art, and based upon K'ung Fû-tsze's teachings, humans have quite consistently been depicted as serious, thoughtful, and humble beings. They have been depicted as extremely important in relation to their interactions with other people, and humble in relation to the enormity of the rest of creation. Even in those works of art in which human beings are not present, some sign of meaningful human existence, be it a path, a hut, or an abandoned fishing boat, is usually present. This is invariably a sign, elusive as it might be, that human beings have made a significant difference.

The human beings generally depicted in Chinese art are people of integrity. They are sages, pensive scholars, responsible adults, and people struggling to put in an honest day's work. They are not drawn to depict beauty, but rather, to depict character.

K'ung Fû-tsze was a man deeply concerned about the welfare of society and of the responsibilities of human beings in relation to one another. He held no interest, and certainly no illusions, concerning the concept of immortality. To him, life was here and now, and it was imperitive that each human being do his or her best to make their one brief sojourn on earth the most morally meaningful and valuable one possible.

China's art conveys K'ung Fû-tsze's wisdom that a life lived with morality and with sincere concern for others is to be respected. Accordingly, the individuals portrayed in Chinese art are: plain, yet dignified; small in stature, yet great in character; hard at work, yet not seeking glory; wise, yet not forceful; and always honest, honorable and responsible.

K'ung Fû-tsze believed passionately that although each human being should accept the fleeting nature of his or her existence, each must follow a life path that is meaningful. Each should live his or her life to the highest level of moral integrity. Each must live with principle. Each must seek harmony with all others and with the rest of creation. And each must live with humanitarian compassion and with respect for all others.

Through the simple illustrations within this book, I have sought to capture the essence of K'ung Fû-tsze's wisdom that a life lived with sincerity, integrity, and compassion is truly sacred.

THE ANALECTS

學而 第一

子曰學而時習之不亦說乎
有朋自遠方來不亦樂乎
人不知而不慍不亦君子乎

THE ANALECTS OF CONFUCIUS

DISCOURSES AND DIALOGUES OF K'UNG FÛ-TSZE
COMPILED BY HIS DISCIPLES

BOOK I   HSIO R
To Learn, and Then

CHAPTER I

1. K'ung Fû-tsze said: Is it not pleasant to attain wisdom through consistent effort and dedication?

2. Is it not fulfilling to have friends of honorable character visit from distant lands?

3. Is one not of noble character if one does not take offense when others do not show respect?

The *Confucian Analects* contains the teachings K'ung Fû-tsze expressed through various dialogues he had with his disciples. The *Confucian Analects* was not actually written by either K'ung Fû-tsze or his immediate disciples. It was written by later disciples of his disciples. To fully grasp its messages, one should know something about the context in which they were uttered. Within most chapters of the *Analects*, K'ung Fû-tsze is replying to questions posed by his disciples. Some chapters, however, consist solely of statements by his disciples. Historians feel confident in stating that K'ung Fû-tsze did not actually write the *Analects*. That is because many of the events to which the *Analects* relate occurred well after the time that either K'ung Fû-tsze or his immediate disciples lived. It was only after K'ung Fû-tsze's death that many of his disciples came together to collate, compare, and analyze his teachings. They recognized that K'ung Fû-tsze taught different principles, depending upon the context in which each was given. It was from these teachings, collected and compiled by his disciples, that the *Analects* was born.

The *Analects* is divided into 'books.' As had been the tradition of ancient times, the title of each book referred to the first word or thought of that discourse. Most versions of the *Analects* contain twenty books, although some contain twenty-two. This difference arises because of variations in the division of passages, not because of variations in content. The *Analects* does not develop a continuous flow of thoughts with later passages based on prior ones. Rather, each book and each phrase is an entity unto itself. In Chinese philosophy, wisdom is pure, direct and simple. There is no need to adorn it with an intriguing plot or to place it amidst a flow of events. It is through the straight-forward literary style of the *Analects* that insight into the honest, concerned, and meaningful wisdom of K'ung Fû-tsze can be ascertained.

有子曰其為人也孝弟
而好犯上者鮮矣不好犯上而好作亂者
未之有也君子務本。立而道生
孝弟也者其為仁人本與

CHAPTER II

1. Philosopher Yû said: One who is respectful toward one's parents and siblings, will not be disrespectful toward one's superiors.

Of those who have been respectful toward their superiors, none have been rebellious.

2. One of character seeks to cultivate foundational values. Once these have become firmly established, all of one's future actions will sprout naturally from these.

Are not respect and loyalty towards one's parents and siblings the foundational root of all virtues?

Chapter II: The philosopher Yû was a disciple of K'ung Fû-tsze. (He is the second disciple in the index of disciples later in this book). He was distinguished among the disciples for the strength of his memory and for his love of ancient wisdom. In some respects, he was considered a sage in his own right.

The title of this first book of the *The Confucian Analects* is simply "To Learn, and Then." In it, K'ung Fû-tsze discusses those traits one should develop so as to cultivate an honorable character. Although James Legge, in his 1893 translation of the *Analects* refers to a person on such a path as a "superior man," I prefer to refer to such an individual as: one of virtue, one of honor, or one of character.

Although during K'ung Fû-tsze's life, 2,500 years ago, all of his disciples were male, I have chosen to render this translation gender neutral, wherever possible. Were K'ung Fû-tsze living today, I believe he would have wanted people of all genders to benefit from his teachings. The sixteen chapters of the first book of the *Analects* (Hsio R: To Learn, and Then) teach that one must perfect one's knowledge of honorable and virtuous values in order to cultivate one's character. One must learn from other people of character, and must emulate them in all that is sincere, upright and meaningful. Just as a bird, striving to sustain its flight, must flap its wings at all times, one seeking to cultivate high moral values, must practice them at all times and in all circumstances. One must absorb them into one's character and live them.

In Chinese society, respect for and loyalty towards one's parents is termed filial piety. Filial piety also refers to respect and obedience towards one's older siblings, and all one's older relatives. Once such respect has been cultivated, it becomes part of one's personality. It will manifest in all one's actions. One with filial piety will hold all elders and teachers in respect. K'ung Fû-tsze recognized that those who respect their elders and learn from their teachings avoid making the same mistakes these older relatives made. Hence, it was to help the young that K'ung Fû-tsze taught principles of family loyalty, filial piety, and respect for the wisdom of elders.

3

子曰巧言令色鮮矣仁

曾子曰吾日三省吾身

為人謀而不忠乎

與朋友交言而不信

乎傳不習乎

子曰道千乘之國敬事而信

節用而愛人使民以時

CHAPTER III

K'ung Fû-tsze said: Honeyed words and ingratiating actions are rarely found in one with true virtue.

CHAPTER IV

The philosopher Tsǎng said: Every day I reflect on my actions to ensure that in dealing with others: I have not been insincere; in dealing with friends, I have not been unfaithful; in guiding others, I have not been hypocritical in my advice.

CHAPTER V

K'ung Fû-tsze said: To lead a country of a thousand chariots, one must adhere reverently to responsibility. One must strictly uphold one's promises, must exercise caution in spending, must love one's people, and must employ one's people only during the proper seasons.

Chapter III: K'ung Fû-tsze recognized that words can be empty, slick, sugar-coated, hypocritical and totally false. He was suspicious of praise and flatter, and avoided people who used these. He judged people by their actions, not their words.

Chapter IV: Tsǎng was one of K'ung Fû-tsze's principal disciples. He joined K'ung Fû-tsze when only sixteen years of age. Although he was considered intellectually slow, he was respected for his loyalty and morality. He followed K'ung Fû-tsze's doctrines explicitly and gained his esteem. K'ung Fû-tsze used his assistance when he composed the *Classic of Filial Piety*.

The phrase used at the beginning of many passages of the *Analects*, and referring specifically to K'ung Fû-tsze's teachings, can be translated in several ways. This includes, "the Master said," "the Philosopher said," and "Confucius said." In most instances, I have chosen to use the phrase "K'ung Fû-tsze said." I have done so not to make light of the fact that K'ung Fû-tsze was considered a Master by his disciples, nor to negate the fact that he was a great philosopher, but rather to maintain consistency and to avoid confusion between K'ung Fû-tsze and the other masters and philosophers mentioned within the *Analects*. I have used the Chinese transliteration of the name "K'ung Fû-tsze" rather than the westernized term "Confucius" to ensure that K'ung Fû-tsze is continually revered as an individual of Chinese heritage and as the Father of Chinese philosophy.

Chapter V: K'ung Fû-tsze gives advice to both rulers and to the general populace. The term used in ancient China to refer to a large, powerful nation is, "a country of a thousand chariots." For a country to function at its best, not only must the masses respect their leaders, but these leaders must protect their people. It is particularly important that leaders do not send their people to war if it is not the proper season, i.e. not the proper time, proper situation, or proper cause.

子曰弟子入則孝出則弟謹而信汎愛眾而親仁行有餘力則以學文

子夏曰賢賢易色事父母能竭其力事君能致其身與朋友交言而有信雖曰未學吾必謂之學矣

子曰君子不重則不威學則不固主忠信無友不如己者過則勿憚改

CHAPTER VI

K'ung Fû-tsze said: When at home, respect one's parents. When abroad, be filial. Be sincere and speak only truth. Treat all with respect, yet cultivate friendships only with the virtuous. After fulfilling responsibilities, cultivate oneself through studies.

CHAPTER VII

Tsze-hsiâ said: I believe that one who values one's spouse more for his or her virtue than for his or her physical appearance, who strives to assist one's parents, who devotes one's life to serving one's country, and who keeps one's word in dealing with friends, even if lacking in formal education, is truly a person of wisdom.

CHAPTER VIII

1. K'ung Fû-tsze said: One must be serious to gain the respect of others. If one is not serious, one will not be able to advance one's knowledge.
2. Value faithfulness and sincerity above all virtues.
3. Have no friends of low character.
4. Recognize one's own faults, and do not fear admitting them and correcting them.

Chapter VI: When K'ung Fû-tsze uses the term *when abroad*, he is referring to anytime one is traveling far from home, especially when traveling to distant lands. Filial piety is an extremely important concept in Chinese philosophy. It refers to the respectful, concerned, and obedient manner in which one should act towards one's parents and to those elders filling the role of parents

Chapter VII: Tsze-hsiâ was one of K'ung Fû-tsze's disciples. He was famous both for his knowledge and for his commentaries on several Chinese sacred texts. He lived to a great age, but wept himself blind over the death of his son. He was esteemed by both the masses and the monarchy of that era.

Chapter VIII: K'ung Fû-tsze explains how to cultivate character. If one is not serious, one will not gain the respect of learned colleagues and teachers. Then, others will not want to teach that individual. One must be truthful and sincere in each and every action, and seek the acquaintance of those who conduct themselves similarly. Lastly, one must be honest with oneself, recognize one's own faults, accept responsibility for one's actions, and make changes to correct them.

K'ung Fû-tsze's teachings are concise and to the point. They leave no room for ambiguity. Although K'ung Fû-tsze was a man of few words, he was a man of tremendous integrity. He recognized that one is either truthful, respectful, and sincere, or one is not. There is no middle ground. Words, excuses, or embellishments do not change the underlying truth of one's actions or character.

曾子曰慎終追遠民德歸厚矣

子禽問於子貢曰夫子至於是邦也

必聞其政求之與抑與之與

子貢曰夫子溫良恭儉讓以得

夫子之求之也其諸異乎人之求之與

CHAPTER IX

Philosopher Tsăng said: If those leading a nation conduct funeral rites for their deceased parents with diligence, and adhere to traditional acts of sacrifice with reverence, even long after their ancestors have passed on, the morality of their people will rise to the highest level possible.

CHAPTER X

1. Tsze-ch'in asked Tsze-kung: When K'ung Fû-tsze enters a country, he strives to gain full information concerning its government. Does he request this information or do others offer it to him?
2. Tsze-kung said: K'ung Fû-tsze is gentle, honest, respectful, mild-mannered, and amicable. Hence, others seek to share their knowledge with him. Is not his mode of attaining information different from that of others?

Chinese IX: In traditional Chinese philosophy, there is no belief in an unknown transcendent deity. People believe that the spirits of their deceased relatives return in an invisible form. Just as family members bond together and help one another during their earthly lives, so too, the spirits of deceased ancestors return to help those still living. For the living to continually receive the assistance and guidance of these deceased ancestors, however, they must honor and respect the deceased long after they have passed on. This philosophy is the foundation of Chinese ancestor worship. Those who showed sincere and enduring reverence for deceased members of their family, particularly their own parents, were respected.

K'ung Fû-tsze held a strong belief in ancestor worship. He felt, however, that such worship must be practiced with sincerity. He believed that tradition and ritual were necessary for society to develop a stable foundation. To him, traditional values and rituals gave society its roots. The cultured of society were to cultivate knowledge of the traditions and rituals of their forefathers, and then practice them reverently.

K'ung Fû-tsze believed it particularly important for the monarchy to follow tradition and precisely follow established practices of ancestor worship. A monarch must value and respect the wisdom and traditions of the past for the nation to sustain itself in a civilized fashion. If the leader did not respect his own nation's values, that society would face moral collapse.

Chapter X: Tsze-ch'in and Tsze-kung were minor disciples of K'ung Fû-tsze. This chapter sheds light upon the straight-forward, honest wisdom of K'ung Fû-tsze. It also gives insight into his understanding of human nature. K'ung Fû-tsze recognized that were he to abruptly question strangers about their country, they would question his motives and withhold information. By showing them respect, K'ung Fû-tsze gained their confidence, and then their information.

子曰父在觀其志父沒觀其行

三年無改於父之道可謂孝矣

有子曰禮之用和為貴先王之道

斯為美小大由之有所不行

知和而和不以禮節之亦不可行也

有子曰信近於義言可復也恭

近於禮遠恥辱也因不失其親

亦可宗也

CHAPTER XI

K'ung Fû-tsze said: While one's parent's are alive, one's true character is restrained. After one's parents have died, one's true character will sprout forth. If for three years after one's parents' death, one does not deviate in conduct significantly from the values of one's parents, one may be considered an honor to one's family.

CHAPTER XII

1. Philosopher Yû said: For one seeking to follow the rules of propriety, it is beneficial if it is one's true nature to do so. Ancient kings considered true reverence to be an excellent quality within an individual. They recognized that those who were truly respectful in all aspects of their lives, from the greatest to the smallest deeds, were individuals of character.
2. It is not easy to tell if one naturally feels respect for tradition. Some people, knowing that others think highly of respectful actions, feign them. Such actions make a mockery of both tradition and of one's respect for it, and should not be done.

CHAPTER XIII

Philosopher Yû said: When an agreement is made between people, if both parties enter into it with honest intent from the start, it will come to fruition.

If one consistently maintains respect for that which is decent and proper, one will never face shame.

When those upon whom one depends are of honorable character, one can feel peace of mind in making such individuals one's guides and leaders.

Chapter XI: In ancient China, ancestor worship for deceased parents lasted three years. K'ung Fû-tsze explained this from a moral perspective: because a child cannot leave the arms of its parents until it is about three years old and is totally dependent upon parents until then, after the demise of one's parents, one should return this dedication for the same period of time, three years. One was not to engage in frivolous acts or sexual activities for three years after the death of one's father.

Chapter XII: The term "Philosopher Yû" refers to K'ung Fû-tsze's disciple Yû Zo (second disciple listed in the Background section of this book). K'ung Fû-tsze notes that a difference exists between sincere reverence and superficial propriety. One who is sincerely respectful will manifest reverence in every aspect of his or her life, including the major and minor aspects, and even those never seen by others.

Chapter XIII: An act embarked upon with sincere intent will meet its desired goal.

子曰君子食无求饱居无求安

敏於事而慎於言就有道而正焉

可谓好学也已

子贡曰贫而无谄富而无骄

何如子曰可也未若贫而乐富而好礼者也

子贡曰诗云如切如磋如琢如磨 其斯之谓与

CHAPTER XIV

K'ung Fû-tsze said: One seeking to be truly virtuous will desire neither gratification in food, nor luxury in living; will be sincere in conduct, and careful in speech; and will seek friendships with those having good character. Acting thusly, one will develop an honorable character and will gain true wisdom.

CHAPTER XV

1. Tsze-kung said: What do you think of one who when poor, does not flatter others insincerely; and when rich, is not proud? K'ung Fû-tsze replied: They are both to be commended. Better yet, however, is one who when poor is cheerful; and when rich, does not bend the rules to help oneself.

2. Tsze-kung replied: The *Book of Odes* states, "Delicate jade work requires repetitive, patient filing, carving, and polishing." Is this what you have alluded to about one's continual need to refine one's character?

Chapter XIV: K'ung Fû-tsze teaches that one seeking a virtuous life will not desire fulfillment of the senses or pleasures of the flesh. Such an individual will value wisdom, sincerity, simple truths, and honorable deeds. Such an individual will strive to cultivate friendships with those on similar paths, and will gain from their wisdom. Although K'ung Fû-tsze sought to elevate the ethical values of all in society, those who were in search of deeper understanding and those who sought to carry on his teachings, in particular, were drawn to him.

Chapter XV, Passage 1: Oftentimes, wealth offers people the opportunity to break rules. Only the truly honorable will forgo such privileges and adhere to the same rules as everyone else.

Passage 2: K'ung Fû-tsze advised his disciples to study the *Six Classics*, known collectively as the *Liu Yu*. The *Six Classics* include the *Book of Changes, Book of Odes* [poetry], *Book of History, Book of Rituals, Book of Music*, and the *Spring and Autumn Annals*. They were written before the time of K'ung Fû-tsze and became the foundation for Chinese cultural values. They were studied by all educated individuals during the early years of the Châu dynasty. By the seventh century BCE, as China's feudal system began to disintegrate, the aristocracy lost their status and began to scatter among the masses. By that time, the aristocracy had already become well versed in these classics and began to earn their livings by teaching these to others. These teachers were referred to as the *literati*.

By referring to the carving of delicate jade, Tsze-kung meant that one must develop moral values. Only after these are established can one improve upon them.

K'ung Fû-tsze believed his primary function was to teach the wisdom of ancient China to present day individuals. Because of this, he considered himself a transmitter of knowledge, rather than an originator of it.

子曰賜也始可與言詩已矣
告諸往而知來者
子曰不患人之不己知患不知人也

3. K'ung Fû-tsze said: With one such as Tsze-kung, I can discuss the *Book of Odes*. When I share with him the wisdom of the past, he recognizes how to apply it to the future.

CHAPTER XVI

K'ung Fû-tsze said: Be not upset if others do not understand you. Rather, be upset if you do not understand others.

Chapter XV, passage 3: K'ung Fû-tsze stressed the moral values within the *Six Classics*. Concerning the *Book of Odes*, the ancient *Chinese Book of Poetry*, K'ung Fû-tsze believed that of the numerous poems within this text, the ones from which moral values could be extracted should be studied in depth. The era during which the *Six Classics* were composed, the Chău dynasty, 1122–256 BCE, is considered the golden age of Chinese philosophy. During the early years of this dynasty, numerous small states, clustered along the valley of the Yellow River (in North China), emerged. These small states were linked together through a common bond of allegiance to the Chău royal house. The link was a feudal system of allegiance in which taxes were paid to the monarchy by the people, and safety was afforded the people by the monarchy. When this system began to disintegrate, the Chău dynasty fell from power. Then, with no central focus of control, warfare among the small states erupted. This was followed by a period of political, economic, and social collapse. It was during this turbulent period in China's history that the golden age of Chinese philosophy, and the age of K'ung Fû-tsze (551–479 BCE) emerged.

K'ung Fû-tsze believed that by studying the past, one in search of truth would gain insight into the patterns and cycles of both humanity and of all creation. With such insight, one might attain sufficient wisdom to enable one to predict how humankind's present actions might affect the course of future events.

Chapter XVI summarizes much of the teachings of this first book of the *Analects*. Although one cannot change the world, one can certainly change oneself. Another interpretation of this passage has been: Be not upset if others do not treat you with respect, be upset if you do not treat others with respect.

15

為政 第二

子曰為政以德譬如北辰居其
所而眾星共之

子曰詩三百一言以蔽之曰思無邪

子曰道之以政齊之以刑民免而無恥
道之以德齊之以禮有恥且格

BOOK II WEI CHĂNG
One who Governs

CHAPTER I

K'ung Fû-tsze said: One who governs guided by morality can be compared to the North Polar Star. The North Polar Star stands strong and steady in its place and the other stars turn towards it.

CHAPTER II

K'ung Fû-tsze said: In the *Book of Poetry* there are three hundred pieces, yet one underlying theme embraces all: "Maintain pure and moral values in one's thoughts."

CHAPTER III

1. K'ung Fû-tsze said: Those who follow the law merely to avoid punishment, will merely avoid punishment. They will not cultivate character.

2. Those who follow the law guided by virtue and motivated by their conscience, will truly cultivate moral values. They will live righteously at all times.

This second book of the *Confucian Analects* contains twenty-four chapters. It is termed *One who Governs*. It discusses those qualities and character traits that one seeking to lead a country morally should possess.

Chapter I: In ancient China, the North Star was believed to be located directly over the polar region of the earth. That is why it was referred to as the *North Polar Star*. Although K'ung Fû-tsze describes the *Book of Poetry*, or *Book of Odes*, as containing 300 pieces, it may actually have contained over three thousand pieces. K'ung Fû-tsze removed those which were repetitious and selected 305 which he felt would be useful in instilling values of propriety and righteousness within others. The *Book of Odes* tells of the lifestyles, country life, vegetation, and simple joys of life in China's bygone eras. The odes were written in an unassuming, humble manner and express simple, pure longings of the heart.

17

子曰吾十有五而志於學
三十而立四十而不惑五十而知天命
六十而耳順七十而從心所欲不踰矩

樊遲御子告之曰孟孫問孝於我我對曰
無違樊遲曰何謂也子曰生事之以禮
死葬之以禮祭之以禮

孟懿子問孝子曰無違

CHAPTER IV
1. K'ung Fû-tsze said: By age fifteen, I devoted myself to learning values.
2. By age thirty, I strove to develop these values firmly.
3. By age forty, I gained understanding of these values and no longer questioned them.
4. By age fifty, I recognized my Heaven Destiny.
5. By age sixty, I attained the ability to distinguish what was honorable from what was dishonorable in other people's words.
6. By age seventy, I attained the ability to follow my heart without veering from what was right.

CHAPTER V
1. Măng Î asked the meaning of filial piety. K'ung Fû-tsze said: It is not being disobedient.
2. Later, as Fan Ch'ih was driving, K'ung Fû-tsze said: Măng Î asked me about filial piety. I told him: It is not being disobedient.
3. Fan Ch'ih asked: What did you mean? K'ung Fû-tsze replied: When one's parents are alive, serve them according to all rules of propriety. At the time of one's parents' deaths, bury them according to all rules of propriety. Thereafter, long after their demise, continue to sacrifice to them, following all rules of propriety.

Chapter IV: K'ung Fû-tsze said he was not an individual gifted with wisdom at birth, but simply one who had worked to learn wisdom and cultivate it. He felt that he was led on such a life path not because he was above others, but because it was the will of Heaven. In Chinese philosophy, the term Heaven Destiny does not refer to the conscious will of a God or a supernatural force. Rather, it refers to the natural order of the universe, or simply put: 'The Way Things Are.' By age forty, K'ung Fû-tsze felt he knew the proper time and place to apply the proper actions. By age fifty, he felt that Heaven had chosen a specific life path for him. By age sixty, he felt he could intuitively recognize truth within himself, and by age seventy, he felt that his values had been so deeply ingrained, that he no longer needed to think about them. They flowed naturally.

Chapter V: Filial piety refers to respecting and honoring one's parents, one's elder family members, and one's elder siblings. Respect for one's parents and ancestors must continue long after their demise.

Măng Î was a great officer and head of one of the three ruling families of the state of Lû, K'ung Fû-tsze's home state. He was a man of character and was given the posthumous title, 'The mild and virtuous one.'

孟武伯問孝子曰父母唯其疾之憂

子游問孝子曰今之孝者是謂能養

至於犬馬皆能有養不敬何以別乎

子夏問孝子曰色難有事弟子服其勞

有酒食先生饌曾是以為孝乎

子曰吾與回言終日不違如愚

退而省其私亦足以發回也不愚

CHAPTER VI

Măng Wû asked the meaning of filial piety. K'ung Fû-tsze said: Parents suffer if their children become ill.

CHAPTER VII

Tsze-yû asked the meaning of filial piety. K'ung Fû-tsze said: People, nowadays, believe that filial piety means supporting one's parents. Yet people support even dogs and horses. Is it not the act of offering reverence that distinguishes filial piety from the mere act of offering sustenance?

CHAPTER VIII

Tsze-hsiâ asked the meaning of filial piety. K'ung Fû-tsze said: The essence of filial piety lies in the feelings behind one's actions. If children bear the burden of their parents' problems joyfully, and also permit their parents to share in the joy of their own lives, this is filial piety.

CHAPTER IX

K'ung Fû-tsze said: I spoke with Hûi an entire day. He listened silently while I taught. Others might have thought he was simple. After he left, I observed his conduct while away from me. He fully followed my teachings. Hûi is not simple.

Chapters VI, VII, and VIII: To K'ung Fû-tsze, filial piety was important for many reasons. He felt it was the substance that bound society together and gave it stability. It created a continuous thread of respect and humbleness that passed on from the older to the younger members of each generation. K'ung Fû-tsze told Măng Wû, a learned disciple, it meant that one who is concerned about one's parents will take care of oneself. That is because one's parents suffer if their children become ill or if their children die. K'ung Fû-tsze told Tsze-yû that it meant one must not merely support one's parents in their old age, but one must also offer them comfort and respect. In addition, K'ung Fû-tsze felt that one who possessed filial piety should invite one's parents to partake in their lives so as to share in their joys.

Chapter IX: Hûi was K'ung Fû-tsze's favorite disciple. K'ung Fû-tsze recognized that his silence was not the silence of one who was simple, but rather the silence of one who was a deep thinker. At age twenty-nine, Hûi's hair turned completely white. At age thirty-two, Hûi died. K'ung Fû-tsze grieved tremendously over his death.

子曰視其所以觀其所由察其所安人焉廋哉人焉廋哉

子曰溫故而知新可以為師矣

子曰君子不器

子貢問君子子曰先行其言而後從之

子曰君子周而不比小人比而不周

子曰學而不思則罔思而不學則殆

CHAPTER X

K'ung Fû-tsze said:

1. Observe one's actions.

2. Analyze one's motives.

3. Take notice of what one does for pleasure.

4. How can one conceal one's character?

5. Can one conceal one's character?

CHAPTER XI

K'ung Fû-tsze said: One who is able to apply one's knowledge of the past to guide one's actions in the future is fit to lead others.

CHAPTER XII

K'ung Fû-tsze said: The accomplished scholar is not a mere tool.

CHAPTER XIII

Tsze-kung asked about character. K'ung Fû-tsze replied: One with character puts one's ideas into action prior to speaking or bragging about them.

CHAPTER XIV

K'ung Fû-tsze said: One of character feels compassion for all, and does so without prejudice. One without character is biased and does not care equally about all.

CHAPTER XV

K'ung Fû-tsze said: Knowledge without thought is learning that is wasted. Thought without knowledge is dangerous.

Chapter X: K'ung Fû-tsze explains how to judge the character of others. Simple observation of their actions is not sufficient. One must gain insight into their underlying motives. Insight into the character of others can be attained by observing how they conduct themselves during their leisure time. This is when pressure is off and they do not feel that others are observing and judging them. This is the time their true character will be revealed.

Chapter XI through XV: One who has studied solely to learn a trade is not a true scholar. A true scholar is one who seeks a broad foundation and scope of knowledge, and thus gains wisdom.

子曰攻乎異端斯害也已

子曰由誨女知之乎知之為

知之不知為不知是知也

子張學干祿子曰多聞闕疑

慎言其餘則寡尤多見闕殆

慎行其餘則寡悔言寡尤

行寡悔祿在其中矣

CHAPTER XVI

K'ung Fû-tsze said: The incursion of strange doctrines can be harmful. If such doctrines are studied, they must be analyzed with critical thought and penetrating questions.

CHAPTER XVII

K'ung Fû-tsze said: Yû, Do you want me to tell you about knowledge? To possess true knowledge is to know what you know, and to admit what you do not know. Only through such a process will one attain true knowledge.

CHAPTER XVIII

1. Tsze-chang sought to attain a position in government.
2. K'ung Fû-tsze advised him: Listen intently. Disregard that which seems dubious. Speak discretely of the rest. Thusly, you will avoid blame.

Observe all situations carefully. Disregard all that is dangerous for you to know, and carry out the rest cautiously. Then you will avoid regrets.

Governmental positions are attained by those who make fewer errors in both speech and conduct.

Chapter XVI: Historians have yet to determine the exact nature of the strange doctrines to which K'ung Fû-tsze is referring.

Chapter XVIII: Tsze-chang was a native of Ch'ăn. He was considered a man of merit who did not boast, and who acted humbly even towards the helpless. In K'ung Fû-tsze's era, governmental positions were highly respected and were difficult to obtain. Only one respected for one's honor and intelligence was able to procure a position in government.

哀公問曰何為則民服

孔子對曰舉直錯諸枉則民服

舉枉錯諸直則民不服

季康子問使民敬忠以勸

如之何子曰臨之以莊則敬孝慈

則忠舉善而教不能則勸

或謂孔子曰子奚不為政

子曰書云孝乎惟孝友于兄弟

施於有政是亦為政奚其為為政

CHAPTER XIX
Duke Âi asked: What must I do to lead my people? K'ung Fû-tsze replied: Promote the honest and dismiss the dishonest. Recognizing your integrity, your subjects will remain loyal. If you advance the dishonest and dismiss the honest, your subjects will not remain loyal.

CHAPTER XX
Chî K'ang asked how a ruler could create a society in which the people remain reverent to the monarchy and act virtuously toward one another. K'ung Fû-tsze replied: If a leader presides with dignity, all will return this dignity with respect. If a leader presides with faithfulness and kindness, all will return this kindness by acting with intelligence. If a leader appropriately advances those who are capable and assists those of limited capabilities, all will seek to perform honestly to the best of their abilities.

CHAPTER XXI
1. An individual approached K'ung Fû-tsze and questioned: Sir, why are you not employed in government?
2. K'ung Fû-tsze replied: Have you read what the *Shû Ching* says about filial piety? It says that one should fulfill one's responsibilities as a son and a brother, and such values will permeate throughout society. All of one's actions, even those outside of governmental employment, affect the functioning of the entire nation. One need not hold office to effect change in one's government.

Chapter XIX: Duke Âi was the honorary title of the duke of Lû (494–468 BCE). K'ung Fû-tsze advised him during his first sixteen years in office, the period just prior to K'ung Fû-tsze's death.

Chapter XX: Chî K'ang was head of one of the three great families of Lû. K'ung Fû-tsze taught that when one practices goodness, others rejoice in acting similarly. Thus it is, that wise and benevolent actions disseminate throughout a society.

Chapter XXI: K'ung Fû-tsze believed that to govern, the wisest course was to examine the *Shû Ching*, or the *Chinese Classic* termed the *Book of History*. This is one of the *Six Chinese Classics*, the others being the *Book of Changes, Book of Odes, Book of Rituals, Book of Music*, and the *Spring and Summer Annals*. The *Shû Ching* teaches that even those performing the humblest of tasks contribute to the welfare of society. One need not hold a position of status to fulfill one's responsibility to society.

子曰人而無信不知其可也大車無輗小車無軏其何以行之哉子張問十世可知也子曰殷因於夏禮所損益可知也周因於殷禮所損益可知也其或繼周者雖百世可知也子曰非其鬼而祭之諂也見義不為無勇也

CHAPTER XXII

K'ung Fû-tsze said: I do not know how those without principle can get on. Can a carriage function without a cross-bar to yoke its oxen, or a cart move forward without a brace to yoke its horses?

CHAPTER XXIII

1. Tsze-chang asked K'ung Fû-tsze if he thought that the lofty doctrines of their society would be remembered ten generations later.
2. K'ung Fû-tsze replied: The Yin dynasty was founded upon the moral principles of the Hsiâ dynasty, more or less with minor changes. The Châu dynasty was founded upon the moral principles of the Yin dynasty, more or less with minor changes. It stands to reason that the moral values cultivated during our present times will be followed and perpetuated amongst future generations, even a hundred generations into the future.

CHAPTER XXIV

1. K'ung Fû-tsze said: It is insincere to sacrifice to a spirit that is not one's own.
2. It is cowardly not to defend righteousness when righteousness is in danger of being lost.

Chapter XXIII: K'ung Fû-tsze had faith that great principles of morality within a society would be passed on continuously from generation to generation, as they had been passed on throughout the three great dynasties of China: the Hsiâ, the Yin, and the Châu. When K'ung Fû-tsze uses the term "present times" he is referring to the Châu dynasty.

Chapter XXIV: In Chinese society, one offers reverent sacrifice to one's own deceased ancestors. Just as one's family members help one another when living, it is believed that deceased members continue to help the living members after their demise. Hence, to sacrifice to the ancestors of someone else is quite odd and not meaningful.

八佾第三

孔子謂季氏八佾舞於庭

是可忍也孰不可忍也

三家者以雍徹子曰相維辟公

天子穆穆奚取於三家之堂

子曰人而不仁如禮何人而不

仁如樂何

BOOK III PÂ YÎH
Eight Rows of Dancers

CHAPTER I

K'ung Fû-tsze was upset that the head of the Chî family had positioned eight rows of pantomime dancers to perform ancestor worship in his courtyard. K'ung Fû-tsze said: If he can resort to this, what will he not resort to next?

CHAPTER II

At the culmination of the sacrifice, as sacrificial vessels were being removed from the temple, the three families recited the *Yung Ode*. K'ung Fû-tsze questioned the use of the passage: "Assisted by Princes, the Son of Heaven is reverent and serious." K'ung Fû-tsze did not feel it was appropriate for the three families to recite this in their ancestral hall.

CHAPTER III

K'ung Fû-tsze said: Of what use are rituals to the welfare of a nation, if its ruler is not benevolent? Of what use is music, if its ruler is not kind?

Chapter 1: K'ung Fû-tsze was upset because the head of the Chî family, Jisun Yiru, a minister of Lû, violated tradition by employing an excessive number of dancers at a funeral service. He employed eight rows of eight dancers each to perform an ancient royal dance. Only the monarch was supposed to use so many dancers when offering sacrifices to Heaven. According to Chău rites, the monarch could employ eight rows of dancers, the duke six rows, and the ministers four rows. Since Jisun Yiru was a minister, he should have employed only four rows. K'ung Fû-tsze accused him of being presumptuous and of flouting tradition by using so many dancers.

Chapter II: The three noble families of Lû (the Mensun Shi, Shusun Shi, and Jisun Shi families) used a specific ode known as the *Yung Ode* while performing sacrifices. The *Yung Ode* is from the *Book of Poetry*. It was supposed to be used only by the emperor because the emperor was considered divine. The emperor was considered the son of Heaven. K'ung Fû-tsze considered the use of this ode by the three families to be sacrilegious.

Chapter III: K'ung Fû-tsze advises rulers that although they may put on an act of morality and reverence by using rituals and music, if they are not kind to the needy people over whom they rule, those ancestors they are worshiping will see right through their disingenuous practices.

31

林放問禮之本子曰大哉問

禮與其奢也寧儉喪與其易也

寧戚

子曰夷狄之有君不如諸夏之亡也

季氏旅於泰山子謂冉有曰

女不能救與對曰不能子曰嗚呼

曾謂泰山不如林放乎

子曰君子無所爭必也射乎

揖讓而升下而飲其爭也君子

CHAPTER IV

1. Lin Fang asked K'ung Fû-tsze what he believed was most important during ceremonies.

2. K'ung Fû-tsze replied: That is an excellent question.

3. During festive ceremonies, simplicity is better then extravagance. During mourning ceremonies, sincere sorrow is better than concern over following details.

CHAPTER V

K'ung Fû-tsze said: Even though the primitive tribes of the East and the North have princes, they are not as civilized as our society. That is because we have an ancient and wise tradition.

CHAPTER VI

The head of the Chî family was preparing to offer sacrifice to the T'âi Mountain. K'ung Fû-tsze asked Zan Yû: Can you not save him from doing this? Zan Yû replied that he was not able to. Then K'ung Fû-tsze said: How tragic! Does he not think that the spirit of the T'âi mountain is wise enough to know when one who is praying to it is not the one who is supposed to.

CHAPTER VII

K'ung Fû-tsze said: One who has cultivated values will not seek confrontation. Some have said that even cultured individuals can be confrontational, such as when they do archery. K'ung Fû-tsze replied: archers bow and respectfully cup their hands towards their competitors when they ascend and descend the arena. When the sport is over, they even drink together. Therefore, even during competition, those who are cultivated do not harbor confrontational thoughts.

Chapter IV: Lin Fang was a wise disciple of K'ung Fû-tsze's and was from his own home state of Lû. He was an expert on the rites of the Lû region.

Chapter V: K'ung Fû-tsze was a firm believer that tradition was the backbone of a society. Famous princes would come and go, but a society's traditions would endure, and would serve to make it civilized and hold it together.

Chapter VI: The T'âi Mountain was one of five great mountains in Chinese literature. According to tradition, only emperors were permitted to offer sacrifices to the god of the T'âi Mountain. The head of the Chî family, Jisun Shi, was presumptuous when he offered sacrifice to this mountain. Zan Yû had been one of K'ung Fû-tsze's disciples, but now he worked for the Chî family. Sarcastically, K'ung Fû-tsze asked him if his master did not think the god would know who was sacrificing to it.

子夏問曰巧笑倩兮美目盼兮素以為絢兮何謂也子曰繪事後素曰禮後乎子曰起予者商也始可與言詩已矣

子曰夏禮吾能言之杞不足徵也殷禮吾能言之宋不足徵也文獻不足故也足則吾能徵之矣

子曰禘自既灌而往者吾不欲觀之矣

CHAPTER VIII

1. Tsze-hsiâ questioned the meaning of a verse from the *Book of Odes*, "The dimples of her enchanting smile and the beautiful black and white of her eyes! These are like flowers painted upon a white background."

2. K'ung Fû-tsze replied: It is only because the purity of her character radiates through, that such external characteristics as her dimples and eyes can appear beautiful.

3. Shang questioned: Must not ritual be based upon benevolence? K'ung Fû-tsze replied elatedly: Ah, Shang understands deeper meanings. Now I can begin to discuss the *Odes* with him.

Chapter IX

K'ung Fû-tsze said: I can speak of the ceremonies of the Hsiâ dynasty, but not of those from the people of Chî. They left almost no records. I can speak of the ceremonies of the Yin dynasty, but not of those from the people of Sung. They, too, left almost no records. Because the ancient sages of both Chî and Sung left such meager records, knowledge that could have been gained by studying the past has been lost.

CHAPTER X

K'ung Fû-tsze said: I have no wish to look on at the Great Sacrifice after the pouring out of libation.

Chapter VIII, passage 2: The external characteristics referred to in this verse are the woman's dimples and her eyes. K'ung Fû-tsze felt that if the woman appeared beautiful, it was only because her pure character shone through her eyes.

Chapter IX: K'ung Fû-tsze laments that during prior eras, people did not always recognize the value of maintaining written records of their ancient wisdom. Therefore, they did not do so. This occurred following the Hsiâ dynasty (c. 2200–1750 BCE) and the Yin (Shang) dynasty (c. 1750–1100 BCE). Hence, much of the wisdom of antiquity had been lost.

Chapter X: K'ung Fû-tsze states that as soon as it was polite for him to leave the Great Sacrifice, he would. This was a sacrifice to ancestors that was only to be performed by the emperor of the Châu dynasty (c. 1110–249 BCE). The emperor was considered the Son of Heaven and was believed to have special dispensation from Heaven. During this part of the sacrifice, the emperor was to call upon the spirits to descend, and the spirits would respond. Sometimes, however, people of lower status performed this sacrifice. K'ung Fû-tsze could not bear to watch such presumptuous acts, particularly when they involved such reverent events.

或問禘之説子曰不知也知其説

者之於天下也其如示諸斯乎指其掌

祭如在祭神如神在子曰吾不與祭如不祭

王孫賈問曰與其媚於奧寧媚於竈

何謂也子曰不然獲罪於天無所禱也

Chapter XI

When an individual asked K'ung Fû-tsze to explain the meaning of the Great Sacrifice, K'ung Fû-tsze humbly replied: I do not know. Those who truly understood it were probably capable of explaining All under Heaven, just as one who is capable of reading this, pointing to his palm.

CHAPTER XII

1. K'ung Fû-tsze sacrificed to his deceased ancestors and to all the spirits as if they were still alive.
2. K'ung Fû-tsze said: If I do not attend the sacrifices personally, I would feel as though I had not offered sacrifice at all.

CHAPTER XIII

1. Wang-Sun Chiâ asked: What is the meaning of the ancient saying, "It is better to pay tribute to the kitchen god then to the god that dwells in the southwest corner of the room?
2. K'ung Fû-tsze said: I do not agree with this. One who offends Heaven has no one upon whom to depend.

Chapter XI: The term *All under Heaven* refers to all on earth. In K'ung Fû-tsze's era, this referred specifically to the Chinese empire. K'ung Fû-tsze respected the traditions and wisdom of the past, even if some of the underlying meanings of ancient traditions had been lost over time. He felt that if ancient sages, such as those sages of antiquity who possessed the ability to read palms and to predict the future, had recognized the benefits of these sacrifices, he would not question them. He accepted and respected such traditions out of reverence for the wisdom of the ancients.

Chapter XII: K'ung Fû-tsze sincerely believed in sacrificing to both the spirits of his own ancestors and to the spirits of those he was supposed to sacrifice to in his official capacity. If he did not attend the sacrifices, and had others go in his place, he would have felt as though he had not attended. So he attended all sacrifices in person.

Chapter XIII: Wang-Sun Chiâ was minister of Wei. He asked if it was better to pay tribute to the god of the southwest corner of the room than to the god of the kitchen. The god of the kitchen was a minor god. Wang-Sun Chiâ questioned this because ancient tradition taught that the southwest corner of the room was a revered place. The manner in which ancient Chinese homes were constructed made the southwest region the coziest nook of the house and, hence, the place of honor. Any god that dwelled there was considered superior. K'ung Fû-tsze said that there is no need to curry favor with any god. One should conduct oneself respectfully to all. One cannot fool the gods. Heaven knows all.

子曰周監於二代郁郁乎文哉吾從周

子入大廟每事問或曰

孰謂鄹人之子知禮乎入大廟每事問

子聞之曰是禮也

子曰射不主皮為力不同科古之道也

子貢欲去告朔之餼羊子曰

賜也爾愛其羊我愛其禮

CHAPTER XIV

K'ung Fû-tsze said: The Châu dynasty had the benefit of the wisdom of the two prior dynasties. Its culture was full and rich. I adhere to the principles of the Châu dynasty.

CHAPTER XV

When K'ung Fû-tsze entered the Grand Temple, he asked many questions. Someone said: Who says that the son of the man of Tsâu knows the rules of propriety! He enters the temple and asks about everything. When K'ung Fû-tsze heard this remark, he replied: I ask my questions because of my sincere wish to learn.

CHAPTER XVI

K'ung Fû-tsze said: In archery, it is not the penetration of the leather that is of greatest importance, for all people do not possess equal strength. Such thoughts are no longer accepted.

CHAPTER XVII

1. Tsze-kung wished to do away with the sacrifice of sheep within the ancestral temples at each new moon.
2. K'ung Fû-tsze said: Tsze-kung, I appreciate your love of sheep. But I value the tradition of ancient teachings and ceremonies.

Chapter XIV: The two dynasties immediately preceding the Châu dynasty were the Hsiâ and Shang (or Yin) dynasties. Their traditions were respected for their honor and wisdom. The Châu dynasty, founded upon many of these principles, benefited when it followed the traditions of these two prior dynasties.

Chapter XV: The Grand Temple was a temple built in honor of the duke of Châu. K'ung Fû-tsze's father had been governor of Tsâu. Therefore, some referred to K'ung Fû-tsze as the son of the man of Tsâu. In this chapter, someone questioned K'ung Fû-tsze's respect for the temple because he asked questions when in it. K'ung Fû-tsze replied that he asked these questions out of his sincere desire to learn. Hence his questions were a sign of his respect for the Grand Temple, not disrespect.

Chapter XVI: K'ung Fû-tsze's statement about archery relates to all aspects of life. One cannot place value on another's actions solely by the outcome. One must judge others by the sincerity of their attempt. All are not gifted with the same abilities.

Chapter XVII: The emperor issued official calendars each year showing the dates of the new moons. On each new moon, each prince was to slaughter a sheep and conduct a prayer ceremony. K'ung Fû-tsze believed that although some questioned the practice of sheep slaughter, such traditional practices must not be abandoned. He felt that continuation of the entire ritual would ensure that the prayers that accompanied the ritual would not be forgotten over time.

子曰事君盡禮人以為諂也

定公問君使臣臣事君如之何

孔子對曰君使臣以禮臣事君以忠

子曰關雎樂而不淫哀而不傷

哀公問社於宰我宰我對曰

夏后氏以松殷人以柏周人以栗曰使

民戰栗子聞之曰成事不說遂事不諫既往不咎

CHAPTER XVIII
K'ung Fû-tsze said: Some may say that those who serve the ruler faithfully adhering to the rules of propriety are disingenuous.

CHAPTER XIX
Duke Tíng asked: How should a prince employ his ministers, and how should ministers serve their prince. K'ung Fû-tsze answered: A prince should treat his ministers with respect. Ministers should serve their prince with loyalty.

CHAPTER XX
K'ung Fû-tsze said: The *Kwan Tsü* conveys joy without resorting to sensual terms, and conveys melancholy without resorting to vulgar terms.

CHAPTER XXI
1. Duke Âi asked Tsâi Wo: What trees should be planted to grow wood to create alters to the *Spirits of the Soil*? Tsâi Wo replied: During the Hsiâ dynasty, they planted pine; during the Yin dynasty, cypress; and during the Châu dynasty, chestnut. The reason for planting chestnut trees was to instill fear.
2. When K'ung Fû-tsze heard these words of Tsâi Wo, he believed Tsâi Wo was mocking the past. K'ung Fû-tsze said: It is useless to talk of prior actions; useless to argue about what is finished; and useless to lay blame on those of the past.

Chapter XVIII: K'ung Fû-tsze responded to those who ridiculed the rites and ceremonies of the monarchy. K'ung Fû-tsze believed that tradition contributed those values to a society that would hold it together. He responded that his actions were based upon honest values, and not upon dishonest goals of currying favor.

Chapter XIX: Duke Ting was a minister in the province of Lû.

Chapter XX: The poem *Kwan Tsü* is one of the ancient odes from the *Chinese Classics*. K'ung Fû-tsze praises it because it conveys both love and melancholy, yet never resorts to base language. It conveys these messages while remaining morally high.

Chapter XXI: The Chinese character for "chestnut tree" is the same character as for the word "terror." K'ung Fû-tsze ridiculed Tsâi Wo for insinuating that the monarchy planted chestnut trees to instill fear in the people. K'ung Fû-tsze felt that people of any later generation can never fully understand the actions and values of those of prior generations. Hence, they should not ridicule them.

子曰管仲之器小哉或曰

管仲儉乎曰管氏有三歸官事不攝焉得儉

然則管仲知禮乎曰邦君樹塞門

管氏亦樹塞門邦君為兩君之好有反坫

管氏亦有反坫管氏而知禮孰不知禮

子語魯太師樂曰樂其可知也

始作翕如也從之純如也皦如也繹如也以成

CHAPTER XXII

1. K'ung Fû-tsze said that Kwan Chung had some limitations in character.

2. Someone asked: Is it that Kwan Chung is stingy? K'ung Fû-tsze replied: In his palace in *San Kwei*, he employs separate employees for each chore. How can he be considered stingy?

3. Someone asked if Kwan Chung followed the rules of propriety? K'ung Fû-tsze replied: Princes place screens to block people from peering behind their gates. Kwan Chung does the same. Also, when two Princes meet, they place their inverted cups on stands. Kwan Chung does the same. If he does not follow the rules of propriety, who does?

CHAPTER XXIII

The Grand Musician of Lû said that one must possess natural instincts to conduct a musical piece. At the commencement of a performance, all instruments must begin in unison; during the performance, all must play in harmony, with pure tone; during the finale, all must blend and finish together melodiously.

Chapter XXII: Kwan Chung was famous in Chinese history. He was prime minister for the Duke of Qi. Although K'ung Fû-tsze agreed that he possessed some character limitations, neither stinginess nor disrespect were among them. Not only was he liberal in employing and paying employees, but he also possessed such respect for the monarchy that he sought to emulate these rulers in his personal life.

Chapter XXIII: This passage concerning the great musician of Lû reflects the importance K'ung Fû-tsze placed upon culture. Although it is not a dialogue between K'ung Fû-tsze and another individual, it is a statement K'ung Fû-tsze considered important. K'ung Fû-tsze valued the wisdom of those who were both cultured and personally disciplined.

儀封人請見曰君子之至於斯也

吾未嘗不得見也從者見之出曰

二三子何患於喪乎天下之無道也久矣

天將以夫子為木鐸

子謂韶盡美矣又盡善也

謂武盡美矣未盡善也

子曰居上不寬為禮不敬

臨喪不哀吾何以觀之者

CHAPTER XXIV

The officer at the border of the state of Î asked to be introduced to
K'ung Fû-tsze. He said: When individuals of superior virtue pass
through, I never miss the privilege of meeting them. K'ung Fû-tsze's
followers arranged for them to meet. After the meeting, the border
officer stated: My friends, do not be distressed that your master
K'ung Fû-tsze has lost his official position. The kingdom has been
without truth and righteousness for so long that Heaven will now use
K'ung Fû-tsze as a bell with a wooden tongue.

CHAPTER XXV

K'ung Fû-tsze said that the music of sage King Shâo was perfect
in form and pure in sentiment, yet the music of King Wû of Châu,
although of perfect form, was not pure in sentiment.

CHAPTER XXVI

K'ung Fû-tsze said: High offices filled by stingy people; ceremonies
performed without reverence; mourning conducted without sorrow!
I cannot bear to witness any of these.

Chapter XXIV: Î was a small town on the border of Wei in Honan province. K'ung
Fû-tsze left civil service and began to wander and spread his teachings in such loca-
tions. The border officer recognized that K'ung Fû-tsze could no longer serve his
government because it had lapsed into a state of moral decline. The guard felt that
Heaven Destiny had guided K'ung Fû-tsze to leave office so that he could serve as
a bell, to herald and rouse the people to righteousness.

Chapter XXV: K'ung Fû-tsze believed that the moral values of a society were expressed through its music. He used the example of the music of sage-king Shâo. A
specific piece from that era, *The Succession,* was perfect in both form and meaning.
King Shun was elevated to the throne by King Yao because he was a man of fine
character and wisdom. Conversely, King Wû of the Châu dynasty rose to power
seizing the throne by force. K'ung Fû-tsze thought that King Wû's music, such as
The Military Exploits, reflected this fall from morality. K'ung Fû-tsze stated that
although the piece was of perfect form, it reflected a lack of purity in sentiment.

Chapter XXVI: K'ung Fû-tsze believed that each and every aspect of the government was significant in ensuring the continuing welfare of the society and its people. Officials must be benevolent, reverent, and sincere in each and every one of
their actions.

子曰里仁為美擇不處仁焉得知

子曰不仁者不可以久處約不可以長處樂仁者安仁知者利仁

子曰唯仁者能好人能惡人

子曰苟志於仁矣無惡也

子曰富與貴是人之所欲也不以其道得之不處也貧與賤是人之所惡也不以其道得之不去也君子去仁惡乎成名君子無終食之間違仁造次必於是顛沛必於是

BOOK IV   LÎ ZĂN
Virtue in Society

CHAPTER I
K'ung Fû-tsze said: It is by its virtuous conduct that a society defines its character. If, in choosing a place to live, one does not consider it essential to live where virtue prevails, how can such an individual be considered wise?

CHAPTER II
K'ung Fû-tsze said: Those without virtue will endure neither in poverty nor in wealth. Although they may make an attempt to follow an honorable path, only those with true virtue will do so instinctively.

CHAPTER III
K'ung Fû-tsze said: Only from one who is truly virtuous can praise or ridicule be trusted.

CHAPTER IV
K'ung Fû-tsze said: The truly virtuous will never be unethical.

CHAPTER V
1. K'ung Fû-tsze said: Although all desire riches and honor, if these cannot be obtained honorably, one with true virtue will not seek these. Although all dislike poverty and low status, if these cannot be avoided honorably, one with true virtue will accept these.
2. If one believed to be honorable forsakes virtue, how can such an individual be considered truly honorable?
3. A truly honorable individual does not forsake virtue even for the few moments it takes to eat a bowl of rice. Whether that individual's face is up or down, he or she will cling to virtue.

Chapter I: Just as one should seek qualities of virtue in choosing one's friends (Book I, Chapter VIII), so too, K'ung Fû-tsze taught that one should seek to live where virtue prevails. K'ung Fû-tsze observed that during times of extreme economic upturn or downturn, those without virtue would succumb to temptation. If wealthy, such individuals would use power unethically to further their economic gain. If poor, such individuals would sustain their existence unethically. In either situation, those without virtue would succumb.

Chapter V: The phrase describing an individual's face being up or down is referring to the times one is facing: good times or bad times.

子曰我未見好仁者惡不仁者 好仁者

無以尚之惡不仁者其為仁矣

不使不仁者加乎其身有能一日用其力於仁矣乎

我未見力不足者蓋有之矣我未之見也

子曰人之過也各於其黨觀過斯知仁矣

子曰朝聞道夕死可矣

子曰士志於道而恥惡衣惡食者未足與議也

子曰君子之於天下也無適也無莫也義之與比

CHAPTER VI

1. K'ung Fû-tsze said: I have never encountered an individual who is truly virtuous, nor one who is truly evil. One who is truly virtuous, values nothing above it. Such an individual practices virtue so completely that no evil can enter his or her life.
2. Does there exist one with the inner strength to devote every day of one's life fully to virtue? I have not met one with such strength!
3. Possibly such an individual exists. But I have yet to meet one without fault.

CHAPTER VII

K'ung Fû-tsze said: One's faults are characteristic of the social class to which one belongs. By observing an individual's faults, it can be determined the class of society to which that individual belongs.

CHAPTER VIII

K'ung Fû-tsze said: One who attains understanding of the Way in the morning, can die in peace that same evening.

CHAPTER IX

K'ung Fû-tsze said: One in search of true virtue, yet ashamed of poor food and clothing, is not yet ready to receive true virtue.

CHAPTER X

K'ung Fû-tsze said: One with true understanding has not closed his or her mind either for or against anything in the world. Such an individual will simply follow what is righteous.

Chapter VI and VII: K'ung Fû-tsze advises people not to feel their virtue is superior to that of others. He states that he has never met anyone without fault. Although the faults of all people differ, and some may appear worse than others, these differences are merely manifestations of the varying backgrounds of each individual.

Chapter VIII: K'ung Fû-tsze expresses his longing to understand the meaning of existence and of humankind's place within it. He believed that if he were to attain such understanding, his life would be fulfilled.

Chapter IX: One who has not progressed beyond concern for one's own comfort and prestige is not ready to understand higher truths.

Chapter X: One with true understanding recognizes that there is no objective right or wrong in the world, but only varying perspectives of these. One with true understanding will listen to the views of others, and seek only truth.

子曰君子懷德小人懷土君子懷刑小人懷惠

子曰放於利而行多怨

子曰能以禮讓為國乎何有不能以禮讓為國如禮何

子曰不患無位患所以立不患莫己知求為可知也

子曰參乎吾道一以貫之曾子曰唯子出門人問曰何謂也曾子曰夫子之道忠恕而已矣

CHAPTER XI

K'ung Fû-tsze said: One without character thinks of comfort; one with character thinks of virtue. One without character thinks of those favours obtainable through manipulation of the law; one with character thinks of the noble virtues of the law.

CHAPTER XII

K'ung Fû-tsze said: In the end, one who always seeks selfish gains will succumb to disgrace.

CHAPTER XIII

K'ung Fû-tsze said: If a ruler can control himself, what problem can he have governing the kingdom? If a ruler cannot control his own conduct, how can he possibly govern the kingdom?

CHAPTER XIV

K'ung Fû-tsze said: One should say, I am not concerned that I have not attained glory. I am concerned that I may not be worthy of it. I am not concerned that I have not attained recognition. I am concerned that I may not be worthy of it.

CHAPTER XV

1. K'ung Fû-tsze said to Shǎn: There is one underlying principle that pervades all my other doctrines. His disciple Tsǎng said that he recognized this in K'ung Fû-tsze's teachings.
2. When K'ung Fû-tsze left, the other disciples asked: What did K'ung Fû-tsze mean by that? Tsâng replied: K'ung Fû-tsze's one pervading doctrine is, "Be true to the principles of human kindness and act with compassion towards all. There is nothing higher."

Chapter XV is one of the most important passages in the *Confucian Analects*. To K'ung Fû-tsze, the greatest virtue one can possess is *Moral Kindness*. This virtue has been also termed *Humane Reciprocity* or *Loyal Forgiving*. The virtue of *Moral Kindness* teaches one to treat all people with the same human kindness that one would wish to be shown to oneself, and that one should not do to others that which one does not wish done to oneself. Although K'ung Fû-tsze is known for his teachings concerning the virtues of loyalty, discipline, ritual, and filial piety, the virtue that he held closest to his heart, and without which he felt all the rest of the virtues were worthless, was *Moral Kindness*.

子曰君子喻於義小人喻於利

子曰見賢思齊焉見不賢而內自省也

子曰事父母幾諫見志不從又敬不違勞而不怨

子曰父母在不遠遊遊必有方

子曰三年無改於父之道可謂孝矣

CHAPTER XVI

K'ung Fû-tsze said: The thoughts of one of character dwell upon righteousness. The thoughts of one without character dwell upon money.

CHAPTER XVII

K'ung Fû-tsze said: Observing those of high character, one should strive to become like them. Observing those of low character, one should reflect inwards and examine oneself.

CHAPTER XVIII

K'ung Fû-tsze said: In serving one's parents, one can disagree, but one should do so respectfully. If one's parents do not accept one's suggestions, one should still show them great reverence, but not abandon one's moral convictions. If one's parents inflict punishment, accept this willingly.

CHAPTER XIX

K'ung Fû-tsze said: While one's parents are alive, one should not travel far. If travel is necessary, one should inform others of one's intended destination.

CHAPTER XX

K'ung Fû-tsze said: If for three years after the death of one's parents, one does not deviate from their values, one will have bestowed an honor upon them.

Chapter XVII: K'ung Fû-tsze directs others to search within, rather than without, concerning the ills of the world.

Chapter XIX: Consistent with his belief in filial piety, K'ung Fû-tsze advised children not to travel far so that if their parents need their assistance, they will be available. If distant travel is unavoidable, children should inform others of their destination so they can be reached in an emergency.

Chapter XX: This philosophical concept of filial piety and respect for the values of one's parents is similar to those expressed in Book I, Chapter XI.

子曰父母之年不可不知也一則以喜一則以懼

子曰古者言之不出恥躬之不逮也

子曰以約失之者鮮矣

子曰君子欲訥於言而敏於行

子曰德不孤必有鄰

子游曰事君數斯辱矣朋友數斯疏矣

CHAPTER XXI

K'ung Fû-tsze said: One should be forever mindful of one's parents' ages, and should reflect upon their advanced ages with thoughts of both joy and fear.

CHAPTER XXII

K'ung Fû-tsze said: In ancient times, those who were wise did not speak in haste. They were mindful lest the only results they might be able to achieve might not live up to their words.

CHAPTER XXIII

K'ung Fû-tsze said: Those who proceed with caution seldom make incorrect choices.

CHAPTER XXIV

K'ung Fû-tsze said: One with character is slow in speech and sincere in conduct.

CHAPTER XXV

K'ung Fû-tsze said: One with virtue need not fear isolation, for such an individual will attract others of kindred spirit.

CHAPTER XXVI

Tsze-yû said: One who ridicules one's superiors will fall into disfavor. One who criticizes one's friends will end up alone.

Chapter XXI: One should keep one's parents reverently in one's thoughts. One should be mindful that they are growing older, feeling both joy that they have attained longevity, and fear that their time of death is soon approaching. Such mindfulness will instill one with a continuous sense of reverence and appreciation for one's parents.

Chapter XXII sheds light upon two fundamental principles of Chinese philosophy. The first principle is that words can be devoid of substance. Only actions hold substance. The second principle is that it is shameful to boast of or exaggerate about one's achievements. One who is wise will never do either of these.

Chapter XXIII: K'ung Fû-tsze teaches self-restraint, carefulness, and attention to detail. One who proceeds with caution will not only avoid mistakes, but will live in peace.

子謂公冶長可妻也雖在縲絏之中非其罪也以其子妻之

子謂南容邦有道不廢邦無道免於刑戮以其兄之子妻之

子謂子賤君子哉若人魯無君子者斯焉取斯

子貢問曰賜也何如子曰女器也曰何器也曰瑚璉也

BOOK V   K'UNG-YÊ CH'ANG
Disciple and Son-in-law

CHAPTER I

1. K'ung Fû-tsze said that Kung-yê Ch'ang could marry, for although he had been put in bonds, he was not guilty of any crime. Kung Fû-tsze gave his own daughter to him in marriage.

2. K'ung Fû-tsze said of Nan-Yung: If the country is governed honestly, Nan Yung will remain in office. If the country is not governed honestly, he will leave office and not become involved in any actions that would cause him either retribution or disgrace. Kung Fû-tsze gave his elder brother's daughter to him in marriage.

CHAPTER II

K'ung Fû-tsze said that, indeed, Tsze-chien was a man of superior virtue. But had there not been others of virtuous character in Lû from whom he must have learned? Otherwise, how could he have attained such character?

CHAPTER III

Tsze-kung asked: How would you describe me? K'ung Fû-tsze replied: You are a valuable tool to me. Tsze-kung asked: What sort of a tool? K'ung Fû-tsze replied: A gemmed-studded sacrificial vessel.

Chapter I: Kung-yê Ch'ang had been one of K'ung Fû-tsze's disciples. Although he had been imprisoned, K'ung Fû-tsze knew he had not committed any crime and that he was a man of character. When choosing a man for his own daughter to marry, K'ung Fû-tsze chose Kung-yê Ch'ang. This showed that K'ung Fû-tsze valued character much more than he valued wealth.

Passage 2: K'ung Fû-tsze chose Nan Yung, another man of character, and also one of his disciples, to marry the daughter of his elder brother. This was the daughter of his crippled brother, Măng-p'î. Nan Yung was of such character that he would not take part in a dishonest government.

Chapter II: Tsze-chien was one of K'ung Fû-tsze's disciples. He held an administrative position in the government. He was a man of integrity and chose his friends wisely, making sure they were of honorable character.

Chapter III: Tsze-kung, seeking reassurance from K'ung Fû-tsze, asked him to describe his character. K'ung Fû-tsze's described Tsze-kung as a very precious sacred vessel, the type used during grain offerings in the royal ancestral temples.

或曰雍也仁而不佞子曰焉用佞禦人以口給屢憎於人

不知其仁焉用佞

子使漆雕開仕對曰吾斯之未能信子說

子曰道不行乘桴浮於海從我者其由與

子路聞之喜子曰由也好勇過我無所取材

孟武伯問子路仁乎子曰不知也又問

子曰由也千乘之國可使治其賦也不知其仁也求也何如

子曰求也千室之邑百乘之家可使為之宰也不知其仁也赤也何如

子曰赤也束帶立於朝可使與賓客言也

不知其仁也

CHAPTER IV

1. Someone said that although Yung was truly virtuous, he was not articulate.

2. K'ung Fû-tsze replied: What is the use of being articulate, if one's words are not truthful? Those who are smooth talkers, generally bring hatred upon themselves. I do not know one who is truly virtuous who is a smooth talker.

CHAPTER V

K'ung Fû-tsze was hoping that Ch'î-tiâo K'âi would enter official office. Ch'î-tiâo K'âi replied: I am not yet sure of my capabilities. K'ung Fû-tsze was pleased that he was so humble.

Chapter VI

K'ung Fû-tsze, dejected, said: My teachings do not seem to change anything. I should get on a raft and drift out to sea. If I did, Yû would join me. Hearing this, Yû expressed joy, upon which K'ung Fû-tsze said: Yû is too daring. He does not always exercise judgment.

CHAPTER VII

1. Măng Wû asked K'ung Fû-tsze if he considered Tsze-lû perfectly virtuous. K'ung Fû-tsze said: I do not know.

2. Măng Wû asked again. K'ung Fû-tsze replied: He can be trusted to manage taxes in a kingdom of a thousand chariots, but I do not know if he is perfectly virtuous.

3. Măng Wû asked : What about Ch'iû? K'ung Fû-tsze replied: Ch'iû can be trusted to govern a city of a thousand families and a hundred chariots, but I do not know if he is perfectly virtuous.

Chapter IV: K'ung Fû-tsze states that the glib of tongue are seldom virtuous.

Chapter V: Ch'î-tiâo K'âi may be referring to the *Book of History* when stating he did not possess full understanding of it. K'ung Fû-tsze believed that to lead wisely, one must study events of the past to gain understanding of the presnt.

Chapter VI: K'ung Fû-tsze did not actually mean that he was going to abandon civilization and drift aimlessly on a raft. He was expressing disappointment that his teachings had not achieved all he hoped they would. Yû felt proud that K'ung Fû-tsze recognized his faithfulness. K'ung Fû-tsze, however, sought to teach Yû that being daring was not as valuable as being cautious.

Chapter VII: K'ung Fû-tsze recognized that although an individual may be trusted to collect taxes, govern large nations (nations of a thousand chariots), and handle foreign affairs, no one can be certain that the individual is truly virtuous.

子謂子貢曰女與回也孰愈對曰賜也何敢望回

回也聞一以十賜也聞一以知二子曰弗如也吾與女弗如也

宰予晝寢子曰朽木不可雕也糞土之牆不可杇也

於予與何誅子曰始吾於人也聽其言而信其行

今吾於人也聽其言而觀其行於予與改是

子曰吾未見剛者或對曰申棖

棖也慾焉得剛

4. Măng Wu asked: What about Ch'ih? K'ung Fû-tsze replied: Ch'ih can be trusted to stand in court in his official sash girt and speak with visitors and guests. But I do not know if he is perfectly virtuous.

CHAPTER VIII
1. K'ung Fû-tsze said to Tsze-kung: Who do you believe is superior, yourself or Hûi?
2. Tsze-kung replied: I dare not compare myself with Hûi. Hûi hears one fact, and knows ten. I hear one fact and know only a second.
3. K'ung Fû-tsze said: I agree. You are not equal to him. Nor am I.

CHAPTER IX
1. Tsâi Yü was asleep during the day. K'ung Fû-tsze said: One cannot carve with wood that is rotten, nor plaster with soil that is dirty. Is there any use in my reprimanding him?
2. K'ung Fû-tsze said: Initially, I would listen to people's words, and believed they would follow through in their conduct. Now, I listen to people's words, and scrutinize their conduct. From observing Tsâi Yü, I have made this change.

CHAPTER X
K'ung Fû-tsze said: I have yet to meet one with the strength of his or her convictions. Someone asked: How about Shăn Ch'ang? K'ung Fû-tsze said: Ch'ang is driven by passion. How can anyone driven by passion be considered an individual of strength and conviction?

Chapter VIII: Hûi had been K'ung Fû-tsze's favorite disciple. He was thirty years younger than K'ung Fû-tsze and also from the state of Lû. Hûi was a man of peace. He dreamed of assisting a king who could lead without war, rather than a prince who would glory in war. When twenty-nine years of age, Hûi's hair turned white. At age thirty-two, he died. Upon his death, K'ung Fû-tsze wept. K'ung Fû-tsze told Tsze-kung that he was not equal to Hûi, but added that neither was he.

Chapter IX: Tsâi Yü was lazy. K'ung Fû-tsze felt that one must change one's character before one can change one's actions. It was by observing Tsâi Yü's failure to follow through on his word, that K'ung Fû-tsze recognized the need to judge people not by their words, but by their deeds.

Chapter X: Shăn Ch'ang was one of K'ung Fû-tsze's disciple. K'ung Fû-tsze used him as an example of a man driven by passions. K'ung Fû-tsze recognized that one led by passion may be provoked to fall from a virtuous path.

子貢曰我不欲人之加諸我也

吾亦欲無加諸人子曰賜也非爾所及也

子貢曰夫子之文章可得而聞也

夫子之言性與天道不可得而聞也

子路有聞未之能行唯恐有聞

子貢問孔文子何以謂之文也子曰敏而好學

不恥下問是以謂之文也

子謂子產有君子之道四焉

其行己也恭其事上也敬其養民也惠其使民也義

CHAPTER XI

Tsze-kung said: What I do not want done to me, I will not do to others. K'ung Fû-tsze told Tsze-kung that he had not achieved this.

CHAPTER XII

Tsze-kung said: K'ung Fû-tsze's life is his teaching. His teachings are not mere discourses on the nature of humankind or the Way of Heaven. They are guidelines for living a life of pure, sincere virtue.

CHAPTER XIII

When Tsze-lû learned rules of conduct, he feared he might not be able to put them into practice before learning newer ones.

CHAPTER XIV

Tsze-kung asked: On what basis did Kung-wăn receive the honorary title *Wăn*? K'ung Fû-tsze said: He was hard working and valued knowledge. He was not too proud to ask for information or to receive it from those beneath him.

CHAPTER XV

K'ung Fû-tsze said: Tsze-ch'an possessed four qualities of a superior individual. In conduct, he was humble. In serving superiors, he was respectful. In giving, he was generous. In leading, he was just.

Chapter XI: This expresses the golden rule of reciprocity: Do unto others only that which you wish done unto yourself. K'ung Fû-tsze held people to a high standard in how they should treat others. He told his disciple Tsze-kung that he had not yet achieved this.

Chapter XII: K'ung Fû-tsze did not just preach ethical principles, he lived them. He did so in every aspect of his life, even down to the most ordinary and simplest of actions. His life was his teachings.

Chapter XIII: K'ung Fû-tsze's disciple Tsze-lû recognized the value of a strong moral foundation. He sought to ensure that his moral value system possessed a firm foundation, prior to building upon it.

Chapter XIV: The title Wăn means *One of Culture*. Kung-wăn received this title posthumously. K'ung Fû-tsze stated that he earned it because he truly valued knowledge and was not too proud to ask for it from those lower than himself.

Chapter XV: Tsze-ch'an had been chief minister of the state of Chăng. K'ung Fû-tsze wept at his death, and told of his virtuous qualities. Tsze-ch'an was humble, respectful, generous, and just.

子曰晏平仲善與人交久而敬之

子曰臧文仲居蔡山節藻梲何如其知也

子張問曰令尹子文三仕為令尹無喜色三已之無慍色

舊令尹之政必以告新令尹何如子曰忠矣曰仁矣乎

曰未知焉得仁崔子弒齊君陳文子有馬十乘棄

而違之至於他邦則曰猶吾大夫崔子也違之

則又曰猶吾大夫崔子也違之之一邦

子曰清矣曰仁矣乎曰未知焉得仁

CHAPTER XVI
K'ung Fû-tsze said: Yen P'ing acted with wisdom concerning friendships. Even if he knew people a long time, he showed them the same respect he had shown them when he first met them

CHAPTER XVII
K'ung Fû-tsze said: In his house, Tsang Wăn, an officer in the state of Lû, kept a large tortoise. He also kept carvings of hills and duckweed on the pillars and structural beams. Can he be considered wise?

CHAPTER XVIII
1. Tsze-chang said: A minister named Tsze-wăn took office three times. At no time did he express pride. He lost office three times. At no time did he express displeasure. When he left office, he taught the minister who was about to replace him well. What would you say about him? K'ung Fû-tsze replied: I would say he was extremely loyal. Did he have perfect virtue? I do not know. Who can say?
2. Tsze-chang continued: The officer of Ch'ûi killed the prince of Ch'î. Recognizing that dishonorable people would now rule, although he owned forty horses, Ch'ăn Wăn left all his wealth behind and fled the state of Ch'î. Upon entering the next state, he found the leaders to be just as dishonorable as the officers of Ch'ûi. So he left and went to another state. Noting the same, he left this state as well. What would you say of him? K'ung Fû-tsze replied: He was a man of honor. Did he have perfect virtue? I do not know. Who can say?

Chapter XVI: Yen P'ing had been a principal minister of Ch'î. K'ung Fû-tsze tells of his wisdom. He treated those with whom he had grown familiar with the same respect as he had the first day he met them.

Chapter XVII: Tsang Wăn, a minister of Lû, was considered a man of wisdom. K'ung Fû-tsze, however, questioned this. The state of Ts'âi was known for its large tortoises. Tortoises were used for divination. K'ung Fû-tsze condemns Tsang Wăn for thinking that just bringing a tortoise into his house could bring him luck.

Chapter XVIII: K'ung Fû-tsze did not take the liberty of declaring one perfectly virtuous lightly. Tsze-wăn felt neither pride nor shame upon gaining or losing his position. He recognized that one always encounters success and failure in life. Nevertheless, one must always do one's best. K'ung Fû-tsze, however, could not say Tsang Wăn was perfectly virtuous in all aspects of life. Similarly, although Ch'ăn Wăn would not reside in a state of questionable morality, K'ung Fû-tsze could not say he was perfectly virtuous. Who can truly judge the virtue of another?

季文子三思而後行子聞之曰再斯可矣

子曰甯武子邦有道則知邦無道則愚
其知可及也其愚不可及也

子在陳曰歸與歸與吾黨之小子狂簡
斐然成章不知所以裁之

伯夷叔齊不念舊惡怨是用希

CHAPTER XIX

Chî Wăn thought three times before acting. Upon hearing this, K'ung Fû-tsze said: Twice is sufficient.

CHAPTER XX

K'ung Fû-tsze said: When morality prevailed in his country, Ning Wû acted with wisdom. When immorality prevailed, he acted like an aimless fool. Acting thusly, he was not forced to take part in the immoral activities of the state. Others may equal him in wisdom, yet none can equal him in foolishness.

CHAPTER XXI

In Ch'ăn, K'ung Fû-tsze said: Let us return. Let us return. The young disciples of my school have become arrogant and impetuous. Though they have acquired skills and knowledge, they have failed to develop basic virtues of self-discipline and self-cultivation.

CHAPTER XXII

K'ung Fû-tsze said: Po-î and Shû-ch'î harbored no resentment against others. Because of this, no one resented them.

Chapter XIX, K'ung Fû-tsze states that although one must think carefully before making decisions, one should be able to distinguish the moral from the immoral quickly.

Chapter XX: Ning Wû was a minister of the state of Wei, 700 BCE. When his prince was driven from the throne, other members of the court rushed out to save themselves. He, alone, rushed in to save the prince. His unwavering loyalty saved the prince. The prince was reinstated to the throne. Ning Wû was a man of principle who would not partake in immoral activities.

Chapter XXI: K'ung Fû-tsze had been in Ch'ăn three times. During his last visit, he was over the age of sixty. He expressed his dismay that his disciples had become conceited concerning their knowledge. What good is knowledge if it is not tempered by patience and humbleness, and possessed by those of character?

Chapter XXII: Po-î and Shû-ch'î were two brothers. They left society to live in seclusion in the mountains rather then remain under the rule of a despotic conqueror. K'ung Fû-tsze used them to exemplify the principle that as one gives, so too, one shall receive. One who neither judges nor resents others, will not be judged or resented by others.

子曰孰謂微生高直或乞醯焉乞諸其鄰而與之

子曰巧言令色足恭左丘明恥之

丘亦恥之匿怨而友其人左丘明恥之丘亦恥之

顏淵季路侍子曰盍各言爾志

子路曰願車馬衣輕裘與朋友共敝之而無憾顏淵曰願無伐善無施勞子

路曰願聞子之志子曰老者安之朋友信之少者懷之

CHAPTER XXIII

K'ung Fû-tsze said: Some say Wei-shang Kâo is righteous. When a beggar asked him for vinegar, he gave some to him. But it was not his own vinegar. Actually, he begged this from a neighbor. It was this vinegar, not his own, that he gave to the beggar.

CHAPTER XXIV

K'ung Fû-tsze said: Slick words, a contrived appearance, and excessive respect—Tso Ch'iû-ming would not lower himself to this. Nor would I. To conceal resentment and feign friendliness—Tso Ch'iû-ming would not lower himself to this. Nor would I.

CHAPTER XXV

1. Yen Yüan and Tsze-Lû were close to K'ung Fû-tsze. He said to them: Come and tell me what you wish in your hearts.
2. Tsze-lû said: I would like to share chariots, horses, clothes, and fine furs with friends, and see them wear them out.
3. Yen Yüan said: I would like that I would never brag of my achievements and not burden others with my honors.
4. Tsze-lû asked K'ung Fû-tsze: I would like to hear your wishes. K'ung Fû-tsze replied: I wish that I could give comfort to the aged; faithful companionship to my friends; and tender care to the young.

Chapter XXIII: K'ung Fû-tsze explains how one who may appear righteous may not actually be so. Although Wei-shang Kâo gave vinegar to a beggar, he did not give his own. He begged vinegar from someone else and gave this to the beggar. He kept his own vinegar for himself.

Chapter XXIV: K'ung Fû-tsze discusses the character of Tso Ch'iû-ming. He was an ancient legendary figure who possessed such purity of character that he never feigned respect in word, action, or deed. He expressed all his feelings, both the positive and the negative, honestly.

Chapter XXV gives three examples of humanitarian virtue. Tsze-lû dreamed of sharing all he owned with his friends, even letting them wear these out. Yen Yüan sought to cultivate the virtue of humbleness so that he would never succumb to bragging. K'ung Fû-tsze sought to give selfless service to the aged, to the young, and to his friends.

君子美乎吾未見其過而內自訟者也

子曰十室之邑必有忠信如丘者焉

不如丘之好學也

CHAPTER XXVI

K'ung Fû-tsze said: It is hopeless! I have yet to meet one who can recognize one's own faults, and inwardly blame oneself.

CHAPTER XXVII

K'ung Fû-tsze said: Within a hamlet of ten families, there may be some who possess honesty and sincerity. But I have yet to find one who is as devoted to the quest and practice of ethics as I am.

Chapter XXVII: K'ung Fû-tsze express his sadness that he had yet to find an individual seeking to devote his or her life to the study and cultivation of virtue. He was not stating this out of conceit, but out of his sincere wish to meet such an individual.

子曰雍也可使南面

仲弓問子桑伯子子曰可也簡仲弓曰居敬而行簡

以臨其民不亦可乎居簡而行簡無乃大簡乎子曰雍之言然

哀公問弟子孰為好學孔子對曰

有顏回者好學不遷怒不貳過不

幸短命死矣今也則亡未聞好學者也

子華使於齊冉子為其母請粟子曰與之釜

請益曰與之庾冉子與之粟五秉子曰赤之適齊也乘肥馬

衣輕裘吾聞之也君子周急不繼富

BOOK VI   YUNG YÊY
Yung Yêy is One Who

CHAPTER I

1. K'ung Fû-tsze said: Yung is a man who is qualified to occupy the position of a prince.
2. Chung-kung asked about Tsze-sang Po-tsze. K'ung Fû-tsze said: He is generally fine, yet he does not pay attention to detail.
3. Chung-kung said: If one is reverently attentive to important issues in governing, yet lax concerning minor issues, one's conduct can be accepted. But if one is lax in one's personal conduct, and also lax in running the government, one's conduct is not acceptable.
4. K'ung Fû-tsze said: Such words are correct.

CHAPTER II

Duke Âi asked K'ung Fû-tsze which of his disciples loved to learn. K'ung Fû-tsze said: Yen Hûi loved to learn. He never felt anger and never repeated a mistake. Unfortunately, his appointed time was short and he passed on. I have not met another like him, nor have I heard of another like him.

CHAPTER III

1. Tsze-hwâ was sent on a mission to Ch'î. Yen begged the disciple Zan for grain for his mother. K'ung Fû-tsze said: Give her a peck. Yen requested more. K'ung Fû-tsze said: Give him a bushel. Zan gave him five hundred weights.
2. K'ung Fû-tsze reprimanded Zan: When Ch-ih traveled to Ch'î, his carriage horses were well fed and he wore fine furs. The virtuous should help the suffering and not add wealth to the rich.

Chapter I discusses those character traits desirable in an honorable leader. K'ung Fû-tsze said that Yung would meet the qualifications of a great leader and could take a seat facing south. In ancient China, a leader was to sit facing south, to govern facing the brightest direction. K'ung Fû-tsze agreed that although Tsze-sang Po-tsze did not pay close attention to detail, this was not a major fault. His lack of ability to control his own character, however, was.

Chapter II: K'ung Fû-tsze discusses his favorite disciple, Yen Hûi. K'ung Fû-tsze states that it was his destiny to die young.

Chapter III: K'ung Fû-tsze did not disagree with giving charity, but reprimanded Zan because he knew these beggars were actually wealthy. Alms should be given to those who truly suffered poverty, not to those who feign it.

原思為之宰與之粟九百辭子曰毋以與爾鄰里鄉黨乎

子謂仲弓曰犂牛之子騂且角雖欲勿用山川其舍諸

子曰回也其心三月不違仁其餘則日月至焉而已矣

季康子問仲由可使從政也與子曰由也果於從政乎何有曰賜也達於從政乎何有曰求也藝於從政乎何有

季氏使閔子騫為費宰閔子騫曰善為我辭焉如有復我者則吾必在汶上矣

3. K'ung Fû-tsze appointed Yuan Sze governor of his town and of-fered to give him nine hundred measures of grain. Sze declined.
4. K'ung Fû-tsze said: Do not decline. Take this grain and distribute it amongst the poor in your small hamlets and villages.

CHAPTER IV
K'ung Fû-tsze said of Chung-kung: If the calf of a brindled cow is red and horned, although people may reject it, the spirits of the mountains and rivers will not.

CHAPTER V
K'ung Fû-tsze said: For three months, nothing entered Hûi's mind except perfect virtue. Others may be able to sustain such virtue for several days or weeks, but none can sustain it longer than that.

CHAPTER VI
Chî K'ang asked if Chung-yû was fit for a position in government. K'ung Fû-tsze said: Yû is clear thinking. What difficulty would he have in a government position? K'ang asked: Is Ts'ze fit for a posi-tion in government? K'ung Fû-tsze said: Ts'ze is intelligent. What difficulty would he find in the government? Asked about Ch'iû, K'ung Fû-tsze said: Ch'iû possesses diverse abilities.

CHAPTER VII
The head of the Chî family was sent to ask Min Tsze-ch'ien to as-sume the position as governor of Pî. Min Tsze-ch'ien politely de-clined. He said: If they return with a second request, I shall be forced to retreat to live on the banks of the Wăn River.

Chapter III, passage 3: K'ung Fû-tsze advises Yuan Sze not to neglect the needs of those in your village who are truly impoverished.

Chapter IV: K'ung Fû-tsze tells Chung-kung not to judge people by their parents. Even if a cow was brindled (tawny with streaks or spots), yet it gives birth to a calf that is pure red, the spirits of the mountains and rivers will not reject the calf as a sacrifice.

Chapter VII: Min Tsze-ch'ien would not work for the powerful, but corrupt, Chî family. He would rather retreat to the banks of the Wăn river, separating Ch'î and Lû provinces, rather than accept a position in a corrupt regime.

伯牛有疾子問之自牖執其手曰亡之命矣夫

斯人也而有斯疾也斯人也而有斯疾也

子曰賢哉回也一簞食一瓢飲 在陋巷

人不堪其憂回也不改其樂賢哉回也

冉求曰非不說子之道力不足

子曰力不足者中道而廢今女畫

子謂子夏曰女為君子儒無為小人儒

子游為武城宰子曰女得人焉爾乎曰有澹臺滅明者

行不由徑非公事未嘗至於偃之室也

CHAPTER VIII

Po-niû became ill. When K'ung Fû-tsze visited him, he placed his hand through the window, and said: Po-niû is dying. It is the appointed time of Heaven. How tragic that such a man should be so ill! That such a man should be so ill!

CHAPTER IX

K'ung Fû-tsze said: Hûi was a man of character. With one bamboo bowl for rice, one bowl for liquid, and a home on a miserable, narrow street, his was a situation that others would not endure. Yet he was always joyful. Hûi was a man of character.

CHAPTER X

Yen Ch'iû said: It is not that I do not value your teachings, it is that my strength is insufficient. K'ung Fû-tsze said: Those whose strength is truly insufficient still progress midway. Your inadequacies are your own doing.

CHAPTER XI

K'ung Fû-tsze advised Tsze-hsiâ: To become a scholar, one must be of noble character. Do not follow those who lack it.

CHAPTER XII

K'ung Fû-tsze asked Tsze-yû, the governor of Wû-ch'ǎng: Do you have people of character in your state? Tsze-yû replied: Yes, Tan-t'âi Mieh-ming. He never follows a crooked path and never comes to my office, except for official reasons.

Chapter VIII: Po-niû, a disciple of K'ung Fû-tsze became ill with a disorder termed the *evil disease*. This may have meant leprosy. Because of his illness, others were not permitted to see him. Nevertheless, K'ung Fû-tsze placed his hand through a window as a sign of friendship to Po-niû.

Chapter IX: K'ung Fû-tsze praises Hûi in that he was able to live contentedly even in poverty.

Chapter X: K'ung Fû-tsze does not accept Yen Ch'iû's excuse that he does not possess the strength to study. K'ung Fû-tsze states that even the weak can meet their teacher's efforts half way.

Chapter XII: The governor praises an individual who is so honorable that he comes to his office only for real reasons, and never to win favors.

子曰孟之反不伐奔而殿將入門策其馬
曰非敢後也馬不進也

子曰不有祝鮀之佞而有宋朝之美難乎免於今之世矣

子曰誰能出不由戶何莫由斯道也

子曰質勝文則野文勝質則史文質彬彬然後君子

CHAPTER XIII
K'ung Fû-tsze said: Măng Chih-fan did not boast of achievements.
When the army was retreating from battle and approaching the gate,
he whipped his horse so as not to be last. Yet he was last. Măng
Chih-fan told the others: I was not last because I was brave. I was
last because my horse would not go faster.

CHAPTER XIV
K'ung Fû-tsze said: Nowadays, if one does not possess the glib
tongue of officer T'o, and the good looks of prince Châo of Sung, it
is difficult to get ahead.

CHAPTER XV
K'ung Fû-tsze said: How can people go out, but through the door?
Why do people not follow correct paths. Why are such simple con-
cepts so difficult for people to understand?

CHAPTER XVI
K'ung Fû-tsze said: When one's common mannerisms exceed one's
cultured ones, one will appear crude and rustic. When one's cultured
mannerisms exceed one's earthy ones, one will seem like one who is
selling oneself. When one's cultured and earthy mannerisms are well
balanced, one will be respected.

Chapter XIII: K'ung Fû-tsze discusses the virtue of Măng Chih-fan, an officer from
Lû. It was considered an honor to be the last to return from battle. As the army re-
treated, the last person to continue fighting was considered brave. Although Măng
Chih-fan was last, he did not want to boast, so he said the only reason he was last
was because his horse would not move faster.

Chapter XIV: K'ung Fû-tsze discusses the moral decay of the times. Officer T'o
was glib of tongue, yet was in charge of prayers in the ancestral temple. Prince Châo
committed incest with his half-sister Nan-tsze, and continued with this incest even
after Nan-tsze married Duke Lei of Wei.

Chapter XV: K'ung Fû-tsze's laments that just as it is so obviously simple for people to go out through the door (proceed the correct way), people could not see how
much easier life would be if they just followed the rules (proceed the correct way).

子曰人之生也直罔之生也幸而免

子曰知之者不如好之者好之者不如樂之者

子曰中人以上可以語上也中人以下不可以語上也

樊遲問知子曰務民之義敬鬼神而遠之

可謂知矣問仁曰仁者先難而後獲可謂仁矣

CHAPTER XVII

K'ung Fû-tsze said: Human beings are born to be honorable. If one abandons one's honor, yet still survives, it is merely because one is lucky.

CHAPTER XVIII

K'ung Fû-tsze said: One who knows the truth is not equal to one who appreciates it. One who appreciates the truth is not equal to one who practices it.

CHAPTER XIX

K'ung Fû-tsze said: Deep philosophical concepts can be discussed with those of above average ability. They cannot be discussed with those of below average ability.

CHAPTER XX

Fan Ch'ih asked: What is wisdom? K'ung Fû-tsze replied: To devote oneself sincerely to the needs of others; and, although it is fine to respect the transcendent, to keep far away from it. This is wisdom. Fan Ch'ih asked: What is moral virtue? K'ung Fû-tsze replied: Attending to the responsibilities of one's business, and thinking of success only secondarily. This is moral virtue.

Chapter XVII: K'ung Fû-tsze sought to advise his disciples that one who abandons honor is living dangerously.

Chapter XVIII describes different moral levels one may attain concerning truth: recognizing it, appreciating it, and living it.

Chapter XX: These are two important beliefs K'ung Fû-tsze held concerning attainment of wisdom. The first is that although one should respect religious tradition, one should focus on that over which one has control. K'ung Fû-tsze's goal was to cultivate righteousness within people. He advised people that although they should not abandon their quest to understand the supernatural, it would be better for them to focus on their own responsibilities. His advised people to keep a cautious, respectful distance from the supernatural. The second belief K'ung Fû-tsze held concerning wisdom related to how a wise individual should fulfill responsibilities. One must focus on one's responsibilities and think of gain only later. To K'ung Fû-tsze, this was the only path that was honorable.

子曰知者樂水仁者樂山知者動仁者靜知者樂仁者壽

子曰齊一變至於魯魯一變至於道

子曰觚不觚觚哉觚哉

宰我問曰仁者雖告之曰井有仁焉其從之也子曰何為其然也君子可逝也不可陷也可欺也不可罔也

子曰君子博學於文約之以禮亦可以弗畔矣夫

CHAPTER XXI

K'ung Fû-tsze said: The wise find pleasure in water. The virtuous find pleasure in the hills. The wise are active and joyful. The virtuous are tranquil and attain longevity.

CHAPTER XXII

K'ung Fû-tsze said: If the state of Ch'î improved slightly, it would approach the virtue of the State of Lû. If the state of Lû changed slightly, it would become a State where virtue pervaded all.

CHAPTER XXIII

K'ung Fû-tsze said: How can you refer to this vessel as a sacrificial spouted vessel? Is it not strange to you that there are no spouts?

CHAPTER XXIV

Tsâi Wo said: One with compassion, if told that someone has fallen in a well, will go in after him. K'ung Fû-tsze questioned: Why should one do so? A wise individual will go to the well, but will not be falsely provoked to go down. A wise individual may be coaxed, but not fooled.

CHAPTER XXV

K'ung Fû-tsze said: One with character, who has attained great knowledge and has mastered self-restraint, will not venture into a dishonorable situation.

Chapter XXI: K'ung Fû-tsze observed different natures amongst those who reside within different geographic regions. Those living along the coast wonder what is beyond. Seeking adventure, they journey past their own borders. Those who live inland are content living upon their own soil. They do not seek the excitement of foreign lands. Being content with tranquil lives, they attain peaceful longevity.

Chapter XXII concerns the fate of a nation wherein the people have lost moral values. The states of Ch'î and Lû were in Shantung province. Ch'î was on the northern coast and Lû was in the south. The state of Ch'î had fallen into moral decay.

Chapter XXIII: K'ung Fû-tsze expresses his disappointment that people had changed the traditional shape of the sacrificial vessel, yet referred to it by the same name.

Chapter XXIV advises one to be cautious concerning one's benevolence.

Chapter XXV: K'ung Fû-tsze tells that one who has mastered both one's studies and oneself, will be able to follow a path of righteousness with natural ease.

子見南子子路不說夫子矢之曰

予所否者天厭之天厭之

子曰中庸之為德也其至矣乎民鮮久矣

子貢曰如有博施於民而能濟眾何如可謂仁乎

子曰何事於仁必也聖乎堯舜其猶病諸

夫仁者己欲立而立人己欲達而達人能近取譬

可謂仁之方也已

CHAPTER XXVI

Tsze-lû was displeased that K'ung Fû-tsze had visited Nan-tsze. K'ung Fû-tsze said: If I have acted improperly, Heaven will reject me.

CHAPTER XXVII

K'ung Fû-tsze said: The practice of moderation is a perfect virtue. For a long time now, people have almost given up practicing it.

CHAPTER XXVIII

1. Tsze-kung asked: Would you consider one who bestows great benefits upon one's people to be perfectly virtuous? K'ung Fû-tsze said: Why speak merely of virtue. Such an individual would be a sage. Even Yâo and Shun had not lived up to such a standard.

2. One with perfect virtue, wishing to cultivate oneself, seeks to cultivate others. One with perfect virtue, wishing to develop oneself, seeks to develop others.

3. By striving to elevate the qualities of others, one will attain the ability to recognize what is deficient within oneself. Recognizing one's own deficiencies is a virtue.

Chapter XXVI: K'ung Fû-tsze told Tsze-lû that although he visited Nan-tsze, a woman of questionable character, Tsze-lû had no right to question him. If he had done something wrong, it was not for Tsze-lû to judge. It is for Heaven to judge.

Chapter XXVII relates to the loss of moderation that had occurred in society during that era. In Chinese philosophy, anything carried to an extreme, was considered unhealthy and unwise.

Chapter XXVIII: K'ung Fû-tsze tells Tsze-kung that to become a sage, one need not accomplish a tremendous feat. Just showing benevolence and kindness towards all people constitutes perfect virtue. Even Emperors Yâo and Shun, revered ancient sovereigns, had not been able to achieve this. Yet they were still considered sages.

Passage 2 illustrates the selfless nature of one with perfect virtue. One with perfect virtue strives not only to cultivate oneself, but also to cultivate others.

Passage 3 advises people not to judge others, but to look within themselves. One cannot change others, one can only change oneself. By so doing, one will be on a path toward attainment of perfect virtue.

述而 第七

子曰述而不作信而好古竊比於我老彭

子曰默而識之學而不厭誨人不倦何有於我哉

子曰德之不修學之不講聞義不能徙不善不能改是吾憂也

子之燕居申申如也夭夭如也

子曰甚矣吾衰也久矣吾不復夢見周公

BOOK VII SHÛ R
Transmitting Wisdom

CHAPTER I.

K'ung Fû-tsze said: The wisdom I teach, is not wisdom I have created. It is the wisdom of the ancients that I am merely transmitting from them to you. I trust and cherish the teachings of the ancients. I dare not consider myself like ancient P'ăng.

CHAPTER II

K'ung Fû-tsze said: I view myself as one who silently seeks to accumulate knowledge, voraciously seeks to understand it, and unceasingly strives to share it with others.

CHAPTER III

K'ung Fû-tsze said: If I fail to cultivate virtue, fail to fully analyze what I have learned, fail to progress towards what I know is right, and fail to correct my own faults, that would distress me greatly.

CHAPTER IV

During times of leisure, K'ung Fû-tsze remained calm and content.

CHAPTER V

K'ung Fû-tsze said: My decline is terrible. For a long time, I have not even been able to dream of the duke of Châu.

Chapter I: K'ung Fû-tsze states he is not the originator of his teachings, but rather, a transmitter of it, handing it down from ancient sages to people of his time. He states he is merely a man who recognizes that the lessons of the past become the wisdom of the future. K'ung Fû-tsze studied history and dedicated himself to learning from the past. The identity of ancient P'ăng remains elusive. Some believe he was either: Lâo Tzu; an individual in the writings of Chwang Tzu; or P'ăng Hsien, an ancient sage of the Shang dynasty.

Chapters I, II, and III express K'ung Fû-tsze's humble beliefs that he is only a vehicle transmitting wisdom from the past to the present.

Chapter IV: One learns that K'ung Fû-tsze was a man at peace.

Chapter V: During his later years, K'ung Fû-tsze laments that his teachings had not led to the changes that he had envisioned. Because of this, he lost the dream of a society patterned by individuals such as the duke of Châu. The duke of Châu was a man revered in Chinese history for his concern for the people, his formation of a legal code, and his ability to elevate moral values throughout the empire.

子曰志於道據於德依於仁游於藝

子曰自行束脩以上吾未嘗無誨焉

子曰不憤不啟不悱不發舉一隅不以三隅反則不復也

子食於有喪者之側未嘗飽也 子於是日哭則不歌

CHAPTER VI

1. K'ung Fû-tsze said: Set your mind on duty.
2. Fix your desires firmly on all that is right.
3. Adhere to perfect virtue.
4. Spend your leisure time and find your enjoyment in cultured arts.

CHAPTER VII

K'ung Fû-tsze said: There has been no one, from the men bringing their bundles of dried fish, to those within the highest levels of society, to whom I have refused instruction.

CHAPTER VIII

K'ung Fû-tsze said: I do not open the truth to one who is not eager to learn. I do not help one who is not ready to look within. When I explain one corner of a subject, and one refuses to accept the other three corners from this, I do not repeat my teachings.

CHAPTER IX

1. When near a mourner, K'ung Fû-tsze never ate a full meal.
2. K'ung Fû-tsze never sang on the same day in which he had wept in mourning.

Chapter VI: K'ung Fû-tsze guides people on how to mature their characters fully. The cultured arts to which he is referring were ceremonies, music, architecture, chariot driving, the study of characters, and the study of arithmetic.

K'ung Fû-tsze would teach all who sought to learn, even those who could only reimburse him with dried fish. Because sincere teachers, such as K'ung Fû-tsze, would accept dried fish as payment, the wages of a teacher became known as the money of dried fish.

Chapter IX: At all times, K'ung Fû-tsze respected the deceased and those in mourning.

子謂顏淵曰用之則行舍之則藏惟我與爾有是夫

子路曰子行三軍則誰與子曰暴虎馮河死而無悔者

吾不與也必也臨事而懼好謀而成者也

子曰富而可求也雖執鞭之士吾亦為之如不可求從吾所好

子之所慎齊戰疾

子在齊聞韶三月不知肉味曰不圖為樂之至於斯也

CHAPTER X

1. K'ung Fû-tsze told Yen Yüan: Only you and I, when called to office, fulfilled our duties. Only you and I, when no longer called to office, accepted our dismissal.

2. Tsze-lû inquired: If you were leading the military of a great State, who would you trust to work with you?

3. K'ung Fû-tsze said: I would not trust one who would attack a tiger unarmed, who would cross a river without a boat, or who would die without regret. My colleague must be one who proceeds with caution, who accepts a change in plans when it is prudent to do so, and who follows through with everything responsibly.

CHAPTER XI

K'ung Fû-tsze said: If the search for riches were a worthwhile pursuit, I would race a chariot to attain it. But because I do not believe the search for riches to be a worthwhile pursuit, I will follow a different path in search of that in which I believe.

CHAPTER XII

K'ung Fû-tsze exercised great caution concerning issues of fasting, fighting, and illness.

CHAPTER XIII

When in Ch'î, K'ung Fû-tsze listened to the music of Shâo. For the following three months, he had no interest in the taste of flesh. He had never before known that music could be so captivating.

Chapter X: K'ung Fû-tsze praises Yen Yüan stating that when called to duty he accepted gracefully, and when called to resign, he acquiesced gracefully. Tsze-lû was jealous and turned the conversation toward bravery. K'ung Fû-tsze rebuked his daring attitude and said that even during war, he would not want a comrade who was daring.

Chapter XII tells that K'ung Fû-tsze recognized the significance of sacrificial fasting, of declaring war, and of protecting one's health. He took none of these lightly.

Chapter XIII tells of the period when K'ung Fû-tsze, at thirty-six years of age, was traveling from Lû to Ch'î. He found the level of culture manifest within the music so magnificent that his senses were enraptured. His interest in all mundane activities, such as the consumption of food, paled compared to this.

舟有曰夫子為衛君乎子貢曰 諾吾將問之入

曰伯夷叔齊何人也曰古之賢人也曰怨乎

曰求仁而得仁又何怨出曰夫子不為也

子曰飯蔬食飲水曲肱而枕之樂亦在其中矣

不義而富且貴於我如浮雲

子曰加我數年五十以學易可以無大過矣

子所雅言詩書執禮皆雅言也

CHAPTER XIV

1. Yen Yû asked Tsze-kung: Does K'ung Fû-tsze hold the ruler of Wei in respect? Tsze-kung said he would ask him.

2. Tsze-kung asked K'ung Fû-tsze: What do you think of the characters of Po-î and Shû-ch'î? K'ung Fû-tsze said: They were ancient men of worth. Tsze-kung asked: Did they have any regrets concerning their actions? K'ung Fû-tsze replied: They valued virtue, and followed it. Hence, there was nothing for them to regret. On hearing this, Tsze-kung left, saying: K'ung Fû-tsze does not support me.

CHAPTER XV

K'ung Fû-tsze said: With just coarse rice to eat, only water to drink, and with only my bent arm as a pillow, without even trying, I find joy. To me, wealth and glory gained unethically are valueless. They are as fleeting as a floating cloud.

Chapter XVI

K'ung Fû-tsze said: If more years were added to my life, I would devote fifty of them to the study of the *Yî*. Only then, might I be able to live without faults.

CHAPTER XVII

The topics on which K'ung Fû-tsze frequently gave discourse were the *Book of Odes*, the *Book of History*, and the *Rules of Propriety*. He spoke frequently on each of these.

Chapter XIV: The eldest son of Duke Ling of Wei plotted to kill his notorious stepmother, Nan-tsze. Because this plot was discovered, he was forced to flee the country. Later, when Duke Ling died, the son of this eldest son seized power. K'ung Fû-tsze felt that the young son should have relinquished the throne to his father, the rightful heir. He used the examples of Po-î and Shû-ch'î as men of character. Each gave up his throne and his life to do what was morally correct.

Chapter XVI: At age sixty-eight, K'ung Fû-tsze retired to Lû to study the *Yî* (also known as the *I Ching* or the *Book of Changes*) and other classics. He wrote a full analysis of the *I Ching* that has remained a valuable analysis of it to this day. K'ung Fû-tsze recognized that only with intense study of ancient classics might he attain full virtue.

Chapter XVII: K'ung Fû-tsze taught the ancient classics frequently: These include the *Shih Ching* (*Book of Odes*), the *Shu Ching* (*Book of History*), and the *Li Ching* (*Book of Rites*). He valued the wisdom of the ancients and sought to pass it on to others.

葉公問孔子於子路子路不對子曰女奚不曰其為人也

發憤忘食樂以忘憂不知老之將至云爾

子曰我非生而知之者好古敏以求之者也

子不語怪力亂神

子曰三人行必有我師焉擇其善者而從之其不善者而改之

子曰天生德於予桓魋其如予何

CHAPTER XVIII

1. The duke of Sheh asked Tsze-lû about K'ung Fû-tsze. Tsze-lû did not respond.

2. K'ung Fû-tsze said: Why did you not tell him that my Master is simply one who when on a quest for knowledge, forgets his food; one who when joyful in his attainment of knowledge, forgets sorrows; and one who, when enraptured with his understanding of knowledge, does not even notice old age coming.

CHAPTER XIX

K'ung Fû-tsze said: I am not one who was born with knowledge. I am one who values the wisdom of the ancients, and am sincere in searching for it from their teachings.

CHAPTER XX

K'ung Fû-tsze never spoke of supernatural events, acts of violence, rebellion, or spiritual beings.

CHAPTER XXI

K'ung Fû-tsze said: When I am walking with two other individuals, I consider both of them my teachers. I observe their virtues so as to emulate them. I observe their faults so as to avoid them.

CHAPTER XXII

K'ung Fû-tsze said: Heaven produced the virtue that is in me. What can Hwan-T'ûi do to me?

Chapter XVIII: K'ung Fû-tsze describes himself as a simple man who delights in the pursuit, attainment, and understanding of knowledge.

Chapter XX lends insight into those subjects K'ung Fû-tsze preferred to discuss and those he did not. He did not like to discuss transcendent, supernatural, or spiritual matters. Although he held great respect for the mysteries of the unknown, he preferred to discuss those subjects over which humankind had control. One may not be able to change the supernatural, but one can surely change oneself.

Chapter XXII relates to an event that occurred when K'ung Fû-tsze was passing through Sung on his way from Wei to Ch'ăn (possibly in Ch'ăn-châu in Honan province). He and his disciples had been performing ceremonies under a large tree. An officer of Sung hired Hwan-T'ûi, a powerful ruler, to pull down a tree to kill K'ung Fû-tsze. K'ung Fû-tsze remained calm. He had faith that Heaven did not want him to die for he had not yet completed the mission Heaven planned for him.

子曰二三子以我为隐乎吾无隐乎尔

吾无行而不与二三子者是丘也

子以四教文行忠信

子曰圣人吾不得而见之矣得见君子者斯可矣

子曰善人吾不得而见之矣得见有恒者斯可矣亡而为有

虚而为盈约而为泰难乎有恒矣

子钓而不纲弋不射宿

子曰盖有不知而作之者我无是也多闻择其善者而从之

多见而识之知之次也

CHAPTER XXIII

K'ung Fû-tsze asked his disciples: Do you think I harbor secrets? I hide nothing from you. It has been my way not to do anything that I cannot reveal to you.

CHAPTER XXIV

There were four things K'ung Fû-tsze taught: Letters, ethics, that which was useful, and truthfulness.

CHAPTER XXV

1. K'ung Fû-tsze said: I need not meet a sage. I would be content to meet one of true sincerity and true virtue.
2. K'ung Fû-tsze said: I need not meet one who is great. I would be satisfied to meet one who possesses constancy.
3. One possessing constancy: Though without, would not pretend to have; though empty, would not pretend to be full; though poor, would not pretend to be wealthy.

CHAPTER XXVI

K'ung Fû-tsze fished with a fishing rod, not a net. He shot arrows at birds in flight, not at birds perched to roost.

CHAPTER XXVII

K'ung Fû-tsze said: Some act without thinking. I do not. I listen intently, observe, and reflect upon what I see. I select what seems right, and follow it. By acting thusly, by listening to and observing others, I gain wisdom secondarily.

Chapter XXIII tells that K'ung Fû-tsze lived what he taught. Hence, he had nothing to hide.

Chapter XXIV: K'ung Fû-tsze was a practical man. He taught his disciples reading, morality, subjects that were practical, and truthfulness.

Chapter XXV tells of K'ung Fû-tsze's practical nature. Rather than meet a great individual, he would prefer to meet a good one. Rather than meet one who had achieved sudden fame, he would rather meet one who was consistent and faithful.

Chapter XXVI: When fishing or hunting, K'ung Fû-tsze only took that amount he needed. He would take only one fish, not sweep a net to take many. He did not take the life of an animal for mere sport.

Chapter XXVII: K'ung Fû-tsze longed to meet a person with no pretenses. He appreciated people he could trust.

互鄉難與言童子見門人惑子曰與其進也不與其退

也唯何甚人潔己以進與其潔也不保其往也

子曰仁乎遠哉我欲仁斯仁至矣

陳司敗問昭公知禮乎孔子曰知禮孔子退

揖巫馬期而進之曰吾聞君子不黨乎君取於吳

為同姓謂之吳孟子君而知禮孰不知禮

巫馬期以告子曰丘也幸苟有過人必知之

子與人歌而善必使反之而後和之

CHAPTER XXVIII

1. It had been difficult dealing honorably with the people of Hû-hsiang. A young man from Hû-hsiang sought a meeting with K'ung Fû-tsze. K'ung Fû-tsze's disciples were hesitant to arrange it.

2. K'ung Fû-tsze said: I will meet with him. If one seeks my presence, I accept that person for the best in him. I do not look to find the worst. One must not judge harshly. Although people may wash their hands before visiting, and one receives them, can one ever be sure that their hands have always been clean?

CHAPTER XXIX

K'ung Fû-tsze said: Is virtue beyond one's reach? No, it is not. If one just seeks to be virtuous, it is right there within one's grasp.

CHAPTER XXX

1. The minister of justice of Ch'ăn asked K'ung Fû-tsze if the duke of Châo was a man of propriety. K'ung Fû-tsze said he was.

2. After K'ung Fû-tsze left, the minister bowed, came forward to Wû-mâ Ch'î, and said: I have heard that one of character is not biased. Can one who is biased still have character? The duke of Châo married a daughter of the house of Wû, a woman with his same surname. He concealed this by calling her: "The elder Tsze of Wû." The duke must have known the rules. If he did not, then who did?

3. When Wû-mâ Ch'î told this to K'ung Fû-tsze, K'ung Fû-tsze said: I feel fortunate that people easily know my faults.

CHAPTER XXXI

If K'ung Fû-tsze was with people who were singing well, he would ask them to repeat the song, so that he might sing along.

Chapter XXVIII: K'ung Fû-tsze never refused anyone who sought his teachings. He recognized that one never truly knows the past conduct of any individual, even those who are most respected. Hence, one should never judge anyone in advance.

Chapter XXX: K'ung Fû-tsze stated that Duke Châo, a man from his own state of Lû, was virtuous. The minister, however knew that Duke Châo had married a woman of the same surname. This was forbidden. The minister knew K'ung Fû-tsze was not truthful. K'ung Fû-tsze was not upset, because all this showed was that he would not ridicule the sovereign of his own state. K'ung Fû-tsze considered being loyal more important than discussing the details of his sovereign's personal relationships. Hence, K'ung Fû-tsze accepted this criticism lightly.

子曰文莫吾猶人也躬行君子則吾未之有得

子曰若聖與仁則吾豈敢抑為之不厭誨人不倦

則可謂云爾已矣公西華曰正唯弟子不能學也

子疾病子路請禱子曰有諸子路對曰有之

誄曰禱爾於上下神祇子曰丘之禱久矣

子曰奢則不孫儉則固與其不孫也寧固

子曰君子坦蕩蕩小人長戚戚

子溫而厲威而不猛恭而安

CHAPTER XXXII

K'ung Fû-tsze said: In letters I may be equal to others. But in character, I have not yet attained the high level of those who always live up to what they profess.

CHAPTER XXXIII

K'ung Fû-tsze said: I dare not equate myself to a sage or to one who has attained perfect virtue. I am simply one who strives unceasingly to attain virtue, and who teaches others without tire. I am nothing more. Kung-hsî Hwâ said: These are just the qualities we, your disciples, value in you.

CHAPTER XXXIV

K'ung Fû-tsze was gravely ill. Tsze-lû requested leave to pray for him. K'ung Fû-tsze said, Can such prayers really help? Tsze-lû replied: They can. The Eulogies state: "We pray to the spirits of the upper and lower worlds." K'ung Fû-tsze said: Then I have been praying for quite a long time.

CHAPTER XXXV

K'ung Fû-tsze said: Immoderation leads to lack of discipline. Frugality leads to stinginess. It is not as bad to be stingy as it is to lack discipline.

CHAPTER XXXVI

K'ung Fû-tsze said: One of character is content and peaceful. One without character always finds cause for discontent.

CHAPTER XXXVII

K'ung Fû-tsze was humble, yet dignified; awe inspiring, yet peaceful; serious, yet tolerant.

Chapter XXXII: K'ung Fû-tsze admits that although he had acquired a tremendous amount of scholarly knowledge, he had not yet perfected his own character to the level he sought.

Chapter XXXIV: Tsze-lû asked leave to pray for K'ung Fû-tsze. K'ung Fû-tsze was hesitant to let him go. He said that prayer is needed for one who needs to repent. He felt that his life had been one long prayer, and there was no reason to specifically perform prayer now. He felt at peace.

泰伯第八

子曰恭伯其可謂至德也已矣三以天下讓民無得而稱焉

子曰恭而無禮則勞慎而無禮則葸勇而無禮則亂直而無禮則絞君子篤於親則民興於仁故舊不遺則民不偷

曾子有疾召門弟子曰啟予足啟予手詩云戰戰兢兢如臨深淵如履薄冰而今而後吾知免夫小子

BOOK VIII   T'ÂI-PO
Eldest son of King T'âi

CHAPTER I

K'ung Fû-tsze said: It may be said that T'âi-po attained the highest level of virtue. Three times, he declined the kingdom. After this, he quietly left the region, without explaining his ideals to anyone. He left without telling others so that others would not praise him.

CHAPTER II

1. K'ung Fû-tsze said: Respectfulness, in one without moral values becomes mere protocol. Rules, in one without moral values becomes intimidation. Courage, in one without moral values becomes defiance. Candidness, in one without moral values becomes rudeness.
2. When those in positions of responsibility treat their families well, the rest of society will all respect one another. When those in positions of responsibility never neglect old friends, the rest of society will care for one another.

CHAPTER III

When the philosopher Tsăng became ill, he called the disciples of his school, and said: Uncover my feet and hands. It is written in the *Book of Poetry*: We should live carefully and cautious, as if on the edge of a steep chasm or on thin ice. I have acted thusly. Now and hereafter, my children, I will depart from the burdens of this body.

Chapter I discusses the self-sacrificing virtues of T'âi-po. T'âi-po was the eldest son of King T'âi. T'âi-po did not approve of his father's aggressive actions. King T'âi sought to hand the throne down to his sagely grandson, Ch'ang, the son of his third son. T'âi-po, recognized the sagely qualities of Ch'ang, so he, too, wanted the throne passed on to him. Because of this, T'âi-po quietly withdrew to live in the barbarian region of the north. Ch'ang eventually attained the throne and became King Wăn, founder of the Châu dynasty.

Chapter II: K'ung Fû-tsze explains that formality, devoid of moral values, is hypocritical.

Chapter III: The ailing philosopher Tsăng wanted his disciples to be cautious and careful concerning their own health. He told them to uncover his hands and feet to observe how he had cared for his health during his life. He was respectful of the body given him by his parents. He considered caring for his health an act of filial piety.

曾子有疾，孟敬子問之。曾子言曰：「鳥之將死，其鳴也哀；人之將死，其言也善。君子所貴乎道者三：動容貌，斯遠暴慢矣；正顏色，斯近信矣；出辭氣，斯遠鄙倍矣。籩豆之事，則有司存。」

曾子曰：「以能問於不能，以多問於寡；有若無，實若虛，犯而不校。昔者吾友嘗從事於斯矣。」

曾子曰：「可以託六尺之孤，可以寄百里之命，臨大節而不可奪也。君子人與？君子人也。」

曾子曰：「士不可以不弘毅，任重而道遠。仁以為己任，不亦重乎？死而後已，不亦遠乎？」

CHAPTER IV

1. Philosopher Tsăng was extremely ill. Măng Chăng inquired about his health.

2. Tsăng said: When a bird is about to die, its notes are mournful. When a human is about to die, his words are truthful.

3. There are three principles of conduct that one in a position of responsibility should follow: be neither violent nor rash in action; be neither vulgar nor improper in speech; and be sincere in conduct. As for the protocols of sacrifice, leave these to the officials.

CHAPTER V

Philosopher Tsăng sought to teach his disciples about his friend who: though wise, graciously accepted advice from those with less wisdom; though gifted, acted respectfully towards those less gifted; though able to live in abundance, preferred to live in simplicity; though possessing great knowledge, respected the knowledge of others; though offended, did not seek retribution.

CHAPTER VI

The philosopher Tsăng asked: Do you not consider one who can be trusted to care for an orphan prince, who is able to rule a state of a hundred lî, and who is capable of adhering to principle even in times of crisis, to be a fine individual? Certainly, this is a fine person.

CHAPTER VII

1. Philosopher Tsăng said: A scholar must be broad-minded in outlook and strong in character. For a scholar's responsibilities are heavy and his journey is long.

2. Moral virtue is a burden a scholar must bear. It ceases only at death. Is this not a long, heavy burden?

Chapters III through VII concern the philosopher Tsăng. He was one of K'ung Fû-tsze's principal disciples. Though he was considered slow in natural abilities, K'ung Fû-tsze admired him for his filial piety and morality.

Chapter V is describing the character of Yen Yüan, a friend of philosopher Tsăng. Yen Yüan, although imprisoned in wood shackles, remained a man of impeccable character.

Chapter VII: In ancient China, scholars filled many official government positions. These scholars were responsible for analyzing events of the past to determine how the ruler should lead the country in the future.

子曰興於詩立於禮成於樂

子曰民可使由之不可使知之

子曰好勇疾貧亂也人而不仁疾之已甚亂也

子曰如有周公之才之美使驕其吝其餘不足觀也已

子曰三年學不至於穀不易得也

子曰篤信好學守死善道危邦不入亂邦不居天下有道則見無道則隱邦有道貧賤焉恥也邦無道富且貴焉恥也

CHAPTER VIII

1. K'ung Fû-tsze said: Through the *Odes*, one's mind is awakened.
2, Through the *Rules of Propriety*, one's character is established.
3. Through *Music*, one's culture is refined.

CHAPTER IX

K'ung Fû-tsze said: Although people can be guided towards a path, they can not be made to follow it.

CHAPTER X

K'ung Fû-tsze said: The daring, when faced with poverty, will rebel. The non-virtuous, when faced with adversity, will rebel.

CHAPTER XI

K'ung Fû-tsze said: Although one may possess many of the honorable qualities of the duke of Châu, if one is either proud and stingy, these beneficial qualities lose their value.

CHAPTER XII

K'ung Fû-tsze said: It is rare to find one who has pursued a path of self-cultivation for three years, who has not attained virtue.

CHAPTER XIII

1. K'ung Fû-tsze said: One who seeks to be sincere and virtuous throughout one's entire life, has lived honorably.
2. Such an individual will never falter or waver in purpose. When a moral government is in power, such an individual will rise to the top. When an immoral government is in power, such an individual will retreat from any participation in it.

Chapter VIII: K'ung Fû-tsze tells of the importance of attaining knowledge of ancient classics in the development of one's character.

Chapter X is a lesson to rulers. Although insubordination may emerge from amongst the ranks of the rebellious poor, during times of adversity, it may also emerge from absolutely any individual who lacks values.

Chapter XI tells how important K'ung Fû-tsze thought it was for one to avoid negative qualities such as pride and stinginess.

子曰不在其位不謀其政

子曰師摯之始關雎之亂洋洋乎盈耳哉

子曰狂而不直侗而不愿悾悾而不信吾不知之矣

子曰學如不及猶恐失之

子曰巍巍乎舜禹之有天下也而不與焉

3. When a country is governed ethically, one may feel ashamed if one is poor and unrecognized. When a country is governed unethically, one should feel ashamed if one attains riches and status.

CHAPTER XIV
K'ung Fû-tsze said: One who does not bear the responsibility for running the government, should not interfere with how others do.

CHAPTER XV
K'ung Fû-tsze said: When the music director Chih entered office, the finale of the *Kwan Tsü* became magnificent and pleasing to the ears.

CHAPTER XVI
K'ung Fû-tsze said: I find it difficult to deal with those who are self-assued, yet not forthright; uneducated, yet not attentive; direct, yet not really sincere.

CHAPTER XVII
K'ung Fû-tsze said: Search for knowledge as if you can never attain enough. Cling to it as though you may lose it.

CHAPTER XVIII
K'ung Fû-tsze said: How nobly did Shun and Yü rule the empire. They never sought personal gain for themselves.

Chapter XIII, passage 3 tells that one may feel ashamed of being poor when a nation is run morally, because one may not have contributed to its growth. But one should feel ashamed of having amassed riches when a nation is governed unethically, because one's profits may have been obtained corruptly.

Chapter XIV: Unless one strives to be part of the solution to a problem, one should not blame others who are trying to solve it.

Chapter XV: It has been difficult for scholars to interpret the meaning of this chapter. It may relate to K'ung Fû-tsze's belief that one may obtain insight into the moral values of a society by listening to its music.

Chapter XVI: K'ung Fû-tsze laments the difficulties in dealing with those who are neither gifted in abilities nor honorable in character.

Chapter XVIII: Emperor Shun assumed the throne in 2255 BCE and Emperor Yü in 2205 BCE. Neither attained the throne through inheritance, but rather because of their talents and virtuous characters.

子曰大哉堯之為君也巍巍乎唯天為大唯堯則之

蕩蕩乎民無能名焉巍巍乎其有成功也煥乎其有文章

舜有臣五人而天下治武王曰予有亂臣十人

孔子曰才難不其然乎唐虞之際於斯為盛有婦人焉

九人而已三分天下有其二以服事殷周之德

其可謂至德也已矣

子曰禹吾無間然矣菲飲食而致孝乎鬼神

惡衣服而致美乎黻冕卑宮室而盡力乎溝洫

禹吾無間然矣

CHAPTER XIX

1. K'ung Fû-tsze said: Yâo was an excellent and noble sovereign. Although Heaven is sublime, Yâo approached it. His character was so pure, that people could not describe it.

2. His accomplishments were majestic and his regulations virtuous.

CHAPTER XX

1. With only five ministers, Shun was able to govern his empire well.

2. King Wû said: I have ten capable ministers.

3. K'ung Fû-tsze said: Capable people are difficult to find. Only during the dynasties of T'ang and Yü were there more capable people than during the Châu dynasty. During the Châu dynasty, the monarchy could not find more than nine able male ministers. Therefore, they made a woman the tenth minister.

4. King Wăn ruled two thirds of the empire, yet he always remained respectful of the doctrines of the Yin dynasty. The house of Châu attained the highest level of virtue.

CHAPTER XXI

K'ung Fû-tsze said: I find no crevice in the character of Yü. He consumed coarse food and drink. He showed the utmost piety towards his ancestors. The garments he wore every day were poor, yet the cap and apron he wore for sacrifices were elegant. For his home, he chose a low, common house. He expended all his resources constructing ditches and water channels for the people. I find no crevice in the character of Yü.

Chapter XX: Ministers who were both capable and honorable were few. The five ministers of the Shun dynasty were the superintendents of works, agriculture, instruction, justice, and lands. The female minister during King Wû's reign was either his mother or wife. The meaning of the fourth passage remains obscure.

Chapter XXI praises the virtuous ruler Yü. The term "no crevice" means no flaws. Yü lived selflessly, showing respect both to his ancestors and to his people. The ditches and water channels he funded delineated the boundaries of fields and also communicated with larger conduits of water. During times of drought, they were used for irrigation. During times of flood, they served as conduits to carry off excess flood waters.

子罕言利與命與仁

達巷黨人曰大哉孔子博學而無所成名子聞之
謂門弟子曰吾何執執御乎執射乎吾執御矣

子曰麻冕禮也今也純儉吾從眾拜下禮也
今拜乎上泰也雖違眾吾從下

BOOK IX TSZE HAN
The Master Seldom

CHAPTER I

The subjects about which K'ung Fû-tsze seldom engaged in conversation were: matters of finance, the decisions of Heaven, and criticisms of the virtue of others.

CHAPTER II

1. An individual from the village of Tâ-hsiang said: Great indeed is the philosopher K'ung! His learning is extensive, but he is not famous for any skill in particular.
2. K'ung Fû-tsze heard this and asked his disciples: What skill shall I practice? Shall I practice chariot driving, or shall I practice archery? I will practice chariot driving.

CHAPTER III

1. K'ung Fû-tsze said: In ancient times, a linen cap was used during ceremonies. Now a silk cap is used. It is economical and has become standard practice.
2. During ancient times, the rules of ceremony prescribed that one bow to the prince from below the platform. Now the rules of ceremony prescribe bowing only after ascending the platform. I find that presumptuous. So I continue to bow from below.

Most of the chapters in Book IX deal with K'ung Fû-tsze's teachings, character, and mode of living.

Chapter I: K'ung Fû-tsze's concerns were oriented towards the cultivation of morality and integrity. He was not concerned with mundane or superficial issues. His goal was the advancement of humankind. He was beyond discussions concerning finances. He believed that people should leave the role of Heaven to Heaven, and concentrate on refining their own characters. He also felt that it was virtually impossible to determine if any individual possessed perfect virtue.

Chapter II: K'ung Fû-tsze mocks the words of the person who said he was not famous for anything in particular. K'ung Fû-tsze felt his teachings of virtue and morality were of greater significance than excelling in one skill.

Chapter III: K'ung Fû-tsze was not adverse to changing with the times, but only if such an action was not sacrilegious. He considered bowing to the monarchy from a position equal to or higher than his position to be sacrilegious.

子絕四毋意毋必毋固毋我

子畏於匡曰文王既沒文不在茲乎天之將喪斯
文也後死者不得與於斯文也天之未喪斯文也
匡人其如予何

大宰問於子貢曰夫子聖者與何其多能也子貢曰
固天縱之將聖又多能也子聞之大宰知我乎
吾少也故多賤鄙事君子多乎哉不多也
牢曰子云吾不試故藝

CHAPTER IV

The four negative traits that K'ung Fû-tsze had succeeded in eliminating from his character were: harboring foregone conclusions, holding unswerving prejudices, being stubborn, and having an ego.

CHAPTER V

1. K'ung Fû-tsze left the state of K'wang in fear.
2. K'ung Fû-tsze said: After the death of King Wăn, I have dedicated my life to cultivating virtue.
3. If Heaven had wished me and my message to perish, then I, a mere mortal, would have perished. It is Heaven that has given me this cause. If Heaven does not wish truth to perish, what can the people of K'wang do to harm me?

CHAPTER VI

1. A high officer asked Tsze-kung: May one not say that your Master, K'ung Fû-tsze, is a sage? How diverse are his abilities.
2. Tsze-kung said: Certainly Heaven has endowed him with a multitude of abilities. He is like a sage.
3. K'ung Fû-tsze, hearing the conversation, questioned: Does this officer really know me? When I was young, my means were humble. To sustain myself, I learned many trades, mostly common ones. Heaven gave me responsibilities. I fulfilled all of these with sincerity. Heaven gave me responsibilities. Through hard work and sincere effort, I turned these into abilities.
4. Lâo stated that K'ung Fû-tsze said: It was only because I had no official employment, that I acquired so many skills.

Chapter V discusses an incident that occurred in the state of K'wang. K'wang was probably a border town along the banks of the Yellow River, between the states of Wei and Cheng. K'ung Fû-tsze had been mistaken for an officer from the state of Lû because he resembled him. The situation became worst because his driver also become involved in an altercation with a person in K'wang. K'ung Fû-tsze was captured and imprisoned for five days. After his escape, K'ung Fû-tsze felt that Heaven had saved him, because It did not want the truth he was teaching to perish.

Chapter VI: K'ung Fû-tsze dispels the notion that neither he, nor anyone else seeking to live virtuously, has been endowed with these qualities by Heaven. He said he was just a common man who, lacking skill in one trade, ended up learning several. He merely sought to follow a virtuous life and felt that such was within the reach of all people.

子曰吾有知乎哉無知也有鄙夫問於我空空如也

我叩其兩端而竭焉

子曰鳳鳥不至河不出圖吾已矣夫

子見齊衰者冕衣裳者與瞽者

見之雖少必作過之必趨

顏淵喟然歎曰仰之彌高鑽之彌堅瞻之在前

忽焉在後夫子循循然善誘人博我以文

約我以禮欲罷不能既竭吾才

如有所立卓爾雖欲從之末由也已

CHAPTER VII

K'ung Fû-tsze asked: Do I truly possesses knowledge? I do not think so. It may only seem that way because if people without knowledge of a subject ask me a question, I research it, look at it from all perspectives, and explain all of these as best I can.

CHAPTER VIII

K'ung Fû-tsze said: The Făng bird has not come; The river sends forth no map. There is no chance of enlightenment for humankind!

CHAPTER IX

When K'ung Fû-tsze saw a person in mourning clothes, a person in official garments, or a person who was blind, even if they were younger than him, he would rise up. If he were walking, he would pass them quickly, as a sign of respect.

CHAPTER X

1. Yen Yüan praised K'ung Fû-tsze's doctrines, saying: Each time I study them, they seem more profound. Each time I bore into them, they seem more solid. Each time I try to grasp them, they seem to extend further.

2. K'ung Fû-tsze, in an orderly, skilful manner, draws in his students. He opens their minds to learning, and leads them to self motivation.

3. When I tried to abandon the study of his doctrines, I could not do so. When I felt my abilities waning, an elusive lure pulled me back in. Though I sought to follow and grasp all of them, I could not.

Chapter VII: K'ung Fû-tsze lays aside claims that he possesses great wisdom, stating that his only gift is his desire to share what he knows with others.

Chapter VIII: K'ung Fû-tsze tells of his disappointment by comparing it to a legend. The legend tells that when a sage finally ascends to the throne, and moral principles prevail, a Făng bird will appear. The Făng is the male of a species of bird called the phoenix. This sighting will be the sign that a golden age in which righteousness will triumph throughout the world, has begun. The legend goes on to say that after the phoenix appears, a dragon horse, an animal with the head of a dragon and the body of a horse, with specific markings on its back, will emerge from the Yellow River. It will be carrying a magical map that guides the sage in interpreting the hexagrams of the *I Ching*. K'ung Fû-tsze said he sees no sign of the Făng.

Chapter X is a discussion by Yen Yüan, also called Hûi. He was K'ung Fû-tsze's favorite disciple. He greatly valued K'ung Fû-tsze's teachings.

子疾病子路使門人為臣病間曰久矣哉由之行詐也

無臣而為有臣吾誰欺欺天乎且予與其死於臣之手也

無寧死於二三子之手乎且予縱不得大葬予死於道路乎

子貢曰有美玉於斯韞匵而藏諸求善賈而沽諸子曰

沽之哉沽之哉我待賈者也

子欲居九夷或曰陋如之何子曰

君子居之何陋之有

子曰吾自衛反魯然後樂正雅頌各得其所

CHAPTER XI

1. K'ung Fû-tsze became very ill. Tsze-lû asked his disciples to pretend they were ministers.

2. After remission of his illness, Kung Fû-tsze said: Tsze-lû has been deceitful, pretending I have ministers when I do not. Who does he think he is fooling? One cannot fool Heaven.

3. Moreover, I have no desire to die in the hands of ministers. I prefer to die amongst you, my disciples. Although I may not obtain an official funeral, it is not as though I am dying alone on the road.

CHAPTER XII

Tsze-kung asked: If one has a valuable gem, should one place it in a case and save it, or should one sell it for a good price? K'ung Fû-tsze said: Sell it. Sell it. But wait for a good price.

CHAPTER XIII

1. K'ung Fû-tsze considered going to live amongst the nine wild tribes of the east.

2. Someone said: They are quite savage. Why would you consider this? K'ung Fû-tsze said: If someone with higher values were to dwell amongst them, would not their primitive values abate?

CHAPTER XIV

K'ung Fû-tsze said: I returned from Wei to Lû. By then the culture had reformed so that the music played at royal festivals and at eulogies to the rulers of the various dynasties was used appropriately.

Chapter XI tells of a time when K'ung Fû-tsze had become very ill. His disciples thought he might die and sought to give him the recognition they felt he deserved. They pretended to be ministers of the state, rather than just disciples. When K'ung Fû-tsze recovered, he told them that he did not want such glory. He preferred to die amongst his disciples, those he cherished.

Chapter XII shows what a practical individual Kung Fû-tsze was. He saw no sense in hiding gems. The funds these gems commanded could be put to practical use. One must not rush to squander one's assets, but wait for a good price and use them wisely.

Chapter XIV tells that when K'ung Fû-tsze returned to his home state of Lû at an older age, he felt content hearing the royal music being played correctly. He believed this indicated that a high standard of morality and propriety had been attained.

子曰出則事公卿　入則事父兄喪事不敢不勉

不為酒困何有於我哉

子在川上曰逝者如斯夫不舍晝夜

子曰吾未見好德如好色者也

子曰譬如為山未成一簣止吾止也譬如平地

雖覆一簣進吾往也

子曰語之而不惰者其回也與

子謂顏淵曰惜乎吾見其進也未見其止也

CHAPTER XV

K'ung Fû-tsze stated: When away, serve your ministers faithfully. When at home, serve your father and elder brothers dutifully. When at funeral rites, pay attention to detail. When drinking, do not become overcome by wine. I wonder if I, too, have attained these virtues?

CHAPTER XVI

Standing by a stream, K'ung Fû-tsze said: All of life passes by just like this, never ceasing day or night!

CHAPTER XVII

K'ung Fû-tsze said: I have yet to meet one who loves virtue as much as one loves beauty.

CHAPTER XVIII

K'ung Fû-tsze said: The process of learning is like that of building a hill. If one stops even with one basket left to go, it is as though one has gone down to the ground level and must start over again. But if one is consistent, each time trudging upward, even if only throwing one more basketful of earth each time, one will succeed.

CHAPTER XIX

K'ung Fû-tsze said: Once having made a promise, Hûi has never gone back on his word.

CHAPTER XX

K'ung Fû-tsze said: Hûi advances constantly. I have never seen him stop in his progress.

Chapter XV: K'ung Fû-tsze searches within himself as to whether or not he has attained the levels of virtue and respect that he has preached to others.

Chapter XVI: K'ung Fû-tsze reflects on the perpetual flow of life, stopping for no human being.

Chapter XVII: K'ung Fû-tsze speaks honestly and directly. He states that he has yet to meet an individual who preferred virtue over beauty.

Chapter XVIII: K'ung Fû-tsze encourages students not to disrupt their studies, lest when they commence them again, they may need to start at the beginning.

Chapter XIX: This praise of Hûi may have been given after his death.

子曰苗而不秀者有矣夫秀而不實者有矣夫

子曰後生可畏焉知來者之不如今也

四十五十而無聞焉斯亦不足畏也已

子曰法語之言能無從乎改之為貴巽與之言能無說乎

繹之為貴說而不繹從而不改吾末如之何也已矣

子曰主忠信毋友不如己者過則憚勿改

子曰三軍可奪帥也匹夫不可奪志也

子曰衣敝縕袍與衣狐貉者立而不恥者其由也與

不忮不求何用不臧子路終身誦之子曰是道何足以臧

K'ung Fû-tsze said: There are cases where a blade sprouts, yet a plant does not grow. There are cases where a flower blossoms, yet a fruit does not come forth.

CHAPTER XXII
K'ung Fû-tsze said: Treat the young with respect. One does not know if their achievements will someday equal, or even exceed, one's own. Only when an individual reaches the age of forty or fifty will the extent of one's achievements become apparent.

CHAPTER XXIII
K'ung Fû-tsze said: One should not recoil from hearing firm words of advice. But they are of no value if one does not heed them and improve one's conduct. One prefers gentle words of advice. But they are of no value if one is merely pleased with the sound of these words, and does not delve into their significance and follow them.

CHAPTER XXIV
K'ung Fû-tsze said: Hold faithfulness and sincerity as one's most valuable virtues. Have no friends whose characters are not equal to one's own. When one recognizes one's own faults, one should not fear abandoning them.

CHAPTER XXV
K'ung Fû-tsze said: The commander of a State may be carried off, but the will of an individual of character, even if that individual is of humble status, can never be taken.

CHAPTER XXVI
1. K'ung Fû-tsze said: Yû, dressed in tattered robes of quilted hemp, even when standing beside men dressed in furs, was not ashamed of his status. Who can equal this?

Chapter XXI: One must proceed on with one's mission, even though one may never know if the intended goal will be met.

Chapter XXII: One should treat the young with respect. Their lack of achievement is only a manifestation of their youth. Only years later will it be known if their achievements surpass one's own.

子曰歲寒然後知松柏之後彫也

子曰知者不惑仁者不憂勇者不懼

子曰可與共學未可與適道可與適道未可與立

可与立未可與權

唐棣之華偏其反而豈不爾思室是遠而子曰未之思也夫何遠之有

遠之有

2. Yû does not dislike anyone. He does not seek to acquire possessions for himself. How can he not but be considered virtuous?
3. Tsze-lû kept repeating the words of an *Ode*. K'ung Fû-tsze said:
Such actions alone are not sufficient to constitute perfect virtue.

CHAPTER XXVII

K'ung Fû-tsze said: When the cold weather sets in, the pine and the
cypress are the last to lose their leaves.

CHAPTER XXVIII

K'ung Fû-tsze said: With wisdom, one overcomes confusion. With
virtue, one overcomes indecision. With strength of character, one
overcomes fear.

CHAPTER XXIX

K'ung Fû-tsze said: There are some with whom one may study, but
with whom one may not have the same values. There are some with
whom one may hold the same values, but with whom one may not
follow the same lifestyle. There are some with whom one may follow the same lifestyle, but with whom one cannot agree on every
issue.

CHAPTER XXX

1. How the flowers of the aspen-plum tremble and remain alone!
Do I ever stop thinking of you? But, alas, I cannot see you for your
house is too far.
2. K'ung Fû-tsze said: If he truly loved her, the distance would not
have been too great.

Chapter XXVI, passage 3: K'ung Fû-tsze states that by reciting words from an *Ode*,
one cannot attain excellence. Excellence is attained through action, not words.

Chapter XXVII: One can be judged best by one's actions during times of adversity
(such as during cold, lean winters).

Chapter XXIX: People have various relationships with others in different aspects of
their lives. One cannot expect to agree with others on all issues.

Chapter XXX relates to a passage from the *Book of Odes*. Although the passage
sounds romantic, K'ung Fû-tsze saw right through it. He said that if the young man
really loved the young woman, he would have managed to see her no matter how
great the distance separating them.

孔子於鄉黨恂恂如也似不能言者

其在宗廟朝廷便便言唯謹爾

朝與下大夫言侃侃如也與上大夫言誾誾如也

君在踧踖如也與與如也

君召使擯色勃如也足躩如也揖所與立左右手

衣前後襜如也趨進翼如也賓退必復命曰賓不顧矣

BOOK X HEANG TANG
The Village

CHAPTER I

1. In his village, K'ung Fû-tsze was unassuming and humble. He barely spoke.
2. In the ancestral temple or in the court of the prince, he was well known. He spoke on every issue with detailed, careful confidence.

CHAPTER II

1. In the court, when with officers of the lower rank, his speech was friendly and mild. With those of the higher rank, his speech was serious and direct.
2. When the sovereign was present, his speech was respectful and extremely refined. He remained composed and cautious.

CHAPTER III

1. When the prince called upon K'ung Fû-tsze to receive a visitor, his demeanor changed. He moved his legs slowly and spoke so quietly that he barely seemed to breathe.
2. He leaned towards the other officers with whom he stood, and moved both his arms as needed. At all times, he kept the front and back folds his robe politely adjusted.
3. He advanced forward, moving his arms with firm and brisk regularity.
4. When the guest departed, he would report to the prince, saying: The visitor is no longer turning.

Book X contains several of K'ung Fû-tsze's personal and professional characteristics. It describes his demeanor in various situations.

Chapters I and II: When at home in his village of Lû and with those of lower rank, K'ung Fû-tsze was mild and affable. In court, he remained serious and respectful.

Chapter III: K'ung Fû-tsze's position in court was one of high rank. He received visitors from other states, usually princes, and spoke cautiously, leaning closely towards other officers as he relayed messages. He maintained his dignity at all times. After such meetings, guests were to turn around repeatedly and bow while leaving. The host was to remain stationary until the bowing had been completed. When the guests had finished, and when they had moved far enough away so they could no longer turn around to see or hear the prince, K'ung Fû-tsze would inform the prince that the guest was no longer turning (around bowing).

入公門鞠躬如也如不容立不中門行不履閾

過位色勃如也足躩如也其言似不足者

攝齊升堂鞠躬如也屏氣似不息者出降一等逞顏色

怡怡如也沒階趨進翼如也復其位踧踖如也

執圭鞠躬如也如不勝上如揖下如授勃如戰色

足蹜蹜如有循享禮有容色私覿愉愉如也

CHAPTER IV

1. Upon entering the palace gate, K'ung Fû-tsze bent his body lower than was needed, as if the gate was too low to admit him.
2. While standing, K'ung Fû-tsze did not remain in the middle of the gateway. While passing in and out, he did not step on the threshold.
3. When passing the prince's palace, even when no one was in, K'ung Fû-tsze's demeanor changed. He moved slowly and spoke so quietly that his voice was barely audible.
4. When ascending the reception hall, K'ung Fû-tsze held his robe up with both hands, bent his body, and held his breath, as though he dare not breathe.
5. When the reception was over, as soon as he descended even one step, he began to relax. When he reached the bottom step, he would move rapidly to his quarters, swinging his arms. Only after he entered his quarters, would he totally relax.

CHAPTER V

1. When carrying the jade tablet of the ruler, K'ung Fû-tsze bent his body as though barely able to bear its weight. He did not hold it higher than his hands while bowing, nor lower than his hands when passing it on to another. His demeanor appeared burdened with responsibility and he shuffled his feet as though unable to lift them off the ground.
2. When presenting official gifts, he remained composed.
3. During private audiences, he remained content and pleasing.

Chapter IV: The royal court had four divisions, each was to be entered through its own gate. K'ung Fû-tsze bent his body in reverence, lower than needed, when passing through them. One side of each gate was for ingress and the other side for egress. Only the ruler was permitted to stand in the middle of the gate or on the threshold. K'ung Fû-tsze adhered to all these acts of propriety. Prior to, during, and after receptions, K'ung Fû-tsze always treated the prince with respect.

Chapter V: When carrying the various ritual jade pieces to each of the princes (each piece consistent with the particular prince's status), K'ung Fû-tsze treated each with respect. He never raised his hands higher than the level of the jade piece.

君子不以紺緅飾，紅紫不以為褻服。當暑，袗絺綌，必表而出之。緇衣羔裘，素衣麑裘，黃衣狐裘。褻裘長，短右袂。必有寢衣，長一身有半。狐貉之厚以居。去喪，無所不佩。非帷裳，必殺之。羔裘玄冠不以弔。吉月，必朝服而朝。齊，必有明衣，布。必有齊，必變食，居必遷坐。

CHAPTER VI

1. K'ung Fû-tsze would not wear deep purple or deep red colors in any of his ornamental garments.
2. Even in informal garments, he would not wear pink or red.
3. In warm weather, he used only one garment of coarse or fine texture over an undergarment.
4. He wore a black garment over lamb fur; a white garment over deer fur; and a yellow garment over fox fur.
5. The fur robe of his undergarment was long, with the right sleeve short.
6. He made sure that his sleeping garment was half as long as his body.
7. When at home, he wore thick furs of fox or badger.
8. After periods of mourning, he would carry a small handkerchief and a knife.
9. His undergarment, except when required to be as wide on top as at the bottom, was made of silk cut narrow above and wide below.
10. On condolence visits, he would not wear lamb's fur or a black cap.
11. On the first day of each month he would put on court robes, and present himself at court.

CHAPTER VII

1. While fasting, K'ung Fû-tsze considered it necessary to wear bright, clean linen garments.
2. While fasting, he considered it necessary to restrict his diet and to serenely sit in a different location of his apartment than he usually sat.

Chapter VI describes K'ung Fû-tsze's mode of dress during various occasions. Deep red was created by dipping fabric in red dye three times and black dye twice. When in private, K'ung Fû-tsze preferred garments woven from fibers made of vines of creeping plants. He wore lamb's fur in court and fawn fur in embassies. He wore fox during sacrifices.

Chapter VI continues to describe the sleeping garment K'ung Fû-tsze used when fasting. He carried the small knife after periods of mourning to open knots. When visiting mourners, he would not wear black, because white was the official color of mourning. Even after he retired from office, he presented himself in court on the first of each month, termed the fortunate day of the moon, out of respect.

Chapter VII relates to fasting from wine and herbs, not from all foods.

食不厭精，膾不厭細。食饐而餲，魚餒而肉敗，不食。色惡不食，臭惡不食，失飪不食，不時不食。割不正不食，不得其醬不食。肉雖多，不使勝食氣。唯酒無量，不及亂。沽酒市脯不食。不撤薑食，不多食。祭於公，不宿肉。祭肉不出三日，出三日不食之矣。食不語，寢不言。雖疏食菜羹，瓜祭，必齊如也。席不正不坐。鄉人飲酒，杖者出，斯出矣。鄉人儺，朝服而立於阼階。

CHAPTER VIII

1. K'ung Fû-tsze preferred his rice cleaned well and his meat cut small.

2. He would not eat food decayed from heat or moisture, sour or moldy rice, putrefied fish, or tainted meat. He did not eat anything discolored, foul-smelling, poorly cooked, or out of season.

3. He did not eat meat improperly cut or without its proper sauce.

4. Even when there were large quantities of meat, he did not eat more meat then rice. He did not restrict himself from wine, but he would not drink enough to become confused.

5. He did not drink wine or eat meat exposed in the market.

6. He ate ginger at every meal.

7. He did not eat much.

8. When assisting at temple sacrifice, he did not keep meat overnight. After family sacrifice, he did not keep or eat meat over three days.

9. He did not speak either when eating or when lying in bed.

10. Even when all he had to eat was coarse rice and vegetable soup, he always offered some to his ancestors during worship.

CHAPTER IX

If his mat was not straight, he did not sit on it.

CHAPTER X

1. At village drinking gatherings, K'ung Fû-tsze would leave after those carrying staffs left.

2. If villagers performed ceremonies to drive out spirits, K'ung Fû-tsze would put on court robes and stand on the eastern steps to greet them.

Chapter VIII: The meat referred to was beef, mutton and fish. Before K'ung Fû-tsze ate, he always offered food for ancestor worship. If this food had been left out long enough to decay, however, he would not eat it. He was careful about his health and that was why he did not eat any food that had decayed or that was out of season. He ate ginger, a digestive aid, at every meal. As was Chinese custom, he did not speak while eating.

Chapter IX tells that he did not sit on his mat if it was not in the official position.

Chapter X: K'ung Fû-tsze's respected the villagers. People over age sixty carried staffs. He did not leave before the elders out of respect. The eastern steps were the location from which one greeted guests. K'ung Fû-tsze greeted villagers with respect.

問人於他邦再拜而送之

康子饋藥拜而受之曰丘未達不敢嘗

廄焚子退朝曰傷人乎不問馬

君賜食必正席先嘗之君賜腥必熟

而薦之君賜生必畜之侍食於君君祭先飯

疾君視之東首加朝服拖紳

君命召不俟駕行矣

入大廟每事問

CHAPTER XI

1. When sending a messenger to someone in another state, K'ung Fû-tsze bowed twice while escorting the messenger away.
2. Chî K'ang sent K'ung Fû-tsze a present of medicine. Upon receiving it, K'ung Fû-tsze bowed, but said: I do not know what it is so I dare not taste it.

CHAPTER XII

The stable burned down while K'ung Fû-tsze was at court. When he returned he asked: Have any people been hurt? He did not ask about the financial loss: the horses.

CHAPTER XIII

1. When the prince sent him a gift of cooked meat, he adjusted his mat, tasted the meat, and then gave it away to others. When the prince gave him a gift of raw meat, he cooked it and offered it to his ancestors. When the prince sent him an animal as a gift, he kept it alive.
2. At festivals, the prince offered sacrifice for all. Then people ate the foods. K'ung Fû-tsze tasted everything before the prince did.
3. When K'ung Fû-tsze was ill and the prince visited him, he placed his head to the east. He spread his court robes over him and drew his belt across his waist.
4. When the prince summoned him, K'ung Fû-tsze would proceed on foot immediately, without waiting for his carriage to be yoked.

CHAPTER XIV

When he entered the ancestral temple of the State, K'ung Fû-tsze asked about everything.

Chapter XI: K'ung Fû-tsze bowed twice. One bow was for the messenger and the other was to be relayed from the messenger to the recipient as a sign of respect.

Chapter XIII: Upon receiving a gift from the prince, out of respect, K'ung Fû-tsze would taste it. He would not offer it to his ancestors, however, because it might have already been offered to the ancestors of another. It was the cook's responsibility to taste all food before giving it to the prince. At festivals, out of respect for the prince, K'ung Fû-tsze tasted all foods first to make sure they were safe. Even when he was ill, if the prince visited him, K'ung Fû-tsze would place his head in the proper position for a sick individual, the east, and draw his robes in a respectful manner.

Chapter XIV: K'ung Fû-tsze asked about everything to be sure he followed all protocols correctly.

朋友死無所歸曰於我殯

朋友之饋雖車馬非祭肉不拜寢不尸居不容

見齊衰者雖狎必變見冕者與瞽者雖褻必以貌

凶服者式之式負版者有盛饌必變色而作

迅雷風烈必變

升車必正立執綏車中不內顧不疾言不親指

色斯舉矣翔而後集曰山梁雌雉時哉時哉

子路共之三嗅而作

CHAPTER XV

1. If any of his friends died and there were no relatives to perform a proper burial, K'ung Fû-tsze would say: I will see to the burial.
2. When a friend sent him a present, though it might be a carriage or a horse, he did not bow.
3. The only present he bowed for was sacrificial meat.

CHAPTER XVI

1. When in bed, he did not lie like a corpse. When home, he did not act formal.
2. When he saw any one in mourning attire, even an acquaintance, he remained grave. When he saw an individual wearing official attire, one who was blind, or one in tattered clothes, he would give each a reverent salute.
3. He bowed deeply in front of his carriage to anyone in mourning. He bowed similarly to those carrying the tables of population. When at a banquet, if an abundance of food was set before him, he would rise up and bow to the host as an offer of appreciation.
5. He was concerned if he heard a sudden clap of thunder or a violent wind.

CHAPTER XVII

1. When mounting his carriage, he stood straight and held the cord.
2. When in the carriage, he would not turn his head around fully, not speak too quickly, and not point with his hands.

CHAPTER XVIII

1. Seeing evil intent on a ruler's face, a wise individual rises, continues on, hovers around like a fly, and settles where it is safe.
2. K'ung Fû-tsze recited a poem: There is the hen pheasant on the hill bridge. It waited and waited! Tsze-lû made an offering to it. It sniffed the offering thrice before it rose.

Chapter XV: K'ung Fû-tsze did not bow when his friends sent him gifts. He felt there should be a free flow of gifts between friends. When given a gift of sacrificial meat to offer to deceased ancestors, however, he did bow.

Chapter XVII: K'ung Fû-tsze followed rules of propriety while in his carriage.

Chapter XVIII: Through this poem, K'ung Fû-tsze advises caution. Even a hen hovers carefully around a gift three times, before approaching it.

子曰先進於禮樂野人也後進於禮樂君子也如用之
則吾從先進

子曰從我於陳蔡者皆不及門也
德行顏淵閔子騫冉伯牛仲弓　言語宰我子貢政
事冉有季路　文學子游子夏

子曰回也非助我者也於吾言無所不說

子曰孝哉閔子騫人不間於其父母昆弟之言

BOOK XI   HSIEN TSIN
The Former Men

CHAPTER I

1. K'ung Fû-tsze said: Some say that ceremonies and music of former times were simplistic, while ceremonies and music of present times are sophisticated.

2. Were I given the choice, I would prefer those of former times.

CHAPTER II

1. K'ung Fû-tsze said: Of those who were with me in Ch'ăn and Ts'âi, none can be found to enter my door.

2. Those distinguished for virtuous principles and practices were Yen Yüan, Min Tsze-ch'ien, Zan Po-niû and Chung-kung. Those distinguished for abilities in speech were Tsâi Wo and Tsze-kung. Those distinguished for administrative talents were Zan Yû and Chî Lû. Those distinguished for literary accomplishments were Tsze-yû and Tsze-hsiâ.

CHAPTER III

K'ung Fû-tsze said: Hûi is not helpful to me. He agrees with all I say.

CHAPTER IV

K'ung Fû-tsze said: Min Tsze-ch'ien is filial. Others do not speak differently of him than do his parents and brothers.

Book XI deals with the worthiness of various disciples of K'ung Fû-tsze. Four chapters deal with Min Tsze-ch'ien. Because of this, some attribute portions of this book to his disciples.

Chapter I: K'ung Fû-tsze preferred the simplicity of the past.

Chapter II: K'ung Fû-tsze made this statement towards the end of his life. He is reflecting back to the time when his disciples and he were traveling from Ch'ăn to Ts'âi, and officers cut off their food for several days. He is saddened that most of these disciples either live far away in distant lands, or have died.

Passage 2: These ten disciples have all been mentioned in other chapters of the *Analects*.

Chapter III: K'ung Fû-tsze states that he could not learn from Hûi because Hûi did not question him and challenge him to think.

南宮三復白圭孔子以其兄之子妻之

季康子問弟子孰為好學孔子對曰有顏回者好學

不幸短命死矣今也則亡

顏淵死顏路請子之車以為之椁子曰才不才亦各言其子也

鯉也死有棺而無椁吾不徒行以為之椁以吾從大夫之後

不可徒行也

顏淵死子曰噫天喪予天喪予

顏淵死子哭之慟從者曰子慟矣曰有慟乎

非夫人之為慟而誰為

CHAPTER V

Nan Yung frequently repeated lines from the *Odes*, such as: A flaw in a white gem can be ground away, but a flaw in one's words cannot. K'ung Fû-tsze respected Nan Yung and offered the daughter of his elder brother to him in marriage.

CHAPTER VI

Chî K'ang asked which disciples loved to learn. K'ung Fû-tsze replied: Yen Hûi loved to learn. Unfortunately his appointed time was short, and he died young. Now there is no one who values learning as much as he did.

CHAPTER VII

1. When Yen Lû's son Yen Yüan died, he asked K'ung Fû-tsze to sell his carriage for money to purchase an outer coffin for his son.
2. K'ung Fû-tsze said: Everyone loves one's own children, whether they are gifted or not. Yet even when my son Lî died, I did not sell my carriage and walk on foot just to buy an outer coffin. It is still necessary that I retain a carriage in case I am called upon to consult in court.

CHAPTER VIII

When Yen Yüan (Hûi) died, K'ung Fû-tsze said: Heaven has forsaken me. Heaven has forsaken me!

CHAPTER IX

1. When Yen Yüan died, K'ung Fû-tsze mourned greatly. His disciples said, Master, your grief is excessive.
2. Is it excessive? He questioned.
3. If I cannot mourn bitterly for this man, for whom can I mourn?

Chapter V: People should be cautious of what they say. One can never erase one's words once they have been spoken.

Chapter VII: Yen Lû (who had been a disciple of K'ung Fû-tsze himself) asked K'ung Fû-tsze for funds to purchase an expensive casket for his son Yen Yüan. Although Yen Yüan (Hûi) had been K'ung Fû-tsze's favorite disciple, K'ung Fû-tsze still told Yen Lû that one must live within one's means.

Chapters VIII and IX: K'ung Fû-tsze laments the untimely death of his favorite disciple, Yen Yüan (Hûi).

顏淵死門人欲厚葬之子曰不可門人厚葬之

子曰回也視予猶父也予不得視猶子也非我也二三子也

季路問事鬼神子曰未能事人焉能事鬼

曰敢問死曰未知生焉知死

閔子侍側誾誾如也子路行行如也冉有子貢侃侃如也子樂若由也不得其死然

魯人為長府閔子騫曰仍舊貫如之何何必改作子曰夫人不言言必有中

CHAPTER X
1. When Yen Yüan died, the other disciples wanted a great funeral for him. K'ung Fû-tsze objected.
2. Nevertheless, the disciples gave him a great funeral.
3. K'ung Fû-tsze told his disciples: During Hûi's (Yen Yüan) life, he treated me like a father. I did my best to treat him like a son. I feel at peace.

CHAPTER XI
Chî Lû asked about serving the spirits of the dead. K'ung Fû-tsze answered: We do not know how to serve the living, how can we know how to serve the dead? Chî Lû asked, What is death? K'ung Fû-tsze answered: We do not understand life, how can we understand death?

CHAPTER XII
1. The disciple Min stood by the Master's side, gentle and serene. Tsze-lû stood, upright and soldierly. Zan Yû and Tsze-kung both stood, natural and direct. K'ung Fû-tsze was pleased.
2. K'ung Fû-tsze predicted: Yû will not die a natural death.

CHAPTER XIII
1. Some people in Lû sought to dismantle and rebuild the treasury building.
2. Min Tsze-chi'en said: Can it not be repaired keeping its old style, rather than be totally demolished and rebuilt.
3. K'ung Fû-tsze said: This man seldom speaks. When he does, his words are right on target.

Chapter X: When Yen Yüan died, K'ung Fû-tsze did not want a large funeral for him because his family was poor. K'ung Fû-tsze believed one should live within one's means.

Chapter XI: K'ung Fû-tsze believed that one should take care of that which is in one's control, and let that which is beyond one's control, take care of itself.

Chapter XII: K'ung Fû-tsze thought that Yû was of such noble character that he would not abandon the sovereign even though revolution was inevitable. K'ung Fû-tsze knew he would die defending his ruler.

Chapter XIII: K'ung Fû-tsze agreed with Min Tsze-chi'en. He saw no need to incur excess expenses.

子曰由之瑟奚為於丘之門人不敬子路子曰

由也升堂矣未入於室也

子貢問師與商孰賢子曰師也過商也不及

曰然則師愈與子曰過猶不及

季氏富於周公而求也為之聚斂而附益之

子曰非吾徒也小子鳴鼓而攻之可也

柴也愚參也魯師也辟由也喭

CHAPTER XIV

1. K'ung Fû-tsze said: Why does Yû use his harp to play such music near my door?

2. The other disciples began to lose respect for Yû. K'ung Fû-tsze said: It is alright. Yû is on a path to a higher place. It is just that he has not quite entered its inner sanctuary.

CHAPTER XV

1. Tsze-kung asked who was superior, Shih or Shang. K'ung Fû-tsze said: Shih extends himself far beyond what is expected of him. Shang does not come up to it.

2. Then, said Tsze-kung: Shih is superior, I suppose.

3. K'ung Fû-tsze said: To go too far is as wrong as to fall short.

CHAPTER XVI

1. The leader of the Chî family was more affluent than the duke of Châu. Yet Ch-iû collected taxes for the Chî family to increase their wealth further.

2. K'ung Fû-tsze said: Ch-iû is no disciple of mine. Beat the drums to teach him the folly of his actions.

CHAPTER XVII

1. Ch'âi is simple.

2. Shăn is dull.

3. Shih is superficial.

4. Yû is coarse.

Chapter XIV: The music that Yû was playing was more martial than peaceful. Initially, K'ung Fû-tsze admonishes him, but later he defends him. K'ung Fû-tsze recognizes that Yû was on the road to attaining great wisdom.

Chapter XV: K'ung Fû-tsze tells that too much is as dangerous as too little. Moderation is the best course.

Chapter XVI: K'ung Fû-tsze believes that it is immoral to collect taxes from the poor to give to the rich. The drums were generally beat to herald the people to rise to action.

Chapter XVII: These statements have not been attributed to K'ung Fû-tsze, but rather to a transcriber. They do not match the traits of these disciples.

子曰回也其庶乎屢空賜不受命而貨殖焉億則屢中

子張問善人之道子曰不踐迹亦不入於室

子曰論篤是與君子者乎色莊者乎

子路問聞斯行諸子曰有父兄在如

之何其聞斯行之冉有問聞斯行諸子曰

聞斯行之公西華曰由也問聞斯行諸

子曰有父兄在求也問聞斯行諸子曰聞斯 行之

赤也惑敢問子曰求也退故進之由也兼人故退之

子畏於匡顏淵後子曰吾以女為死矣曰子在回何敢死

CHAPTER XVIII

1. K'ung Fû-tsze said: Hûi has attained almost perfect virtue. He chooses a life of poverty.

2. Ts'ze does not accept the will of Heaven. He seeks to acquire more possessions. Nevertheless, many of his judgments are on target.

CHAPTER XIX

Tsze-chang asked about the conduct of a good person. K'ung Fû-tsze said: A good person seeks neither to follow the masses, nor to enter the chambers of the sages.

CHAPTER XX

K'ung Fû-tsze said: If an individual's conversation appears serious and sincere, we think well of this person. Yet one must look deeper into his or her character to judge if this individual is noble, or if he or she is pretending to be so.

CHAPTER XXI

Tsze-lû asked if he should act immediately upon what he heard. K'ung Fû-tsze said: Consult your father and elder brothers before you immediately carry it out. Zan Yû asked the same question. K'ung Fû-tsze said: Carry it out immediately.

Kung-hsî Hwâ questioned: One asked whether he should carry out what he heard immediately and you said: "Consult your father and elder brothers." Another asked the same and you said, "Carry it out immediately." I am confused. Can you please explain? K'ung Fû-tsze said: One is retiring and slow. So I urged him forward. The other is impulsive. So I kept him back.

CHAPTER XXII

K'ung Fû-tsze fled K'wang in fear of his life. Yen Yüan fell behind. After he caught up with K'ung Fû-tsze, K'ung Fû-tsze said: I thought you died. Yen Yüan replied: While you are still alive, how could I be so presumptuous as to die and leave you?

Chapter XIX: K'ung Fû-tsze extols the traits of a humble, good individual: one guided by conscience, rather than by a quest for praise or glory.

Chapter XXI: This passage is an example of how each of K'ung Fû-tsze's statements must be understood within the context in which each is given.

季子然問仲由冉求可謂大臣與子曰吾以子為異之問

曾由與求之問所謂大臣者以道事君不可則止

今由與求也可謂具臣矣曰然則從之者與子曰弒父與君亦不從也

子路使子羔為費宰子曰賊夫人之子子路曰有民人焉

有社稷焉何必讀書然後為學子曰是故惡夫佞者

CHAPTER XXIII

1. Chî Tsze-zan asked Kung Fû-tsze if he considered Chung Yû and Zan Ch'iû great ministers.

2. K'ung Fû-tsze said: I thought you would ask about great leaders, yet you only ask about Chung Yû and Zan Ch'iû. A great minister is one who serves the prince guided by moral principles. If this cannot be done, a great minister resigns. Yû and Ch'iû should not be considered more than ordinary ministers.

5. Chî Tsze-zan asked: Will a great minister always follow the prince?

6. K'ung Fû-tsze said: Yes, except not when he commands taking the life of a family member or another member of the royalty.

CHAPTER XXIV

1. Tsze-lû helped Tsze-kâo secure the position of governor of Pî.

2. K'ung Fû-tsze said: You have injured another man's son.

3. Tsze-lû said: But in this position, he has many friends as well as numerous altars to the spirits of the land and the grain. Studying from books is not the only path to self-cultivation.

4. K'ung Fû-tsze said: It is because of statements such as these that I dislike smooth talking people.

Chapter XXIII: Chî Tsze-zan is boasting. He aspired to become ruler of Lû. He took two of Kung Fû-tsze's disciples, Chung Yû and Zan Ch'iû, into his service.

Chapter XXIV: Kung Fû-tsze expresses his disapproval of Tsze-lû, for taking the son of another man away from his studies, with the lure of a good job. Kung Fû-tsze believes that taking this job was a short-sighted goal. It offered quick rewards, but little substance. Kung Fû-tsze took the opportunity to tell Tsze-lû that he recognized the dishonesty of his smooth talk.

子路曾皙冉有公西華侍坐

子曰以吾一日長乎爾毋吾以也居則曰

不吾知也如或知爾則何以哉

子路率爾而對曰千乘之國攝乎大國之間加之以師旅

因之以饑饉由也為之比及三年可使有勇且知方也夫子哂之

求爾何如對曰方六七十如五六十求也為之比及三年

可使足民如其禮樂以俟君子

赤爾何如對曰非曰能之願學焉宗廟之事如會同

端章甫願為小相焉

CHAPTER XXV

1. Tsze-lû, Tsǎng Hsi, Zan Yû, and Kung-hsî Hwâ were sitting by K'ung Fû-tsze.

2. K'ung Fû-tsze said to them: Though I am older than you, do not be afraid to speak your mind.

3. K'ung Fû-tsze continued: At times you have said: "We are not recognized." But if you were recognized, what would you like to accomplish?

4. Immediately, and light-heartedly, Tsze-lû replied: Imagine a state of ten thousand chariots positioned between other large states. Imagine it with armies invading it, crippling it with famine. If I were entrusted to govern it, within three years I would instill courage and honor within the people so they could overcome the invaders. K'ung Fû-tsze smiled.

5. Turning to Zan Yû, K'ung Fû-tsze asked: What are your wishes? Zan Yû replied: If only a small territory of fifty, sixty or seventy li square were entrusted to me, within three years, I would instill culture, propriety and music within the masses. Then I would pass the leadership on to one of character from amongst them.

6. K'ung Fû-tsze turned next to Kung-hsî Hwâ: What are your wishes. Kung-hsî Hwâ replied: I do not know if I am capable, but I would like to be a humble worker performing ancestral temple services and assisting the prince as he gives audience to other sovereigns. Dressed in a dark official robe and a black linen cap, I would be his humble assistant.

Chapter XXV, passage 4: Tsze-lû begins to tell K'ung Fû-tsze what he would do if placed in a position of responsibility. Tsze-lû envisions himself in power of a state of ten thousand chariots, and considers that a small state.

Passage 5: Zan Yû states that he would like to instill values within a small territory of fifty to seventy li square (an area of several square miles), and then pass leadership on to one of their own.

Passage 6: Kung-hsî Hwâ says that he would like to be a humble worker performing ancestral temple services, and assisting the prince as he gives audience to other sovereigns.

點爾何如鼓瑟希鏗爾舍瑟而作對曰異乎三子者之撰

子曰何傷乎亦各言其志也曰莫春者春服既成冠者五六人

童子六七人浴乎沂風乎舞雩詠而歸

夫子喟然歎曰吾與點也

三子者出曾皙後曾皙曰夫三子者之言何如

子曰亦各言其志也已矣曰夫子何哂由也

曰為國以禮其言不讓是故哂之唯求則非邦也與

安見方六七十如五六十而非邦也者唯赤非邦也與

宗廟會同非諸侯而何赤也為之小孰能為之大

7. Lastly, K'ung Fû-tsze asked Tsăng Hsî [Tien]: What are your wishes? Tien paused from playing the lute. While it was still vibrating, he set it aside, and rose. My wishes differ from the lofty ideals of the others. K'ung Fû-tsze said: That is not a problem. Please tell your wishes. Tien responded: Towards the last month of spring, with the flora of the season fading, I would like to go with five or six graduated young men, and six or seven boys, and wash in the waters of the Î River. I would enjoy the breeze among the rain altars and return home singing. K'ung Fû-tsze heaved a sigh and said: I give my approval to Tien.

8. After the other three left, Tsăng Hsî remained behind. He asked, What do you think of the words of our three friends? The Master replied: They each said what was in their minds.

9. Tsăng Hsî questioned: Why did you smile?

10. K'ung Fû-tsze replied: To rule a State necessitates humbleness. Tsze-lû's words were far from humble. So I smiled.

11. Tsăng Hsî questioned again: What about the small territory that Zan Yû discussed? K'ung Fû-tsze said: Did you ever see a small territory of sixty or seventy li, or one of fifty or sixty li? If that is a small state, then what is a large state?

12. Once more, Tsăng Hsî inquired: What of the proposal of Kung-hsî Hwâ? Again, K'ung Fû-tsze replied: Only princes deal with ancestral temples and hold audiences with sovereigns. If Kung-hsî Hwâ considers this a humble position, what would he consider an exalted one?

Passage 7: Tsăng Hsî states that if he were to attain recognition, he would merely like to go with colleagues to wash his hands and clothes in the river Î. This was a custom signifying the washing away of evil spirits. Rain altars were sites where summer sacrifices were held. K'ung Fû-tsze approved of Tsăng Hsî's aspirations because they were humble.

Passages 9 and 10: Tsze-lû dreamed of ruling a state of ten thousand chariots, and considered this a humble aspiration. K'ung Fû-tsze felt that a state of ten thousand chariots was not small. Hence, these aspirations were not humble.

Passage 11: Zan Yû dreamed of ruling a state of fifty to seventy li. He considered this small. K'ung Fû-tsze felt that a state of fifty to seventy li was not small.

Passage 12: Kung-hsî Hwâ dreamed of working at ancestral temples. However, only princes dealt with ancestral temples and held audiences with sovereigns. This was not a humble aspiration either.

顏淵問仁子曰克己復禮為仁一日克己復禮

天下歸仁焉為仁由己而由人乎哉顏淵曰請問其目

子曰非禮勿視非禮勿聽非禮勿言非禮勿動

顏淵曰回雖不敏請事斯語矣

仲弓問仁子曰出門如見大賓使民如承大祭

己所不欲勿施於人在邦無怨在家無怨仲弓曰

雍雖不敏請事斯語矣

BOOK XII YEN YÜAN
Conversation with Yen Yüan

CHAPTER I

1. Yen Yüan asked K'ung Fû-tsze to explain how one may attain perfect virtue. K'ung Fû-tsze replied: If one conquers oneself and lives a life of propriety, one may attain perfect virtue. If for even one day, one conquers oneself and returns to propriety, all under Heaven will ascribe perfect virtue to such an individual. Perfect virtue develops within one's heart. It cannot be learned from others.

2. Yen Yüan asked: Please tell me the steps one must follow to attain perfect virtue. K'ung Fû-tsze replied: Do not look at what you know it is improper to see; do not listen to what you know it is improper to hear; do not say what you know it is improper to say; do not act in ways that you know it is improper to act. Yen Yüan then said: Though I lack intelligence and strength, I will make it my goal to practice these teachings.

CHAPTER II

Chung-kung asked how one may attain perfect virtue. K'ung Fû-tsze said: When abroad, treat all people as thought they were distinguished guests. Treat all people as though you were assisting at a great sacrifice. Do not treat others as you would not wish to be treated yourself. Acting thusly, neither your family nor strangers will speak badly of you. Chung-kung said: Though I lack intelligence and strength, I will make it my goal to practice these teachings.

Book III begins with a conversation between K'ung Fû-tsze and his disciple Yen Yüan. K'ung Fû-tsze gives advice to his disciples concerning perfect virtue, government, and morality. His responses vary, however, depending upon his insight into the character and capability of each disciple.

Chapter I: K'ung Fû-tsze tells Yen Yüan how he may attain perfect virtue. He must subdue his ego, his pride, and his personal desires. He must also refrain from seeing, hearing, saying, or acting in any way he knows to be improper.

When K'ung Fû-tsze uses the phrase 'all under Heaven' he is referring to 'all on earth,' for earth is under Heaven.

Chapter II: K'ung Fû-tsze advises Chung-kung that to attain perfect virtue one must: treat all people as distinguished guests; consider all situations to be as significant as a great sacrifice; and treat all people as one would wish to be treated oneself.

司馬牛問仁子曰仁者其言也訒曰其言也訒

斯謂之仁矣乎子曰為之難言之得無訒乎

司馬牛問君子子曰君子不憂不懼曰不憂不懼

斯謂之君子矣乎子曰內省不疚夫何憂何懼

司馬牛憂曰人皆有兄弟我獨亡子夏曰商聞之矣

死生有命富貴在天君子敬而無失與人恭而有禮

四海之內皆兄弟也君子何患乎無兄弟也

CHAPTER III

1. Sze-mâ Niû asked how one may attain perfect virtue.
2. K'ung Fû-tsze said: One with perfect virtue is cautious and slow to speak.
3. Cautious and slow to speak! Niû asked: How does this relate to perfect virtue? K'ung Fû-tsze said: If one recognizes the deeper meanings and complexity of a situation, can one not be cautious and slow in speech?

CHAPTER IV

1. Sze-mâ Niû asked how one may become a perfect person. K'ung Fû-tsze said: The perfect person harbors neither fear nor anxiety.
2. Niû questioned: Does being without anxiety or fear mean that one possesses character?
3. K'ung Fû-tsze said: If upon searching within oneself, one finds no faults, what has one to fear or feel anxious about?

CHAPTER V

1. Sze-mâ Niû, filled with anxiety, said: All other men have brothers. Only I have none.
2. Tsze-hsiâ said to him: I have heard the following saying;
3. "Death and life have their appointed times. Riches and honors depend upon Heaven."
4. One of character must never fail to reverently control one's conduct. If one is respectful of others and observant of propriety, then all people between the four seas will seek to be one's brother. Hence, one of character need not be distressed that one has no siblings.

Chapter III: K'ung Fû-tsze tells Sze-mâ Niû that one with perfect virtue understands that situations are complex, and therefore, will exercise restraint before speaking.

Chapter IV: K'ung Fû-tsze tells Sze-mâ Niû that if one knows that one has committed no wrong, one can accept any outcome without fear.

Chapter V: Sze-mâ Niû states that he is fearful because he has no brothers (no family). Tsze-hsiâ reassures him that one of character will never be alone. All people welcome an individual with character as a brother.

子張問明子曰浸潤之譖膚

浸潤之譖膚受之愬不行焉可謂明也已矣

受之愬不行焉可謂遠也已矣

子貢問政子曰足食足兵民信

於斯三者何先曰去兵子貢曰必不得已而

之矣子貢曰必不得已而去

信二者何先曰去食自古皆有死民無信不立

棘子成曰君子質而已矣何以文為子貢曰惜乎

夫子之說君子也駟不及舌文猶質也

質猶文也虎豹之鞟猶犬羊之鞟

CHAPTER VI

Tsze-chang asked what makes one intelligent. K'ung Fû-tsze said: One who neither soaks up juicy scandals, nor permits shocking slander to penetrate one's judgement, will have succeeded in becoming wise. One who is totally undaunted by scandals or slander will be capable of making far-sighted judgements.

CHAPTER VII

1. Tsze-kung asked about honorable government. K'ung Fû-tsze said: An honorable government must ensure that people have sufficient food, sufficient weapons, and sufficient confidence in their ruler.
2. Tsze-kung asked: If one of these must be given up, which of the three should be discarded first? K'ung Fû-tsze said: The weapons.
3. Tsze-kung again asked: If one of these remaining two must be given up, which should be relinquished next? K'ung Fû-tsze answered: The food. Since long ago, sages have recognized that death must come to all. But if people have no faith in their rulers, there is no chance for the State.

CHAPTER VIII

1. Chî Tsze-ch'ǎng said: If in evaluating character, only inner qualities are significant. Why look at outward accomplishments?
2. Tsze-kung said: Ah, your words show you are one of character. Yet four horses cannot overtake your tongue.
3. Character defines accomplishments, and accomplishments define character. The hide of a tiger or leopard stripped of its hair, cannot be distinguished from the hide of a dog or cat stripped of hair.

Chapter VI: K'ung Fû-tsze knows that although Tsze-chang favors lofty concepts, he also likes common ones. K'ung Fû-tsze tells him that if he just refrains from thinking about slander and sensational stories, he will gain wisdom.

Chapter VII: K'ung Fû-tsze discusses the importance of an honorable leader. If people have neither food nor weapons, they may die, but they will do so with dignity and peace of mind. If people do not trust their leader, however, chaos will erupt and the country will fall into moral decay.

Chapter VIII: Tsze-kung tells Chî Tsze-ch'ǎng that one searching for truth must think before speaking.
Passage 3: Tsze-kung uses the example of a hide without hair to explain how outward manifestations can be an indication of inner characteristics.

哀公問於有若曰年饑用不足如之何有若對曰
盍徹乎曰二吾猶不足如之何其徹也對曰
百姓足君孰不足百姓不足君孰與足

子問崇德辨惑子曰主忠信徙義崇德也
愛之欲其生惡之欲其死既欲其生
又欲其死是惑也誠不以富亦祗以異

CHAPTER IX

1. Duke Âi asked Yû Zo: This is a year of scarcity, and the returns on expenditure are not sufficient. What should I do?
2. Yû Zo said: Why not simply reduce the tax the people must pay to one-tenth?
3. Duke Âi replied: Even when I have been taxing them two-tenths, my funds are insufficient. How could I function if I only tax them one-tenth?
4. Yû Zo advised: A prince will not suffer if his people have abundance. But if his people are forced to endure suffering, surely, the prince will not be able to enjoy plenty alone.

CHAPTER X

1. Tsze-chang asked: How can one cultivate virtue and recognize delusions? K'ung Fû-tsze said: Hold faithfulness and sincerity as one's primary goals. Strive continually to do what is right. This is the way to cultivate virtue.
2. Sometimes people wish that someone they love might live. Sometimes they wish that someone they hate might not live. Yet wishing that one lives, also means wishing that the same individual dies. Such wishes are delusions.
3. It may not be because one is rich, yet one comes to make a difference.

Chapter IX discusses tithing. In the Châu dynasty, land was divided in allotments and the produce divided so that eight or nine-tenths were distributed among the farmers and one or two-tenths (one or two tithes) were given to the state. Yû Zo advised Duke Âi that if the amount taxed was too steep, farmers would not work vigorously and both the ruler and his people would suffer.

Chapter X: K'ung Fû-tsze states that of all virtues, two are the most meaningful: faithfulness and sincerity. He also tells that much of what people think is a delusion. Sometimes we wish that one we love lives, and that one we hate dies. Yet wishing that one lives, also means wishing that they die, for all that lives must die. Such wishes are delusions. In Confucian philosophy, the appointed times for life and death are beyond human control.

Paragraph 3: This is a line from one of the *Odes*. Its relationship to the rest of the chapter remains elusive.

齊景公問政於孔子孔子對曰君君臣臣父父子子公曰善哉

信如君不君臣不臣父不父子不子雖有粟

吾得而食諸

子曰片言可以折獄者其由也與子路無宿諾

子曰聽訟吾猶人也必也使無訟乎

子張問政子曰居之無倦行之以忠

子曰博學於文約之以禮亦可以弗畔矣夫

CHAPTER XI
1. Duke Ching of Ch'î asked K'ung Fû-tsze about government.
2. K'ung Fû-tsze replied: A government can only function well when the prince acts as a prince, the minister acts as a minister, the father acts as a father, and the son acts as a son.
3. This is so! Said the duke. For when the prince does not act as prince, the minister as minister, the father as father, or the son as son, although I receive my salary, I can not feel peace of mind.

CHAPTER XII
1. K'ung Fû-tsze said: Ah! With only half a word, Yû can settle a dispute.
2. He never went to sleep without fulfilling his promise.

CHAPTER XIII
K'ung Fû-tsze said: In hearing about litigations, I feel like everyone else. What we truly need is a society in which there is no litigation.

CHAPTER XIV
Tsze-chang asked about government. K'ung Fû-tsze said: There is an art to governing. One should work tirelessly to clarify all issues in one's mind, then follow through with unswerving constancy.

CHAPTER XV
K'ung Fû-tsze said: By studying all forms of knowledge in depth, and training oneself to follow the rules of propriety, one will not err from what is right.

Chapter XI: K'ung Fû-tsze states that a country will function well when each and every individual fulfills his or her own responsibility. Duke Ching felt unsettled when he heard this. He knew a coup d'état was brewing within the government.

Chapter XII: K'ung Fû-tsze praises Yû for his ability to understand the merits of a conflict. He was able to do so even when hearing only one side of an argument. Yû was very responsible. He always completed what he promised the same day.

Chapter XIII: K'ung Fû-tsze said that the more he heard about litigation, the more he felt society would be better off resolving issues without litigation.

子曰君子成人之美不成人之惡小人反是

季康子問政於孔子孔子對曰政者正也子帥以正孰敢不正

季康子患盜問於孔子孔子對曰苟子之不欲雖賞之不竊

季康子問政於孔子曰如殺無道以就有道何如孔子對曰

子為政焉用殺子欲善而民善矣君子之德風小人之德草草上之風必偃

子張問士何如斯可謂之達矣子曰何哉爾所謂達者子張對曰

在邦必聞在家必聞子曰是聞也非達也夫達也者

CHAPTER XVI
K'ung Fû-tsze said: One of character seeks to help others cultivate honorable qualities and to eliminate dishonorable ones. One without character does the opposite.

CHAPTER XVII
Chî K'ang asked K'ung Fû-tsze about virtuous government. K'ung Fû-tsze replied: To govern honorably means to rectify that which is wrong. If the individual leading the people is honorable, who will dare to be dishonorable?

CHAPTER XVIII
Chî K'ang, distressed about the number of thieves in the state, asked K'ung Fû-tsze how to do away with them. K'ung Fû-tsze said: If you, yourself, were not greedy, even if you rewarded them to do so, other people would not steal.

CHAPTER XIX
Chî K'ang asked K'ung Fû-tsze about government: What do you think about killing the unprincipled members of society for the welfare of the principled? K'ung Fû-tsze replied: In conducting government, why should you kill at all? If you sincerely desire to do what is good, the people will do good as well. The relations between superiors and inferiors is like that between the wind and the grass. The grass will bend in the direction the wind blows across it.

CHAPTER XX
1. Tsze-chang asked: What qualities should an officer who is considered distinguished cultivate?
2. K'ung Fû-tsze asked: How do you define being distinguished?
3. Tsze-chang replied: Being distinguished means being known amongst those within one's own clan and known throughout the state.
4. K'ung Fû-tsze said: That is notoriety, not distinction.

Chapters XVIII and XIX: K'ung Fû-tsze teaches that society will follow the example set by its leaders.

質直而好義察言而觀色慮以下人在邦必達在家必達

夫聞也者色取仁而行違居之不疑在邦必聞在家必聞

樊遲從遊於舞雩之下曰敢問崇德修慝辨惑子曰

善哉問先事後得非崇德與攻其惡無攻人之惡

非修慝與一朝之忿忘其身以及其親非惑與

樊遲問仁子曰愛人問知子曰知人樊遲未達子曰

舉直錯諸枉能使枉者直樊遲退見子夏曰鄉也

吾見於夫子而問知子曰舉直錯諸枉

5. One of distinction is solid, honest, and loves justice. Such an individual examines people's words, looks at the expressions on their faces, and humbles him or herself before others. Such an individual is respected within his or her own family, as well as throughout the state.

6. One of notoriety assumes the appearance of virtue, but actually acts totally opposite. Such an individual rests comfortably in his or her own mode of behavior, never questioning himself. Such an individual attains notoriety at home and throughout the state.

CHAPTER XXI

1. Fan Ch'ih, meandering with K'ung Fû-tsze under the trees, asked about the altars to rain: How can one cultivate virtue, clear up preconceived resentments, and distinguish between delusions and reality?

2. K'ung Fû-tsze replied: This is truly a good question.

3. Doing what needs to be done should be one's main goal. Success should be merely a secondary outcome. Acting thusly, one will cultivate virtue. Judge one's own faults and do not judge those of others. Acting thusly, one will correct preconceived resentments. Realize that it is not worth a morning's burst of anger to endanger the safety of one's life. One who acts thusly, has been able to distinguish delusion from reality.

CHAPTER XXII

1. Fan Ch'ih asked K'ung Fû-tsze to describe the character of one with true compassion. K'ung Fû-tsze replied: One with true compassion loves all people. Fan Ch'ih asked K'ung Fû-tsze to describe the character of one with true wisdom. K'ung Fû-tsze replied: One with true wisdom understands all men.

2. Fan Ch'ih did not immediately understand these answers.

Chapter XXI: Fan Ch'ih may have been asking K'ung Fû-tsze how one can distinguish between right and wrong. He did not believe that altars to rain spirits were real. K'ung Fû-tsze responded with practical answers. One can clear up the prejudices one has been taught by looking within oneself before judging others. One can recognize that defending one's honor is a delusion, because a minute's worth of honor, is not worth a lifetime of suffering the repercussions of one's rash action.

言乎者真何謂也子夏曰富哉言乎舜有天下選於眾舉

皋陶不仁者遠湯有天下選於眾舉伊尹不仁者遠矣

子貢問友子曰忠告而善道之不可則止毋自辱焉

曾子曰君子以文會友以友輔仁

3. K'ung Fû-tsze said: A leader should promote the just and put aside the unjust. In this way the unjust will seek to become just.
4. Fan Ch'ih left, and seeing Tsze-hsiâ, said to him: A short while ago, I met with our sage K'ung Fû-tsze. I inquired as to the meaning of true wisdom. K'ung Fû-tsze said: Value the just, and put aside all the unjust. Then, the unjust will seek to become just. What did he mean?
5. Tsze-hsiâ said: There is great value in his words.
6. When Shun became head of the kingdom, he selected from among the masses, and chose Kâo-yâo. Those in society who lacked virtue left his kingdom. Similarly, when T'ang became head of the kingdom, he selected from among all the masses, and chose Î Yin. Similarly, all who lacked virtue left his kingdom.

CHAPTER XXIII
Tsze-kung asked: What is the meaning of friendship? K'ung Fû-tsze said: Be sincere in criticizing friends, and use tact in giving guidance. If the friend is unwilling to accept criticism, do not continue, lest you will bring shame upon yourself.

CHAPTER XXIV
The philosopher Tsăng said: Those of character cultivate friendships based upon virtues. Through such friendships, their own virtue increases.

Chapter XXII: K'ung Fû-tsze teaches that if a ruler and those who serve under him govern honorably, society will follow their example. Tsze-hsiâ confirmed this, giving examples of rulers under whose leadership virtue reigned.

Chapter XXIII: To be a good friend, one must tell one's friend when he has taken a wrong path and must constructively guide him. Yet if the friend is not ready to accept such guidance, it is best not to continue giving constructive criticism.

子路問政子曰先之勞之請益曰無倦

仲弓為季氏宰問政子曰先有司赦小過舉賢才

曰焉知賢才而舉之曰舉爾所知爾所不知人其舍諸

子路曰衛君待子而為政子將奚先子曰必也正名乎

子路曰有是哉子之迂也奚其正子曰野哉由也君子

於其所不知蓋闕如也名不正則言不順

BOOK XIII TSZE-LÛ
A Lesson to Tsze-lû

CHAPTER I

1. Tsze-lû inquired how to govern properly. K'ung Fû-tsze said: Go before the people setting an example, and labor unceasingly to alleviate their needs.
2. Tsze-lû asked for further advice. K'ung Fû-tsze answered: Never tire until you fulfill these goals.

CHAPTER II

1. Chung-kung, chief minister to the Head of the Chî family, inquired how to govern properly. K'ung Fû-tsze said: Hire your own officers. When teaching them, overlook their small faults, and raise to office those with virtue and ability.
2. Chung-kung said: How does one recognize those with virtue and ability, so as to raise their positions? K'ung Fû-tsze said: Raise those whose qualities you recognize. If there are those with virtue you fail to recognize, others will not fail to bring their worth before you.

CHAPTER III

1. Tsze-lû said: The duke of Wei has been waiting for you to assist him in governing. What will be the first reform you initiate?
2. K'ung Fû-tsze replied: It will be necessary to clearly define names (or terms).
3. Tsze-lû said: Indeed! I do not see why this is important. Why must names be defined?
4. K'ung Fû-tsze said: You have not been shown the importance of this. One with wisdom remains cautiously reserved about that which one does not understand.

Book XIII book relates to the period when K'ung Fû-tsze was approximately sixty-seven years of age and returned to his home state of Lû. Tsze-lû had been employed in the service of Duke Chû of Wei. Many of the chapters relate to running the government and cultivating character.

Chapter I: K'ung Fû-tsze teaches that one must live by example.

Chapter II, passage 3: K'ung Fû-tsze implies that one must call things as they really are. The duke of Chû became ruler of Wei by stealing the throne from his father. He reversed the proper relationship between prince and king, and also between father and son. Therefore, K'ung Fû-tsze would not work for him unless he first defined himself as son, and returned the throne to his father, the true monarch.

言不順則事不成　事不成則禮樂

不興禮樂不興　則刑罰不中　刑罰不中則民無

所措手足　故君子名之必可言也　言之必可行也

君子於其言　無所苟而已矣

與邊情學稼子曰吾不如老農　情學為圃曰吾不如老圃

樊遲出子曰小人哉樊須也　上好禮則民莫敢不敬

上好義則民莫敢不服　上好信則民莫敢不用情夫如是

則四方之民襁負其子而至矣　焉用稼

5. If names chosen to define things are not correct, then statements resulting from the use of these will not reflect truth. Actions based upon such terms, will not be correct and will not lead to successful outcomes.

6. When actions do not lead to successful outcomes, meaningful activities and culture will not flourish. When meaningful activities and culture do not prevail, rewards and punishments will not be directed towards the proper individuals. When rewards and punishments are not directed properly, the masses will not know how to move hand or foot. Therefore, one with wisdom will ensure that the names he or she uses to define terms are correct. Thusly, the results that emanate from these actions will be appropriate. One with wisdom considers it essential that his or her choice of words is correct.

CHAPTER IV

1. Fan Ch'ih requested that K'ung Fû-tsze teach him farming. K'ung Fû-tsze said: I am not as qualified as an experienced farmer. Fan Ch'ih requested that K'ung Fû-tsze teach him gardening. K'ung Fû-tsze answered: I am not as qualified as an experienced gardener.

2. After Fan Ch'ih left, K'ung Fû-tsze said: He is not an individual who recognizes higher concepts.

3. If a ruler loves propriety, his people will not dare act lowly. If a ruler values faithfulness, his people will not dare act insincerely. Once such a ruler's values are recognized, people will flock to him bearing their children on their backs. One who rules thusly has no need to attain knowledge of husbandry.

Chapter III, passages 5 and 6: K'ung Fû-tsze tells that if a government is founded upon untruths, and uses names and words to manipulate truth, its people will lose sight of meaningful goals and values. They will not know what is expected of them, or even what is right and wrong. Therefore, to govern effectively, leaders must consistently act and speak truthfully.

Passage 6: K'ung Fû-tsze recognized that when people become hopeless, their actions cannot lead to success. Meaningful, cultured, and civilized activities (such as music) will not flourish. Under these circumstances, the people will not even know how to act (how to move their hands and feet).

Chapter IV: Fan Ch'ih is a leader seeking guidance from K'ung Fû-tsze. His concerns, however, are oriented towards husbandry. K'ung Fû-tsze recognizes that Fan Ch'ih needs to cultivate propriety and faithfulness, not crops. When K'ung Fû-tsze uses the expression "bearing children on their backs" he is referring to mothers and nurses strapping children on their back with a length of cloth. In this case, it refers to bringing their children and choosing to live in a virtuous environment.

子曰誦詩三百授之以政不達 使於四方不能專對

雖多亦奚以為

子曰其身正不令而行其身不正雖令不從

子曰魯衛之政兄弟也

子謂衛公子荊善居室始有曰苟合矣少有曰苟完矣

富有曰苟美矣

子適衛冉有僕子曰庶矣哉 冉有曰既庶矣又何加焉曰富之曰既富矣又何加焉曰教之

CHAPTER V

K'ung Fû-tsze said: Though an individual may be able to recite the three hundred *Odes*, if this person, when ruling, does not know how to act when sent on missions to distant lands, or cannot make a speech without notes, what is the use of his or her learning?

CHAPTER VI

K'ung Fû-tsze said: If a leader's personal conduct is upright, his or her government will run effectively without the need to issue orders. If a leader's personal conduct is not upright, although he or she may issue orders, they will not be obeyed.

CHAPTER VII

K'ung Fû-tsze said: The rulers of the states of Lû and Wei are brothers, even in their governments.

CHAPTER VIII

K'ung Fû-tsze said of Ching: He was a descendant of the royal family of Wei. He managed the financial affairs of his family well. When he first began to amass means, he said: This is worth saving. When these funds increased, he said: This is sufficient. When he became rich, he said: This is to be respected.

CHAPTER IX

1. K'ung Fû-tsze went to Wei. Zan Yû was driving his carriage.
2, K'ung Fû-tsze observed: How numerous the people are here!
3. Zan Yû questioned: Since they are so populous, what can be done to help them? K'ung Fû-tsze said: Give them prosperity.
4. And after they have been given prosperity, what should be done next? K'ung Fû-tsze said: Educate them.

Chapter V: K'ung Fû-tsze tells that culture is of no use to a leader if he or she does not know how to apply it to everyday life.

Chapter VII: The leaders of the states of Lû and Wei were brothers. Lû was ruled by Châu-kung and Wei by his brother K'ang-shû. They ruled similarly, reacting positively and negatively to the same situations.

Chapter VIII: K'ung Fû-tsze describes Ching as a wise ruler. When times were good, he saved for lean years. He recognized when he had enough. When he attained wealth, he respected these gains and did not squander it.

子曰苟有用我者期月而已可也三年有成

子曰善人為邦百年亦可以勝殘去殺矣誠哉是言也

子曰如有王者必世而後仁

子曰苟正其身矣於從政乎何有

有不能正其身如正人何

冉子退朝子曰何晏也對曰有政子曰其事也

如有政雖不吾以吾其與聞之

CHAPTER X

K'ung Fû-tsze said: If there were a ruler who would employ me, within twelve months, I would be able to begin instituting change. Within three years, the government would be functioning fine.

CHAPTER XI

K'ung Fû-tsze said: If leaders of honorable character were to govern a country continuously for one hundred years, those with violent tendencies would be transformed and there would be no further need for capital punishment. This is a true statement.

CHAPTER XII

K'ung Fû-tsze said: Even if a ruler of ethical character were to appear, it would still require a full generation for virtue to prevail.

CHAPTER XIII

K'ung Fû-tsze said: If a minister can conquer his own character, what difficulty could he possibly have in running the government? But if a minister cannot correct himself, how can he possibly correct others?

CHAPTER XIV

The disciple Zan returned from court. K'ung Fû-tsze asked him: Why were you late? Zan said he had official business. K'ung Fû-tsze replied: Though I am not presently in office, were there any official business going on, I would have heard of it.

Chapter X: The type of individual to whom K'ung Fû-tsze is referring, under whose employment he could institute change, is a prince or ruler.

Chapter XII refers to the Chinese character for ruler. It is formed by three horizontal parallel lines, joined by one central vertical line. This represents the three forces of Heaven, Earth, and Man. It was believed that a good ruler was sent by Heaven to appear on earth and guide humankind.

Chapter XIV: K'ung Fû-tsze admonishes Zan because he does not believe he is telling the truth. If a governmental meeting had been called, K'ung Fû-tsze, though retired, would have heard of it.

定公問一言而可以興邦有諸孔子對曰言不可以若是其幾也人之言曰為君難為臣不易如知為君之難也不幾乎一言而興邦乎曰一言而喪邦有諸孔子對曰言不可以若是其幾也人之言曰予無樂為君唯其言而莫予違也如善而莫之違也不亦善乎如不善而莫之違也不幾乎一言而喪邦乎

葉公問政子曰近者悦遠者來

子夏為莒父宰問政子曰無欲速無見小利欲速則不達見小利則大事不成

Chapter XV

1. Duke Ting asked: Is there a saying concerning how one can make a country prosper. K'ung Fû-tsze replied: This is difficult to express in one phrase.

2. There is a saying, howerever, that: Although it is difficult to be a virtuous ruler, it is not easy to be a virtuous minister, either.

3. If the ruler and his ministers recognize one another's responsibilities, and work together, how can the country not prosper?

4. Duke Ting asked: Is there a saying concerning how one can recognize when a country is being led to ruin? K'ung Fû-tsze replied: This is difficult to express in one phrase. There is one saying, however, that states: When a ruler declares, "I attain no pleasure in being ruler, except that no one can oppose my words," ruination of the empire cannot be far away.

5. If such a ruler's words are honorable, and no one opposes them, good may follow. But if the ruler's words are dishonorable, and no one opposes them, how can a country avoid falling into ruin?

CHAPTER XVI

1. The duke of Sheh inquired: How can one recognize a virtuous government?

2. K'ung Fû-tsze said: A virtuous government is one in which those who live in the lands under it are content, and those who are far away are attracted to it.

CHAPTER XVII

Tsze-hsiâ, governor of Chü-fû, inquired: What characterizes a virtuous government? K'ung Fû-tsze said: It is one governed by leaders who do not seek to have things done quickly and do not seek small gains. Seeking to have things done quickly prevents their being done thoroughly. Seeking only small gains prevents great gains from being accomplished.

Chapter XV: K'ung Fû-tsze expresses two ancient sayings. The first is: If all facets of the government work together honorably, the country will prosper. The second is: If a ruler is not an individual with character, and seeks only glory, surely that country will fall into ruin.

葉公語孔子曰吾黨有直躬者其父攘羊而子證之孔子

曰吾黨之直者異於是父為子隱子為父隱直在其中矣

樊遲問仁子曰居處恭執事

敬與人忠雖之夷狄不可棄也

子貢問曰何如斯可謂之士矣

子曰行己有恥使於四方不

辱君命可謂士矣曰敢問其次曰宗族稱孝焉鄉黨稱弟焉

曰敢問其次曰言必信行必果硜硜然小人哉抑亦可以

為次矣曰今之從政者何如子曰噫斗筲之人何足算也

CHAPTER XVIII

1, The duke of Sheh told K'ung Fû-tsze: In our community, that individual is considered upright who will bear witness even against his own father, if he has stolen a sheep.

2. K'ung Fû-tsze said: In our part of the country, our view of uprightness is considerably different. A father will conceal the misconduct of his son, and a son will conceal the misconduct of his father. This is considered being upright.

CHAPTER XIX

Fan Ch'ih asked how one may attain perfect virtue. K'ung Fû-tsze said: In private life, one must maintain integrity. In business, one must be respectful and attentive. In dealing with others, one must be just and sincere. Even among those who are rude and uncultivated, one must not abandon one's own values.

CHAPTER XX

1. Tsze-kung asked: What qualities must one possess to be considered the first officer of the prince? K'ung Fû-tsze said: In private life, one must possess personal integrity, and in official matters, one must not disgrace one's prince. Such an individual deserves to be considered for the position as first officer of the prince.

2. Tsze-kung continued: Who may be considered next in rank? K'ung Fû-tsze said: One who is faithful to one's relatives and fraternal to one's fellow-villagers and neighbors.

3. Again the disciple asked: Who may be considered for the next lower rank in society. K'ung Fû-tsze said: One who is sincere in one's word and completes what one say one will. Even if such an individual is common, such an individual may be considered for the next position in rank.

4. Finally, Tse-kung asked: What of those presently engaged in government? K'ung Fû-tsze said: Just a show! They are a basket of useless individuals. They are not worth considering.

Chapter XVIII sheds insight into Chinese culture where allegiance to one's family comes before allegiance to all others.

Chapter XX: K'ung Fû-tsze expresses his dislike for the present administration. He believes they are just figureheads. They are common tools use to fulfill goals.

子曰不得中行而與之必也狂狷乎狂者進取狷者有所不為也

子曰南人有言曰人而無恆不可以作巫醫善夫不恆其德

或承之羞子曰不占而已矣

子曰君子和而不同小人同而不和

子貢問曰鄉人皆好之何如子曰未可也鄉人皆惡之何如

子曰未可也不如鄉人之善者好之其不善者惡之

CHAPTER XXI

K'ung Fû-tsze said: Because I cannot attract disciples who practice moderation, I seek either those who are too impetuous or those who are too cautious. Those who are too impetuous jump in and reveal the truth. Those who are too cautious refrain from making mistakes.

CHAPTER XXII

1. K'ung Fû-tsze said: The people of the south have a saying: One without constancy, can be neither a shaman nor a doctor.
2. One who is not consistent in virtue, will encounter disgrace.
3. K'ung Fû-tsze said: Those who lack constancy, have not patiently and slowly learned from observing the patterns of the past.

CHAPTER XXIII

K'ung Fû-tsze said: An individual with character is gracious, and will not flatter excessively. An individual without character will flatter disingenuously.

CHAPTER XXIV

Tsze-kung asked: What would you say of one who is loved by the entire community? K'ung Fû-tsze replied: For that alone, I would not feel convinced that the individual is good. Tsze-kung asked: What would you say of one who is hated by the entire community? K'ung Fû-tsze replied: For that alone, I would not feel convinced that the individual is bad. Better than either of these is one who is loved by the virtuous and hated by the corrupt.

Chapter XXI touches upon the concept of the Due Mean. Chinese philosophy teaches moderation. It recognizes that anything that reaches an extreme will slow down, stop, and then reverse to the other direction, like a pendulum. The Mean is considered the position of peaceful harmony and equilibrium. K'ung Fû-tsze, though unable to obtain disciples with balanced natures, created harmony by balancing the diverse, yet positive, traits of each.

Chapter XXII: In Chinese culture, both the shaman and the doctor were respected as individuals who could make observations and predict outcomes.
In passage 2, K'ung Fû-tsze quotes from the I Ching. One who does not consistently practice virtue will fall into disgrace. Such an individual has not learned from the lessons of antiquity that immoral actions lead to negative outcomes.

Chapter XXIV: K'ung Fû-tsze teaches that one cannot judge another by the opinions of a third party if one does not know the character of the third party.

子曰君子易事而難說也子曰君子易事而難說也

器之小人難事而易說也說之雖不以道說也

及其使人也求備焉

子曰君子泰而不驕小人驕而不泰

子曰剛毅木訥近仁

子路問曰何如斯可謂之士矣子曰切切偲偲怡怡如也可謂士矣

朋友切切偲偲兄弟怡怡

子曰善人教民七年亦可以即戎矣

子曰以不教民戰是謂棄之

CHAPTER XXV

K'ung Fû-tsze said: One of character is easy to serve, yet difficult to please. If others try to please this individual through unethical actions, they will not succeed. One of character expects from people, only that which is consistent with their capabilities. He accepts their limitations. One without character may seem difficult to serve, yet is actually easy to please. If others try to please this individual through unethical actions, he will be pleased. He expects all to perform equally, regardless of their natural abilities.

CHAPTER XXVI

K'ung Fû-tsze said: One of character is refined, yet not proud. One without character is proud, yet not refined.

CHAPTER XXVII

K'ung Fû-tsze said: Those who are dependable, consistent, sincere, and humble approach perfect virtue.

CHAPTER XXVIII

Tsze-lu asked: What qualities must one possess to be considered a scholar? K'ung Fû-tsze said: One must be earnest, concerned, and kind. Earnest and concerned towards one's friends. Kind towards one's brothers.

CHAPTER XXIX

K'ung Fû-tsze said: Let a virtuous leader teach the people for seven years. Only then should such a leader send his people to war.

CHAPTER XXX

K'ung Fû-tsze said: To lead an uninstructed people to war, is to throw them away.

Chapter XXVI: The individual of character to whom K'ung Fû-tsze is referring is a ruler. A ruler should teach societal and moral responsibilities.

Chapter XXX: K'ung Fû-tsze laments the tragic results that occur when a ruler sends people to war without informing them of the need to wage war and without providing them with the skills needed to survive and to win.

憲問恥 子曰邦有道穀邦無道穀恥也 克伐怨慾不行焉

可以為仁矣 子曰可以為難矣 仁則吾不知也

子曰士而懷居不足以為士矣

子曰邦有道危言危行 邦無道危行言孫

子曰有德者必有言 有言者不必有德 仁者必有勇 勇者不必有仁

BOOK XIV HSIEN WĂN
Hsien Asked

CHAPTER I

Hsien asked: What actions do you consider shameful? K'ung Fû-tsze said: When serving an honorable government, it is shameful to think about salary. When serving a dishonorable government, it is shameful to think about salary. Both of these are shameful.

CHAPTER II

1. Hsien asked: When one has eliminated all pride, all desire for superiority, all resentment, and all greed, will one have attained perfect virtue?
2. K'ung Fû-tsze said: These are lofty and difficult goals, but I do not know if attainment of these alone constitutes perfect virtue.

CHAPTER III

K'ung Fû-tsze said: One who clings to comfort cannot be considered of sagely character.

CHAPTER IV

K'ung Fû-tsze said: In a state that is governed honorably, one may act and speak boldly. In a state that is governed dishonorably, one may act boldly, but had best speak with caution.

CHAPTER V

K'ung Fû-tsze said: Those who possess virtue speak respectfully; but those who speak respectfully may not always possess virtue. Those who possess principle will act with courage; but those who act with courage may not always possess principle.

Book XIV discusses proper goals for princes and high ranking officers. These include cultivation of virtue, avoidance of dishonor, and securing peace for the masses.

Chapter I: It is shameful for one in a responsible, honorable position to be preoccupied with reimbursement. It is also shameful for one pursuing a dishonorable cause to accept reimbursement.

Chapter II: K'ung Fû-tsze held high standards in considering an individual perfectly virtuous. One can not know the true virtue of another until his or her time on earth has been completed.

南宮适問於孔子曰羿善射奡盪舟俱不得其死然禹稷躬稼而有天下夫子不答南适出子曰君子哉若人尚德哉若人

子曰君子而不仁者有矣夫未有小人而仁者也

子曰愛之能勿勞乎忠焉能勿誨乎

子曰為命裨諶草創之世叔討論之行人子羽修飾之東里子產潤色之

CHAPTER VI

Nan-kung Kwo said: Î was a skillful archer and Âo was able to lift a boat onto the land. Yet neither of them died a natural death. Yü and Chî, however, toiled as simple farmers, and over time, they gradually possessed the kingdom. K'ung Fû-tsze remained silent. After Nan-kung Kwo left, K'ung Fû-tsze said: He is a fine man, indeed. He appreciates virtue.

CHAPTER VII

K'ung Fû-tsze said: There have always been noble-minded people who lacked virtue, but there has never been a narrow-minded person who possessed it.

CHAPTER VIII

K'ung Fû-tsze said: Can one love others without seeking to guide them? Can one be loyal to others without seeking to teach them?

CHAPTER IX

K'ung Fû-tsze said: In preparing state documents, P'î Shăn created rough drafts. Shî-shû reviewed them and discussed their contents. Tsze-yü, head of Foreign relations, refined their style. And finally, Tsze-ch'ân of Tung-li added elegance.

Chapter VI: Î and Âo were members of a family of minor princes who lived c. 2200 BCE. Î was Âo's father. In 2145 BCE, they took the life of Emperor Hâu-hsiang. As a result of this, the slain emperor's son killed Âo. Then, a minister, Han Cho killed Î and married his widow. Both Î and Âo lived with violence, and died through violence.

Chî was the emperor's son. Upon becoming emperor, he made great strides in controlling the flow of water and in advancing agriculture. The Châu family traces its thousand year heritage to Chî. Yï was a legendary wise emperor of ancient times. He ascended to the throne through hereditary rights. K'ung Fû-tsze agreed with Nan-kung Kwo that one who lives without honor, will not live long.

Chapter VIII: Loving someone includes helping them to attain values. One cannot be loyal to one's children or one's subjects without teaching them values that will help them preserve their safety and honor.

Chapter IX: The state of Chăng, although small and surrounded by large powerful states, sustained its existence. It did so through the cooperation of its loyal ministers. P'î Shăn created drafts, Shî-shû reviewed them, Tsze-yü refined them, and Tsze-ch'ân finalized them.

或問子產子曰惠人也問子西曰彼哉彼哉問管仲曰人也

奪伯氏駢邑三百飯疏食沒齒無怨言

子曰貧而無怨難富而無驕易

子曰孟公綽為趙魏老則優　不可以為滕薛大夫

CHAPTER X
1. Asked about Tsze-ch'ân, K'ung Fû-tsze said: He was kind.
2. Asked about Tsze-hsî, K'ung Fû-tsze said: That man! That man!
3. Asked about Kwan Chung, K'ung Fû-tsze said: Kwan Chung was a genius. He was able to take three hundred households from the city of Pien without any consequences. The head of the Po family was limited to eating coarse food for the remainder of his life because of this. But because of the ingenuous actions of Kwan Chung, the head of the Po family clan never felt upset or murmured a complaint.

CHAPTER XI
K'ung Fû-tsze said: It is easy for the rich to live without arrogance, but difficult for the poor to live without complaining.

CHAPTER XII
K'ung Fû-tsze said: Măng Kung-ch'o is more than fit to be steward over the affairs of the Châo and Wei family clans. He is not fit, however, to be a great officer for small states such as T'ăng or Hsieh.

Chapter X: Tsze-ch'ân, chief minister of the state of Chăng, was a man of honor. He had four characteristics of an honorable leader. He was just, kind, respectful, and humble.

Tsze-hsî had been chief minister of the state of Ch'û. Although he was offered the position as monarch, he refused this in deference to the rightful heir. Yet K'ung Fû-tsze thought poorly of him because he did not oppose the aggression of the rulers of Ch'û. Tsze-hsî also opposed King Châo of Ch'û when he considered employing K'ung Fû-tsze.

Kwan Chung, chief minister under the Châu dynasty, took the fortune that the Po family had amassed in Pien from them. He did it in such a way, however, that although they lived without wealth for the rest of their lives, they did not complain. Because of this, he has been praised throughout Chinese history.

Chapter XII: During K'ung Fû-tsze's era, the state of Tsin was ruled by three families: the Châo, Wei, and Han clans. K'ung Fû-tsze felt that Măng Kung-ch'o could adequately handle their affairs of these states because they were so large, they were stable and secure. T'ăng or Hsieh were smaller states. Because their existences were threatened by larger states, they actually needed wiser ministers to run them.

子路問成人子曰若臧武仲之知公綽之不欲卞莊子之勇

冉求之藝文之以禮樂亦可以為成人矣曰今之成人者何

必然見利思義見危授命久要不忘平生之言

亦可以為成人矣

子問公叔文子於公明賈曰信乎夫子不言不笑不取乎公明賈

以告者過也夫時然後言人不厭其言樂然後笑人不厭其

笑義然後取人不厭其取子曰其然豈其然乎

Chapter XIII

1. Tsze-lû asked K'ung Fû-tsze to describe the traits of one he would consider perfectly virtuous. K'ung Fû-tsze said: One who possesses the knowledge of Tsang Wû-chung, the generosity of Kung-ch'o, the honor and courage of Chwang of Pien, the abilities of Zǎn Ch-iû, and the knowledge of one who has mastered the rules of propriety and music. This is an individual I would consider perfectly virtuous.
2. K'ung Fû-tsze then added: During present times, however this is not really necessary. Actually, I prefer one who seeing gain, will follow one's conscience; who faced with danger, will give up one's life; and who years later, will still honor a contract. This is an individual I would consider perfectly virtuous.

Chapter XIV

1. K'ung Fû-tsze asked Kung-ming Chiâ about Kung-shû Wǎn: Is it true that your master neither speaks, nor laughs, nor accepts things from others?
2. Kung-ming Chiâ replied: Such statements exaggerate the truth. My master speaks when it is the time to speak, so others do not tire of his speaking. He laughs when there is reason for joy, so others do not tire of his laughing. He acquires possessions when it is consistent with his conscience, so others do not tire of his taking. Facetiously, K'ung Fû-tsze inquired: Really, can that be said of you as well?

Chapter XIII: Tsang Wû-chung had been an officer for the state of Lû prior to K'ung Fû-tsze's era. He declined a position as feudal lord under the duke because he predicted that the duke would be overthrown and killed. Thus, he kept himself safe. His wisdom was so great that he was considered a sage.

Kung-ch'o had been a senior official of the state of Lû. He was respected for his ascetic lifestyle.

Chwang of Pien had been a great officer of the city of Pien. He was famous for his honor and bravery.

Zǎn Ch-iû was one of K'ung Fû-tsze's disciples. He was known for his talents.

Chapter XIV: K'ung Fû-tsze asks Kung-ming Chiâ about his master. Because K'ung Fû-tsze knew he was exaggerating, he asked Kung-ming Chiâ if what he said about his master was true of him as well.

子曰臧武仲以防求為後於魯雖曰不要君吾不信也

子曰晉文公譎而不正齊桓公正而不譎

子路曰桓公殺公子糾召忽死之管仲不死曰未仁乎

子曰桓公九合諸侯不以兵車管仲之力也如其仁如其仁

CHAPTER XV
K'ung Fû-tsze said: Tsang Wû-chung sought to maintain possession of Fang. He asked the duke of Lû to appoint a successor from his family. Although it may be said that this was not a threat, K'ung Fû-tsze believed it was.

CHAPTER XVI
K'ung Fû-tsze said: Duke Wăn of Tsin was cunning and not forthright. Duke Hwan of Ch'î was forthright and not cunning.

CHAPTER XVII
1. Tsze-lû said: Duke Hwan put his brother Chiû to death. Chiû's minister, Shâo Hû, chose to die with him. But Chiû's minister, Kwan Chung, did not. Who can deny that Kwan Chung was deficient in virtue?
2. K'ung Fû-tsze said: After this, Duke Hwan brought all the princes together for negotiations, eliminating the need for chariots or weapons of war. He did so under the guidance of Kwan Chung. Who could match his goodness? Who could match his goodness?

Chapter XV: Tsang Wû-chung had been forced by the Măng family to flee from Lû. As head of the Tsang family, it was his responsibility to ensure that temple sacrifices to ancestors were not neglected. He returned to the city of Fang, a city his family owned, and threatened the monarchy that if they did not permit such sacrifices, he would hold the city siege. K'ung Fû-tsze thought this threat was uncalled for, because the court would have granted him such rights anyway.

Chapter XVI: Duke Wăn of Tsin and Duke Hwan of Ch'î are important figures in China's history. They were the initial two of the five leaders of the empire.

Duke Wăn of Tsin was powerful during the Spring and Autumn period, ruling from 636–628 BCE. K'ung Fû-tsze thought he was crafty because he made other dukes worship his king.

Duke Hwan of Ch'î also served during the Spring and Autumn period, 681–643 BCE. When other states failed to respectfully pay tribute to his kingdom, he sent a peaceful convoy to them. Hence, K'ung Fû-tsze thought he was forthright.

Chapter XVII: K'ung Fû-tsze teaches that one must observe all facets of one's character before passing judgment on that individual. Kwan Chung did not sacrifice his own life when Duke Hwan killed his master Chiû. After this coup, when Duke Hwan assumed the throne, Kwan Chung continued in his position, working for peace. He helped Duke Hwan bring peace to the region by facilitating negotiations with neighboring states. K'ung Fû-tsze felt that Duke Hwan's subsequent honorable actions more then compensated for his initial dishonorable one.

子貢曰管仲非仁者與桓公殺公子糾不能死又相之子曰管

仲相桓公霸諸侯一匡天下民到如今受其賜微管仲

吾其被髮左衽矣豈若匹夫匹婦之為諒也自

經於溝瀆而莫之知也

公叔文子之臣大夫僎與文子同升諸公子聞之曰可以為文矣

子言衛靈公之無道也康子曰夫如是奚而不喪孔子曰仲

叔圉治賓客祝鮀治宗廟王孫賈治軍旅夫如是奚其喪

CHAPTER XVIII

1. Tsze-kung said: I believe Kwan Chung was wanting in virtue. When Duke Hwan took the life of his brother, Chiû, Kwan Chung could not bring himself to die with him. In fact, he became prime minister to Duke Hwan.

2. K'ung Fû-tsze said: Kwan Chung became prime minister to Duke Hwan, helped him become leader of all the princes, and united and rectified the entire kingdom. Down to the present day, people enjoy the benefits of his reign. Were it not for Kwan Chung, we might be wearing our hair bound or our coat lapels buttoned on the left side.

3. Should he have acted as the common boy or girl who commit suicide in a stream or ditch, no one even knowing about his cause?

CHAPTER XIX

1. The officer Hsien had been family minister to Kung-shû Wăn. He ascended to the prince's court along with his former chief, Wăn.

2. K'ung Fû-tsze, hearing this, said: He deserves his title of Wăn.

CHAPTER XX

1. K'ung Fû-tsze spoke about the unethical actions of Duke Ling of Wei. Ch'î K'ang asked: If he is of such character, why has he not lost his throne?

2. K'ung Fû-tsze said: He has Chung-shû Yü to run the department of guests and strangers, T'o to lead prayers and manage the ancestral temples, and Wang-sun Chiâ to lead his army. With honorable officers such as these, how could one lose one's throne?

Chapter XVIII: K'ung Fû-tsze defends Kwan Chung. Although he did not die for his master, this was a minor offense. He more than compensated for it by remaining in office and peacefully unifying the entire nation. Wearing one's hair bound and one's lapels buttoned on the left was considered an uncivilized practice of the primitive tribes of the east.

Chapter XIX: The title *Wăn* means *cultured*. Kung-shû Wăn recommended Hsien for a position in government. When Hsien was elevated to the same level position that Kung-shû Wăn held in court, Kung-shû Wăn was pleased. Because of his lack of envy, K'ung Fû-tsze stated Kung-shû Wăn deserved to be called *cultured*.

Chapter XX: Duke Ling of Wei, 533–492 BCE, was the husband of Nan-tsze, a woman of questionable character. Although Duke Ling was not a man of character himself, he chose capable and honorable individuals to run the government for him. Hence, he was able to maintain his throne.

子曰其言之不怍則為之也難

陳成子弑簡公孔子沐浴而朝告於哀公曰陳恒弑其君請

討之公曰告夫三子孔子曰以吾從大夫之後不敢不告也

君曰告夫三子者之三子告不可孔子曰以

以吾從大夫之後不敢不告也

子路問事君子曰勿欺也而犯之

子曰君子上達小人下達

子曰古之學者為己今之學者為人

CHAPTER XXI
K'ung Fû-tsze said: One who speaks without modesty will find difficulty living up to one's boasting.

CHAPTER XXII
1. Chăn Ch'ăng murdered Duke Chien of Ch'î.
2. K'ung Fû-tsze bathed, went to court, and informed Duke Âi. He said: Chăn Ch'ăng has slain the sovereign. I beg you to punish him.
3. Duke Âi said: Tell the chiefs of the three families about this.
4. K'ung Fû-tsze left, and following behind the procession of great ministers, said: I dare not speak of such matters, yet my prince told me to inform the chiefs of the three families about this.
5. K'ung Fû-tsze went to the chiefs and informed them. They did not do anything. K'ung Fû-tsze said: After informing the individuals who have the responsibility to take action, I will no longer speak of this.

CHAPTER XXIII
Tsze-lû asked how one should serve one's ruler. K'ung Fû-tsze said: Do not oppose him. But if you do oppose him, do it to his face.

CHAPTER XXIV
K'ung Fû-tsze said: The path of one with character is upwards. The path of one without character is downwards.

CHAPTER XXV
K'ung Fû-tsze said: In ancient times, people sought knowledge to cultivate themselves. Nowadays, people seek knowledge to gain the official approval of others.

Chapter XXII: The murder of Duke Chien of Ch'î occurred 481 BCE. K'ung Fû-tsze was already advanced in years. He took a ritual bath of ceremonial purification, fasted, washed his hair in water in which rice had been soaked, and bathed his body with hot water. Then he informed Duke Âi. He considered Duke Chien of Ch'î a man of virtue and tranquility. When he told the chiefs of the three families about the murder, they did not act. K'ung Fû-tsze recognized that he might not know the positions of the other individuals, and should best remain quiet.

Chapter XXIII: K'ung Fû-tsze believes that if one has something negative to say about another individual, one should say it to his face, not behind his back.

蘧伯玉使人於孔子孔子與之坐而問焉曰夫子何為對曰

夫子欲寡其過而未能也使者出子曰使乎使乎

子曰不在其位不謀其政曾子曰君子思不出其位

子曰君子恥其言而過其行

子曰君子道者三我無能焉仁者不憂知者不惑勇者不懼子貢曰夫子自道也

子貢方人子曰賜也賢乎哉夫我則不暇

CHAPTER XXVI
1. Chü Po-yü sent a messenger to K'ung Fû-tsze with friendly inquiries.
2. K'ung Fû-tsze sat down and questioned him: In what is your master presently engaged? The messenger replied: My master seeks to make his faults few, but has not yet succeeded. When the messenger departed, K'ung Fû-tsze said: An excellent messenger! An excellent messenger!

CHAPTER XXVII
K'ung Fû-tsze said: One not holding a position in politics should not ridicule the decisions of those bearing such responsibilities.

CHAPTER XXVIII
The philosopher Tsăng said: The thoughts of one of character will not falter from those thoughts expected of such an individual.

CHAPTER XXIX
K'ung Fû-tsze said: One of character is modest in speech and exceptional in action.

CHAPTER XXX
1. K'ung Fû-tsze said: One of perfect character possesses three great virtues. I have not mastered them. Virtuous, such an individual is free of anxiety. Wise, such an individual is free of confusion. Brave, such an individual is free of fear.
2. Tsze-kung said: Only you say you have not attained these.

CHAPTER XXXI
Tsze-kung had the habit of judging faults and merits of others. K'ung Fû-tsze said: Tsze-kung must have reached a high level of excellence. I do not have time for this.

Chapter XXVI: Chü Po-yü was an officer of the state of Wei and a disciple of K'ung Fû-tsze. He sent this letter to K'ung Fû-tsze after he had returned to Lû. K'ung Fû-tsze was pleased to learn that he was still seeking to improve his character.

Chapter XXXI: Tsze-kung judged others. K'ung Fû-tsze believed one should judge oneself, not others. He was being facetious when he stated that Tsze-kung had reached a high level of excellence.

子曰不患人之不己知患其不能也

子曰不逆詐不億不信抑亦先覺者是賢乎

微生畝謂孔子曰丘何為是栖栖者與無乃為佞乎孔子曰

非敢為佞也疾固也

子曰驥不稱其力稱其德也

或曰以德報怨何如子曰何以報德以直報怨以德報德

Chapter XXXII
K'ung Fû-tsze said: I am not concerned that others do not know me. I am concerned at my own inability to deserve recognition.

CHAPTER XXXIII
K'ung Fû-tsze said: There are individuals who neither anticipate deceit, nor suspect unfaithfulness in others, yet recognize these when these occur. Are not such individuals of wise character?

CHAPTER XXXIV
1. Wei-shăng Mâu asked K'ung Fû-tsze: Why do you keep traveling around? Is it not just because you like to talk?
2. K'ung Fû-tsze said: I do not permit myself idle talk. Rather, it is because I recognize the futility of not attempting to effect change.

CHAPTER XXXV
K'ung Fû-tsze said: A certain horse was called Ch'î, not because of its strength, but because of its good temperament.

CHAPTER XXXVI
1. Someone asked: What do you say about the philosophy: Injury should be repaid with kindness?
2. K'ung Fû-tsze replied: If one repays injury with kindness, then with what will one repay kindness?
3. Repay injury with justice, and repay kindness with kindness.

Chapter XXXII: This important concept is repeated four times in the *Analects*.

Chapter XXXIII: K'ung Fû-tsze respected those who were without suspicion, yet were able to accurately evaluate the character of others.

Chapter XXXIV: Wei-shăng Mâu must have been an older man, or he would not have addressed K'ung Fû-tsze without using his honorific title and he would not have insulted him. K'ung Fû-tsze simply responded that he traveled around teaching, not because he liked to speak, but because, had he not, others would not have an opportunity to gain from the wisdom he sought to share.

Chapter XXXV: K'ung Fû-tsze felt that a famous horse of antiquity that was able to run 1000 lî was able to do so, not because of its strength, but because of its obedience.

Chapter XXXVI: K'ung Fû-tsze gives a straightforward, practical, and honest answer.

子曰莫我知也夫子貢曰何為其莫知子也子曰不怨天不尤人

下學上達知我者其天乎

公伯寮愬子路於季孫子服景伯以告曰夫子固有惑志於

公伯寮吾力猶能肆諸市朝子曰道之將行也與命也

之將廢也與命也公伯寮其如命何

子曰賢者辟世其次辟地其次辟色其次辟言子曰作者七人矣

CHAPTER XXXVII
1. K'ung Fû-tsze said: Alas! No one understands my teachings.
2. Tsze-kung said: What do you mean that no one understands you? K'ung Fû-tsze replied: I do not teach about Heaven, or about how to change others. My teachings concern earthly matters, yet they rise to lofty levels. Only Heaven understands me!

CHAPTER XXXVIII
1. Kung-po Liâo slandered Tsze-lû, a disciple of K'ung Fû-tsze, to Chî-sun. Tsze-fû Ching-po, another disciple, informed K'ung Fû-tsze of this, saying that he feared his master, Chî-sun, might be led astray by Kung-po Liâo. But he said that he had the power to expose Kung-po Liâo's lies in the market and in the court.
2. K'ung Fû-tsze said: If my principles are to advance, it has been predetermined. If my principles are to fail, it has been predetermined. What can the lies of Kung-po Liâo do to harm me?

CHAPTER XXXIX
1. K'ung Fû-tsze said: Some people of virtue renounce the world.
2. Some people of virtue retire because of hostile conditions.
3. Some people of virtue retire because of hostile stares.
4. Some people of virtue retire because of hostile words.

CHAPTER XL
K'ung Fû-tsze said: I knew of seven such individuals.

Chapter XXXVII expresses a fundamental concept of Confucian philosophy: One should not focus on transcendental or theoretical concepts, or seek to change that which is beyond the realm of humankind. In addition, one should not seek to change those people one cannot change. Rather, one should search within onself and seek to live the most simple, just, and moral life one possibly can.

Chapter XXXVIII: Kung-po Liâo slandered Tsze-lû to Chî-sun. (Both Kung-po Liâo and Tsze-lû were employed by Chî-sun). Tsze-fû Ching-po, an officer of Lû, informed K'ung Fû-tsze of this, saying that he still had time to expose Kung-po Liâo for his lies. He mentions the courts and markets because corpses of criminals were placed on display in these sites: corpses of great officers in the courts, and corpses of common people in the market places. K'ung Fû-tsze, however, was not concerned. He knew that Chî-sun was a follower of his teachings and would not be swayed. He had faith that if honorable principles were meant to sustain, they would.

Chapter XL: K'ung Fû-tsze knew seven people of integrity who renounced the world rather than abandon their virtuous values.

子路宿於石門晨門曰奚自子路曰自孔氏曰

是知其不可而為之者與

子擊磬於衛有荷蕢而過孔氏之門者曰有心哉擊磬

乎既而曰鄙哉硜硜乎莫己知也斯己而已矣

則厲淺則揭子曰果哉末之難矣

子張曰書云高宗諒陰三年不言何謂也子曰何必高宗

古之人皆然君薨百官總己以聽於冢宰三年

CHAPTER XLI

Tsze-lû happened to be passing the night in Shih-măn. The gate-keeper asked him where he was from? Tsze-lû said he was from the school of Mister K'ung. The gate-keeper said: Oh, isn't that the same Mister K'ung who knows the futility of the world yet still seeks to change it?

CHAPTER XLII

1. One day in the state of Wei, K'ung Fû-tsze was playing a musical chime stone. A man carrying a straw basket passed the door. The passer-by remarked that the music expressed the heart of one filled with sadness concerning the actions of his country.

2. The passer-by continued, saying that the deep sounds of the chime told of one who had been misunderstood. He felt that if one is misunderstood, one should follow one's own conscience, and abandon employment in government. The passer-by recited the lyrics that accompany the tune: "Deep water must be crossed with one's clothes on; shallow water with one's clothes held up."

3. K'ung Fû-tsze said that the lyrics of the passer-by indicated that he was one who had attained wisdom by experiencing life. Hence, there was no need for him, K'ung Fû-tsze, to teach him.

CHAPTER XLIII

1. Tsze-chang questioned the validity of a passage from the *Shû* which stated that Kâo-tsung did not speak for three years to observe the traditional period of imperial mourning.

2. K'ung Fû-tsze said he wondered why Kâo-tsung was even mentioned, for all the ancients always followed this tradition. When a sovereign died, all officers simply continued to attend to their duties without the need for verbal instruction from the prime minister.

Chapter XLI: The gate-keeper may have been one of the virtuous men who renounced the world and assumed a humble position.

Chapter XLII: The lyrics of the tune were from an ancient *Ode*. The *Ode* advises that if one cannot change a situation, one should adapt to it.

Chapter XLIII: The *Shû* is one of the ancient *Chinese Classics*. It tells that one must mourn one's ancestors for three years after their death. Tsze-chang questioned as to how the government functioned over these three years if Kâo-tsung did not speak. K'ung Fû-tsze responded that words were not necessary because all the officers attended to their duties without having to be told to do so.

子曰上好禮則民易使也

子路問君子子曰修己以敬曰如

斯而已乎曰修己以安人曰如

斯而已乎曰修己以安百姓修己以安

百姓堯舜其猶病諸

原壤夷俟子曰幼而不孫弟長而無述焉老而不死

是為賊　以杖叩其脛

闕黨童子將命或問之曰益者與子曰吾見其居於位也

見其與先生並行也非求益者也欲速成者也

CHAPTER XLIV

K'ung Fû-tsze said that when rulers live adhering to virtuous values, their people will serve them readily.

CHAPTER XLV

Tsze-lû asked what made a person virtuous? K'ung Fû-tsze said: One who cultivates oneself with reverent carefulness will become virtuous. Tsze-lû asked: Is that all? K'ung Fû-tsze replied: One who cultivates oneself inorder to bring peace and happiness to others. Tsze-lû asked: Is that all? K'ung Fû-tsze replied: One who cultivates oneself to bring peace and happiness to all humanity. But even Emperors Yâo and Shun found this difficult.

CHAPTER XLVI

Yüan Zang squatted on his heels awaiting the approach of K'ung Fû-tsze. K'ung Fû-tsze said that as a youth, Yüan Zang had not humbled himself as was befitting a junior. In adulthood, he had not accomplished anything worthy of being handed down. And in old age, he was merely a pest. With this K'ung Fû-tsze gave a friendly tap on Yüan Zang's shank with his staff.

CHAPTER XLVII

1. K'ung Fû-tsze hired a young man from the village of Ch'üeh to carry messages to and from visitors. Someone asked K'ung Fû-tsze if he did so because he thought the lad showed potential.
2. K'ung Fû-tsze replied: It is not because the young man shows potential, but rather because he seeks to fill the seat of an adult too quickly. He wants to walk shoulder to shoulder with his elders, seeking the respect of age, without first cultivating himself.

Chapter XLV: Emperors Yâo and Shun were legendary emperors of the third millennium BCE

Chapter XLVI: Yüan Zang was an eccentric old acquaintance of K'ung Fû-tsze who had become a Taoist. He allowed himself great liberties in conduct. He did not rise respectfully to greet K'ung Fû-tsze. K'ung Fû-tsze tapped him on the shank with his staff in the kindly spirit of an old friend.

Chapter XLVII: K'ung Fû-tsze sought to humble the young man by giving him humbling tasks to guide him on a path of self-cultivation.

衞靈公問陳於孔子。對曰俎豆之事則嘗聞之矣軍旅之事未之學也明日遂行

在陳絕糧從者病莫能興子路慍見曰君子亦有窮乎子曰君子固窮小人窮斯濫矣

子曰賜也女以予為多學而識之者與對曰然非與曰非也予一以貫之

子曰由知德者鮮矣

子曰無為而治者其舜也與夫何為哉恭己正南面而已矣

BOOK XV   WEI LING KUNG
Duke Ling of Wei

CHAPTER I

1. Duke Ling of Wei asked K'ung Fû-tsze to teach him military tactics. K'ung Fû-tsze said that he preferred to direct his teaching toward the practice of sacrifice. He said he had never studied war. The following day, K'ung Fû-tsze left.
2. When he arrived in Chăn, K'ung Fû-tsze's provisions were cut off. His followers, exhausted, became so ill they were unable to rise.
3. His disciple, Tsze-lû, outraged, asked why honorable people, such as they, should suffer such indignities? K'ung Fû-tsze said that, although those with character may be forced to endure such deprivation, those without character, when reduced to such states, would also suffer unbridled license.

CHAPTER II

1. K'ung Fû-tsze asked Ts'ze if he thought that he, K'ung Fû-tsze, had studied tremendously and amassed a great deal of knowledge.
2. Ts'ze replied affirmatively, and asked if this was so.
3. K'ung Fû-tsze said this was not the case. He said that all his wisdom was merely one continuous thread weaving a life of virtue.

CHAPTER III

K'ung Fû-tsze said to Yû: Those who know virtue are few.

CHAPTER IV

K'ung Fû-tsze said: Although Emperor Shun did not exert himself, he governed well. He accomplished this by conducting himself reverently and seriously.

Book XV deals with virtue and honor in one's personal life and in government.

Chapter I: K'ung Fû-tsze tells Duke Ling that his knowledge is of sacrificial ceremonies. He wished to teach the duke propriety, not violence. When he and his men left to travel from Wei to Chăn, the duke of Wei cut off their food supply.

Chapter II: K'ung Fû-tsze's goal was not to amass facts, but rather to cultivate values that would help others lead virtuous lives.

Chapter IV: K'ung Fû-tsze believed that when a leader governs virtuously, his subjects will strive to live similarly.

子張問行子曰言忠信行篤敬雖蠻貊之邦行矣言不忠信行

不篤敬雖州里行乎哉立則見其參於前也在輿則見其

倚於衡也夫然後行子張書諸紳

子曰直哉史魚邦有道如矢邦無道如矢君子者蘧伯玉邦有

道則仕邦無道則可卷而懷之

子曰可與言而不與之言失人不可與言而與之言失言

知者不失人亦不失言

子曰志士仁人無求生以害仁有殺身以成仁

CHAPTER V

1. Tsze-chang asked how one should conduct oneself to be of value to all people.

2. K'ung Fû-tsze said: Be sincere and truthful in speech, and be honorable and careful in deed. Do so even when among the uncivilized tribes of the North and the South. If one's words are not sincere and truthful, and one's deeds are not honorable and careful, one will not be of value even to one's own people.

3. Wherever you go, remember these two principles. Carve them on the yoke of your carriage so that you see them in front of you. Then you may carry them into practice at all times.

4. Tsze-chang wrote these words on the ends of his sash.

CHAPTER VI

1. K'ung Fû-tsze said: The historian, Yü, was a man of honor. Whether good or bad government prevailed, he remained as straightforward as an arrow.

2. Chü Po-yü was a man of even higher character. When good government prevailed, he assumed office. When bad government prevailed, he retired from office. His honorable values were dear to his heart.

CHAPTER VII

K'ung Fû-tsze said: There are those amongst whom one should speak. Not to speak, would be to waste those people. There are those amongst whom one should remain silent. To speak, would be to waste one's words. One who neither errors in wasting people, nor in wasting words, is one with wisdom.

CHAPTER VIII

K'ung Fû-tsze said: One striving to live a virtuous life would prefer death over loss of virtue. Such an individual will sacrifice his or her life to preserve virtue.

Chapter VI: The historian Yü remained dedicated to truth. Whether the government was honorable or dishonorable, he documented all facts truthfully. The government official Chü Po-yü was of even higher integrity. When government was honorable he worked diligently, when government was dishonorable, he resigned.

子貢問為仁子曰工欲善其事必先利其器居是邦也

事其大夫之賢者友其士之仁者

顏淵問為邦子曰行夏之時乘殷之輅服周之冕樂

則韶舞放鄭聲遠佞人鄭聲淫佞人殆

子曰人無遠慮必有近憂

子曰已矣乎吾未見好德如好色者也

子曰臧文仲其竊位者與知柳下惠之賢而不與立也

CHAPTER IX
Tsze-kung asked about the practice of virtue. K'ung Fû-tsze said: An artisan, wishing to work well, must first sharpen his tools. Follow this example. Where ever you are living, surround yourself with the most virtuous officers, and befriend the most virtuous scholars.

CHAPTER X
1. Yen Yüan asked how one should administer government.
2. K'ung Fû-tsze advised: Follow the calendar of Hsiâ.
3. Ride in the state carriage of Yin.
4. Wear the ceremonial cap of Châu.
5. Play the music and incorporate the pantomimes of Shâo.
6. Banish the songs of Chǎng and stay far away from flattering talkers.

CHAPTER XI
K'ung Fû-tsze said: If one is not carefully observant of that which has happened far away; one will find sorrow near at hand.

CHAPTER XII
K'ung Fû-tsze said: It is over! I have not seen one whose love of virtue is as great as one's love of beauty.

CHAPTER XIII
K'ung Fû-tsze said: Were not the actions of Tsang Wǎn those of a man who had stolen his position? He knew the virtue and talents of Hûi of Liû-hsiâ, yet he did not propose that Hûi should stand with him in court.

Chapter X gives examples of virtue in the governments of various dynasties. The calendar of China begins with the Hsiâ dynasty. The state carriage of the Yin dynasty was plain, yet substantial. The ceremonial cap of the Châu dynasty was small. The music and the pantomimes of the Shâo dynasty followed doctrines of the Shun dynasty. The songs of the Chǎng dynasty lacked moral discipline. K'ung Fû-tsze's philosophy teaches one to beware of flattery. It is dangerous.

Chapter XII: It is believed that K'ung Fû-tsze uttered this when he saw the duke of Wei riding in a carriage with Nan-tsze, a woman of questionable character.

Chapter XIII: Tsang Wǎn recognized that Hûi was more capable at performing his job then he was. He did not recommend Hûi for advancement, however, for fear that he would move up the ranks and eventually replace him.

子曰躬自厚而薄責於人則遠怨矣

子曰不曰如之何如之何者吾末如之何也已矣

子曰群居終日言不及義好行小慧難矣哉

子曰君子義以為質禮以行之孫以出之信以成之君子哉

子曰君子病無能焉不病人之不己知也

子曰君子疾沒世而名不稱焉

子曰君子求諸己小人求諸人

Chapter XIV
K'ung Fû-tsze said: One who requires much from oneself and little from others, will not be resented.

Chapter XV
K'ung Fû-tsze said: To those who do not question, "What is correct?" I can offer no guidance.

Chapter XVI
K'ung Fû-tsze said: I find it difficult to understand those who gather together all day without their conversations turning toward righteousness, but speak rather on petty, financial issues. It is difficult to understand their values.

Chapter XVII
K'ung Fû-tsze said: One of character: considers righteousness essential in all matters; performs all adhering to rules of propriety; brings forth all in humility; and completes all with sincerity. Such an individual is indeed virtuous.

Chapter XVIII
K'ung Fû-tsze said: One of character is not distressed if others do not show recognition, but is distressed, rather, by one's own lack of ability to perform things worthy of recognition.

Chapter XIX
K'ung Fû-tsze said: One of character regrets if one cannot leave an honorable legacy.

Chapter XX
K'ung Fû-tsze said: What one without character seeks, is within others. What one of character seeks, is within oneself.

Chapter XVI: It is difficult to teach values to those whose only concern is money.

Chapter XVIII: One should be concerned about one's own competency, not about the opinions and praise of others.

Chapter XIX: One of character does not want one's name remembered for glory. One of character is content merely knowing that one has lived honorably.

子曰君子矜而不爭群而不黨

子曰君子不以言舉人不以人廢言

子貢問曰有一言而可以終身行之者乎子曰其恕乎
己所不欲勿施於人

子曰吾之於人也誰毀誰譽如有所譽者其有所試矣斯民也
三代之所以直道而行也

子曰吾猶及史之闕文也有馬者借人乘之今亡矣夫

CHAPTER XXI

K'ung Fû-tsze said: One of character is dignified and does not squabble. One of character is impartial and is accepting of all.

CHAPTER XXII

K'ung Fû-tsze said: One of character does not esteem others merely because of what they say. One of character does not dismiss what is said merely because of the individual who has said it.

CHAPTER XXIII

Tsze-kung asked: Is there one word one may use to guide one throughout one's life? K'ung Fû-tsze said: Is not "reciprocity" such a word? Do not do to others what you do not want done to yourself.

CHAPTER XXIV

1. K'ung Fû-tsze said: In my dealings with people: Whose errors have I unjustly condemned? Whose good actions have I unjustly praised? If I have sometimes conferred excess praise, it is because I found ground for it within the character of that individual.
2. Leaders of the three dynasties laid the path of righteousness. They supplied the groundwork upon which our civilization has been founded.

CHAPTER XXV

K'ung Fû-tsze said: Years back, historians would leave a blank in their texts. Years back, owners of a horse would lend it to others to ride. People with such virtues no longer exist.

Chapter XXIII: K'ung Fû-tsze states that if people were to use one word to guide their lives, it would be "reciprocity." Do not do to others what you do not want done to yourself.

Chapter XXIV, passage 1: K'ung Fû-tsze hoped that he did not unjustly condemn or praise anyone. He sought to praise people for the sincerity of their attempt, not merely for the outcome.

Chapter XXIV, passage 2: K'ung Fû-tsze is referring to the leaders of the Hsia, Shang, and Châu dynasties for laying a foundation of morality.

Chapter XXV: K'ung Fû-tsze reflects back to the time when historians would record only truth, and leave blanks in the text rather than record something that was not accurate. The meaning of the second half of the passage has been lost to antiquity.

子曰巧言亂德 小不忍則亂大謀

子曰衆惡之必察焉 衆好之必察焉

子曰人能弘道非道弘人

子曰過而不改是謂過矣

子曰吾嘗終日不食終夜不寢以思無益不如學也

子曰君子謀道不謀食耕也餒在其中矣學也祿在其中矣君子憂道不憂貧

CHAPTER XXVI
K'ung Fû-tsze said: Cunning words distort truth. Impatience in small matters destroys great plans.

CHAPTER XXVII
K'ung Fû-tsze said: If many others dislike an individual, one must examine the situation. If many others like an individual, one must examine the situation.

CHAPTER XXVIII
K'ung Fû-tsze said: It is the individual who cultivates virtue, not virtue that cultivates the individual.

CHAPTER XXIX
K'ung Fû-tsze said: To have faults and not strive to correct them, is indeed, to have faults.

CHAPTER XXX
K'ung Fû-tsze said: I neither ate all day, nor slept all night. I rejected my physical needs in an attempt to attain wisdom. It was of no use. I do better studying.

CHAPTER XXXI
K'ung Fû-tsze said: The goal of one of character is not food. It is truth. For those who plough, their fear is loss of profit and even famine. For those seeking wisdom and virtue, their only fear is failing to understand truth.

Chapter XXVII: One must not act blindly in accepting popular judgment.

Chapter XXVIII: One must continually strive to cultivate one's virtue. Once having attained some virtuous traits, one must not become complacent. Virtue does not continue to grow on its own.

Chapter XXX: One's actions should not be aimless. One should not reject one's physical needs just for the sake of renunciation. One's actions should be oriented towards a purpose.

Chapter XXXI: One of character does not seek tangible gain. One of character recognizes that one can never predict fate and, according, does not worry if the future will bring wealth or poverty. Rather, one of character fears only lack of personal integrity and virtue.

子曰知及之仁不能守之雖得之必失之知及之仁能守之不莊以莅

之則民不敬知及之仁能守之莊以莅之動之不以禮未善也

子曰君子不可小知而可大受也小人不可大受而可小知也

子曰民之於仁也甚於水火水火吾見蹈而死者矣

未見蹈仁而死者也

子曰當仁不讓於師

子曰君子貞而不諒

CHAPTER XXXII

1. K'ung Fû-tsze said: If one's knowledge is sufficient to secure gain, but one's virtue not sufficient to maintain it, whatever one has attained, one will lose.

2. If one's knowledge is sufficient to secure gain and one's virtue is sufficient to maintain it, yet one cannot lead with dignity, one will not gain the respect of one's people.

3. If one's knowledge is sufficient to secure gain, and one's virtue is sufficient to maintain it, and one leads with dignity, but does not follow the rules of propriety, one will never reach one's full potential.

CHAPTER XXXIII

K'ung Fû-tsze said: One of high character may not succeed in mundane activities, but will succeed in great ones. One of low character may succeed in mundane activities, but will not succeed in great ones.

CHAPTER XXXIV

K'ung Fû-tsze said: Virtue is more important to the survival of humankind than either fire or water. One treading dangerously amidst fire or water may still sustain one's life, but one lacking virtue will surely succumb to one's folly.

CHAPTER XXXV

K'ung Fû-tsze said: One must consider virtue as necessary for the cultivation of one's character. One cannot delegate the responsibility for cultivation of one's virtue to any other individual, even to one's teacher.

CHAPTER XXXVI

K'ung Fû-tsze said: One with virtuous values is not just strong in one's committment to actions, but is also strong in character.

Chapter XXXIII: The way of a great individual is profound and far-reaching, while the way of the small individual is shallow and short-sighted.

Chapter XXXIV: Fire or water may harm parts of one's body. But lack of virtue will harm every aspect of one's existence.

子曰事君敬其事而後其食

子曰有教無類

子曰道不同不相為謀

子曰辭達而已矣

師冕見及階子曰階也及席子曰席也皆坐

子告之曰某在斯某在斯師冕出子張問曰

與師言之道與子曰然固相師之道也

CHAPTER XXXVII
K'ung Fû-tsze said: In serving his leader, a minister should fulfill his duties reverently and consider remuneration only secondarily.

CHAPTER XXXVIII
K'ung Fû-tsze said: When teaching, one should make no distinction between students based upon their class in society.

CHAPTER XXXIX
K'ung Fû-tsze said: Those treading along different life paths should not lay plans for one another.

CHAPTER XL
K'ung Fû-tsze said: In language, it is just simple clarity that is best.

CHAPTER XLI
1. K'ung Fû-tsze called upon the music-master Mien. Upon his arrival at the steps, K'ung Fû-tsze said: Here are the steps. When he arrived at the sitting mat, K'ung Fû-tsze said: Here is the mat. When all were seated, K'ung Fû-tsze told him who was present.
2. After the music-master Mien left, Tsze-chang asked K'ung Fû-tsze if it was the custom to inform the music-master of such things.
3. K'ung Fû-tsze told him: Certainly, these are the courtesies one should show when directing the blind.

Chapter XLI: The blind were employed in musical professions because their sense of hearing was more acute than that of ordinary individuals.

季氏將伐顓臾冉有季路見於孔子曰季氏將有事於顓臾

孔子曰求無乃爾是過與夫顓臾昔者先王以為東蒙主且

在邦域之中矣是社稷之臣也何以伐為

冉有曰夫子欲之吾二臣者皆不欲也

孔子曰求周任有言曰陳力就列不能者止危而不持顛而

不扶則將焉用彼相矣且爾言過矣虎兕出於柙龜玉毀

於櫝中是誰之過與

冉有曰今夫顓臾固而近於費今不取後世必為子孫憂

BOOK XVI CHÎ SHIH
Chief of the Chî

CHAPTER I

1. The chief of the Chî family was planning to attack Chwan-yü.
2. Zan Yû and Chî-lû met with K'ung Fû-tsze. They said that their leader, Chî, was planning to attack the region of Chwan-yü.
3. K'ung Fû-tsze asked: Are you not at fault?
4. K'ung Fû-tsze continued: Long ago, a former king appointed the ruler of Chwan-yü to preside over the sacrifices to the Eastern Măng Mountains in the midst of our State of Lû. Since then, our ministers have presided over the sacrifices. What right has your chief to attack it?
5. Zan Yû said: It is our master's wish, it is not ours.
6. K'ung Fû-tsze said: The words of Châu Zăn teach: "While one can function effectively, one should hold office. When one is no longer able to do so, one should retire." How can one be an effective guide to a blind man if one does not support him when he stumbles or raise him up when he falls?
7. In addition, your words are not correct. When a tiger or rhinoceros escapes from a cage, when a tortoise shell or piece of jade is damaged in its repository, who is at fault, certainly not the object itself?

Chapter I, paragraph 1: The chief of the Chî family was planning to attack Chwan-yü, a small principality in the state of Lû. This occurred c. 483–482 BCE.

Paragraph 2: Two of this chief's disciples came to tell K'ung Fû-tsze of the impending attack.

Paragraph 3: K'ung Fû-tsze addressed one of the disciples and asked him if he did not think that he, as advisor to his chief, was at fault.

Paragraph 4: K'ung Fû-tsze tells the history of this region. The former king of the Châu dynasty had granted a royalty to the chief of Chwan-yü making him lord of the Măng mountains. As such, he was permitted to preside over sacrifices offered to the hills and rivers of the region. He was minister to the altars of land and grain. K'ung Fû-tsze questioned how anyone could dare attack the chief of Chwan-yü and think of taking this land granted to him by the monarchy?

Passage 6: K'ung Fû-tsze relays the words of a famous historian, Châu Zăn, of the Shang dynasty. He then questions Ch'iû as to why he remained in his official capacity if he was not able to steer his chief from danger.

Passage 7: K'ung Fû-tsze uses these examples to tell the disciples that it was their responsibilities as ministers to the Chî family clan to prevent this attack.

孔子曰求君子疾夫舍曰欲之而必为之辞丘也闻有国有家者不患寡而患不均不患贫而患不安盖均无贫和无寡安无倾夫如是故远人不服则修文德以来之既来之则安之

今由与求也相夫子远人不服而不能来也邦分崩离析而不能守也而谋动干戈于邦内吾恐季孙之忧不在颛臾而在萧墙之内也

8. Zăn Yû said: Even now, Chwan-yü is strongly fortified and is close to Pî. If our chief does not take it, years from now our descendents will regret it.

9. K'ung Fû-tsze said: One of honor would feel contempt for such hypocritical displays of greed, concealed with excuses.

10. There is a saying that rulers of states and chiefs of families need not worry about poverty; but worry rather about uneven distribution of wealth. They need not worry about scarcity of people, but worry rather about discontent and insurrection among the people already there. For where there is equal distribution of goods among all, there will be no poverty. Where there is harmony among all, there will be no scarcity of people. And where there is contentment among all, there will be no insurrection.

11. If outlying small communities do not wish to join a large state, the large state should cultivate its arts, culture, and virtue. Then, sensing its culture and tranquility, the smaller outlying states will be attracted to join it.

12. Now you, Yû and Ch'iû, are assisting your chief in conquering distant peoples. These are people that you have not been able to attract and who resist your conquest. It is the disharmony, moral decay, desire for emigration, and uneven distribution of wealth within your own territory that has led to your problem. Your leader has not been able to create stability within his own state.

13. Now he is planning to invade another state. I fear that the sorrow that will befall the Chî-sun family will not come from the states it is trying to conquer, but rather from the blindness within its own court.

Passage 8: Zăn Yû gives the excuse that the tiny municipality, Chwan-yü, is close to Pî and might someday be a threat to it.

Passage 9: K'ung Fû-tsze tells Zăn Yû that he feels contempt for such a lame excuse offered as a reason to invade another people.

Passage 10: K'ung Fû-tsze tells Zan Yû and Chî-lû that their leader should focus his attention on his own community, rather than on the communities outside it.

Passage 13: K'ung Fû-tsze advises Zan Yû and Chî-lû that even if the chief of the Chî-sun family invades Chwan-yü, this conquest will not endure and his own state will not survive. His monarchy will fall, not because of its conquest, but because of the instability within its own borders.

孔子曰天下有道則禮樂征伐自天子出天下無道則禮樂

征伐自諸侯出蓋十世希不失矣自大夫出五世希不

失矣陪臣執國命三世希不失矣天下有道
則政不在大夫天下有道則庶人不議

孔子曰祿之去公室五世矣政逮於大夫四世矣
故夫三桓之子孫微矣

孔子曰益者三友損者三友友直友諒友多聞益矣
友便辟 友善柔友便佞損矣

CHAPTER II

1. K'ung Fû-tsze said: When honorable government prevails in an empire, ceremonies, music, and defensive military operations proceed from the son of Heaven. When dishonorable government prevails, ceremonies, music, and defensive military operations proceed from the princes. When princes direct the state, in all but a few instances, within ten generations the monarchy loses its power. When great officers of the princes direct the state, in all but a few cases, within five generations the monarchy loses its power. When subsidiary ministers of the great officers direct the state, in all but a few cases, within three generations the monarchy loses its power.
2. Generally, in an empire that is governed well, the government is not in the hands of the officers.
3. Generally, when an empire is governed well, the common people do not feel the need to discuss politics.

CHAPTER III

K'ung Fû-tsze said: For five generations, state revenues have been diverted. For four generations, the government has been in the hands of the great officers. Becuase of this, the descendants of the three sons of Duke Hwan are in a sorry situation.

CHAPTER IV

K'ung Fû-tsze said: Three types of friendships are advantageous and three types of friendships are injurious. Friendship with the upright, the sincere, and the cautious are advantageous. Friendship with those who flatter, those who are coy, and those who are glib of tongue are injurious.

Chapter II: An honorable, virtuous ruler was considered to be the son of Heaven. Descendents and heirs of such rulers, however, were not always considered so.

One in supreme authority should always maintain control of one's power. Violation of this rule would invariably lead to collapse of the empire. The sooner the control was placed in the hands of lower officers, the faster the collapse. In this case, the authority of the princes was usurped by the great officers, and then by the ministers below them.

Chapter III: When the government fell into the hands of lower officers, it collapsed. In 609 BCE, after the death of Duke Wăn of Lû, his rightful heir was killed. The son of a concubine advanced to the throne. It was now five generations since a rightful heir was in control. K'ung Fû-tsze felt that their situation was hopeless. In one more generation, this government would collapse.

孔子曰益者三樂損者三樂：節禮樂；道人之善

樂多賢友益矣樂驕樂；佚遊樂宴樂損

孔子曰侍於君子有三愆言未及之而言謂之躁

言及之而不言謂之隱未見顏色而言謂之瞽

孔子曰君子有三戒少之時血氣未定戒之在色及其壯也

血氣方剛戒之在鬥及其老也血氣既衰戒之在得

孔子曰君子有三畏畏天命畏大人畏聖人之言小人不知天命

而不畏也狎大人侮聖人之言

CHAPTER V

K'ung Fû-tsze said: There are three activities in which people find enjoyment that are advantageous and three that are injurious. Enjoyment in the study of ceremonies and music, in discussing good qualities of others, and in having many worthwhile friends are advantageous. Enjoyment in extravagant pleasures, in idleness, and in feasting are injurious.

CHAPTER VI

K'ung Fû-tsze said: In the presence of distinguished individuals, there are three errors of speech that one should avoid: Rashness, speaking before it is one's turn to speak; bashfulness, not speaking when it is one's obligation to speak; and blindness, speaking without observing the facial expressions of those above oneself.

CHAPTER VII

K'ung Fû-tsze said: There are three impulses that one of character guards against: In youth, when physical powers are not yet settled, against lust. In the prime of life, when physical powers are developed, against quarreling. In old age, when physical powers are weakened, against greed.

CHAPTER VIII

1. K'ung Fû-tsze said: There are three things towards which one of character stands in reverence: The Ordinances of Heaven; the deeds of great men; and the words of sages.
2. One without character does not stand in reverence concerning: The ordinances of Heaven, the deeds of great men, or the words of great sages.

Chapter V: Because ceremonies and music involve principles of propriety and harmony, K'ung Fû-tsze felt that the study of these could not help but be beneficial in the development of one's character

Chapter VIII: 'Ordinances of Heaven' refers to the moral responsibilities humans must uphold to live righteously. In Chinese philosophy, the designation 'great men' does not refer to famous men, but rather to individuals of character, virtue and wisdom.

孔子曰生而知之者上也學而知之者次也困而學之又其次也困而不學民斯為下矣

孔子曰君子有九思視思明聽思聰色思溫貌思恭言思忠事思敬疑思問忿思難見得思義

孔子曰見善如不及見不善如探湯吾見其人矣吾聞其語矣隱居以求其志行義以達其道吾聞其語矣未見其人也

CHAPTER IX

K'ung Fû-tsze said: Those born possessing innate knowledge are the most fortunate individuals. Those who learn and readily acquire knowledge are the next most fortunate. Those who are not bright, yet strive to learn are next. The least fortunate are those who are not bright and do not seek to attain understanding.

CHAPTER X

K'ung Fû-tsze said: There are nine actions concerning which one of character gives thoughtful consideration:
When observing, one of character seeks to see clearly.
When listening, one of character seeks to hear distinctly.
When dressing, one of character seeks to appear benign.
When setting demeanor, one of character seeks to be respectable.
When speaking, one of character seeks to be sincere.
When doing business, one of character seeks to be careful.
When in doubt, one of character seeks to learn from others.
When angry, one of character thinks of repercussions.
When seeking gain, one of character thinks of righteousness.

CHAPTER XI

1. K'ung Fû-tsze said he had heard of those who when contemplating good, pursued it as though it were an unattainable quest; and when contemplating evil, shrank from it as though pulling their hand from boiling water. K'ung Fû-tsze said that he had heard of such individuals, but had yet to meet one.
2. Such individuals often left society to study noble values. They sought to learn righteousness and truth. K'ung Fû-tsze said he heard of such individuals, but had yet to meet one.

Chapter IX: K'ung Fû-tsze did not place himself in the first category. He considered himself to be in the second. He did not create these categories to berate any individuals, but rather to explain the various life paths people chose based upon their innate natures and their values.

Chapter XI: These two sayings had been common during K'ung Fû-tsze's era.

齊景公有馬千駟死之日民無德而稱焉伯夷叔齊

餓死首陽之下民到于今稱之其斯之謂與

陳亢問於伯魚曰子亦有異聞乎對曰未也嘗獨立鯉趨而過庭

曰學詩乎對曰未也不學詩無以言鯉退而學詩他日又獨立鯉

趨而過庭曰學禮乎對曰未也不學禮無以立鯉退而學禮

聞斯二者陳亢退而喜曰問一得三聞詩聞禮

又聞君子之遠其子也

邦君之妻君稱之曰夫人夫人自稱曰小童邦人稱之曰君夫人

稱諸異邦曰寡小君異邦人稱之曰君夫人

CHAPTER XII

1. Duke Ching of Ch'î owned a thousand teams of horses, of four horses in each. But on the day of his death, people could not find any virtues in him to praise. Conversely, Po-î and Shû-ch'î lived humble lives and died of hunger at the foot of the Shâu-yang mountain. Even during K'ung Fû-tsze's time, people continued to praise them.
2. Does this not illustrate the significance of virtue over wealth?

CHAPTER XIII

1. Ch'ăn K'ang asked Po-yü [K'ung Fû-tsze's son]: Have you learned lessons from your father other than those we have been taught?
2. Po-yü replied: No. But one day, my father passed by the hall below with hasty steps. He asked: "Have you learned the *Odes*?" I replied: "Not yet." He said: "If you do not learn the *Odes*, you will not be fit to converse with." I left and studied the *Odes*.
3. Another day, again, I was standing alone. He passed in the hall below with hasty steps and said: "Have you learned the *Rules of Propriety*?" When I replied: "Not yet." he said: "If you do not learn the *Rules of Propriety*, your character will not be established." I left and learned the *Rules of Propriety*.
4. I have heard only these two things from him.
5. Ch'ăn K'ang left quite joyously saying: I asked one question and learned three. I learned about the significance of the *Odes* and the significance of the *Rules of Propriety*, and also that one of character maintains a distinct reserve between his son and himself.

CHAPTER XIV

The wife of the prince of a State was called Fû-zăn [helpmate] by the prince. She referred to herself as Hsiâo T'ung [little girl]. The people of the State called her Chün Fû-zăn [Prince's helpmate], and the people of other States called her either K'wa Hsiâo Chün [our small Princess of little worth] or Chün Fû-Zăn [Prince's helpmate].

Chapter XII tells of the lasting nature of honor, but not of wealth. The second passage refers to a saying from the Chinese classics: *"Truly, men are influenced not by wealth, but by merit."*

Chapter XIII: Through the words of Po-yü, K'ung Fû-tsze's son, one learns that a father must keep a cautious distance of respect between his children and himself.

Chapter XIV: The significance of this passage has been lost to antiquity.

陽貨 第十七

陽貨欲見孔子，孔子不見，歸孔子豚。孔子時其亡也，而往拜之，遇諸塗。謂孔子曰：來予與爾言。曰：懷其寶而迷其邦，可謂仁乎？曰不可。好從事而亟失時，可謂知乎？曰不可。日月逝矣，歲不我與。孔子曰：諾，吾將仕矣。

子曰性相近也習相遠也

BOOK XVII   YANG HO
Minister of the Chî Family

CHAPTER I

1. Yang Ho requested to see K'ung Fû-tsze. K'ung Fû-tsze would
not see him. So, Yang Ho sent K'ung Fû-tsze a gift of a pig. K'ung
Fû-tsze was required to express gratitude to Yang Ho for the gift by
visiting him. He chose a time to visit when he believed Yang Ho
would not be at home. On the way there, however, he met Yang Ho.

2. Yang Ho asked K'ung Fû-tsze to speak with him. He inquired:
Can one who keeps his jewels in his bosom and leaves his country in
disarray be considered benevolent? K'ung Fû-tsze replied: No. Yang
Ho asked: Can one who seeks public employment, yet forgoes the
opportunity of doing so, be considered wise? K'ung Fû-tsze again
replied: No. Then K'ung Fû-tsze said: The days and months are slip-
ping away. The years wait for no one. I will return to office.

CHAPTER II

K'ung Fû-tsze said: All people are born with similar natures. The
way in which each reacts to situations, however, gradually begins
to differ. These actions then become habits. These habits become
habitual patterns. It is these patterns that cause people to differ.

Book XVII: Yang Ho was the principal minister of the Chî family. He was scheming
to appropriate authority of the entire state of Lû to himself.

Chapter I: In order to further his own political aspirations, Yang Ho sought to make
it appear as though he had the support of a great scholar. It had been custom that if
a great officer sent a gift to a scholar, and the scholar was not there to personally
receive it, the scholar must go to the house of the officer to thank him. Yang Ho purposely sent the gift of a pig to K'ung Fû-tsze's house when he knew K'ung Fû-tsze
would not be there. Similarly, K'ung Fû-tsze purposely planned to offer thanks to
Yang Ho when he knew he would not be at home.

In the second passage, Yang Ho was really asking K'ung Fû-tsze if he would return to public office when he assumed power. Although K'ung Fû-tsze said that he
would, after reflecting on this answer, he knew he could not to return to office when
Yang Ho was in power.

Chapter II: K'ung Fû-tsze taught that although all people are born with similar
natures, all react to situations differently. These means of reacting become patterns.
Eventually, these patterns begin to define each individual's nature.

子曰唯上知與下愚不移

子之武城聞弦歌之聲夫子莞爾而笑曰割雞焉用牛刀子游對曰

昔者偃也聞諸夫子曰君子學道則愛人小人學道則易使也

子曰二三子偃之言是也前言戲之耳

公山弗擾以費畔召子欲往子路不說

曰末之也已何必公山氏之之也子曰夫

召我者而豈徒哉如有用我者吾其為東周乎

CHAPTER III
K'ung Fû-tsze said: Only two sorts of individuals never change: Those with the highest of virtues and those with the lowest.

CHAPTER IV
1. K'ung Fû-tsze went to Wû-ch'ăng. There, he heard the sound of stringed instruments and singing.
2. Pleased and smiling, he said: Why use an ox-knife to kill a fowl?
3. Tsze-yû said: Sometime ago I heard you say: "When one of high station is well instructed, he loves men; when one of low station is well instructed, he is easily ruled."
4. K'ung Fû-tsze said: Your words are correct, but I had only said that in jest.

CHAPTER V
1. During a rebellion, Kung-shan Fû-zâo was holding the town of Pî in siege. He invited K'ung Fû-tsze to visit him. K'ung Fû-tsze considered going.
2. Tsze-lû was displeased. He told K'ung Fû-tsze that he considered it traitorous for him to go, and asked K'ung Fû-tsze why he would even consider going to see Kung-shan?
3. K'ung Fû-tsze replied: There must be a reason he invited me. If anyone needs me now, it is the state of eastern Châu.

Chapter IV, Passage 1: K'ung Fû-tsze went to Wû-ch'ăng and observed that the state had changed from a warlike state to a peace-loving one. He observed people rehearsing the rites and music.

Passage 2: K'ung Fû-tsze used this expression to convey the teaching that one need not overreact to a situation.

Passage 3: This expression relates to the youth. If the children of nobility are taught values, later in life, they will respect and care for their people. If the children of commoners are taught virtue, they will become responsible citizens.

Passage 4: K'ung Fû-tsze admitted that he had made this statement, but that he had never realized how true it was.

Chapter V: Kung-shan Fû-zâo had staged a coup d'état of the town of Pî. The original seat of the Châu dynasty was west of Lû, and Pî was in the eastern region of the state. Tsze-lû was upset that K'ung Fû-tsze would visit someone who had committed such a dishonorable act. K'ung Fû-tsze thought that if he went there, he might be able to guide Kung-shan Fû-zâo back to virtue. In the end, however, K'ung Fû-tsze did not go.

241

子張問仁於孔子孔子曰能行五者於天下為仁矣請問之

曰恭寬信敏惠恭則不侮寬則得眾信則人任焉

敏則有功惠則足以使人

佛肸召子欲往子路曰昔者由也聞諸夫子曰親於其身為不

善者君子不入也佛肸以中牟畔子之往也如之何子曰

有是言也不曰堅乎磨而不磷不曰白乎涅而不緇

吾豈匏瓜也哉焉能繫而不食

CHAPTER VI

Tsze-chang asked K'ung Fû-tsze how one might attain perfect virtue. K'ung Fû-tsze said: One with perfect virtue exhibits five characteristics everywhere under Heaven. Tsze-chang begged to know what they were. K'ung Fû-tsze replied: Seriousness, generosity of soul, sincerity, earnestness, and kindness. Being serious, one will be treated with respect. Being generous, one will win the hearts of others. Being sincere, one will gain the trust of others. Being earnest, one will achieve much. Being kind, one will attract the services of others.

CHAPTER VII

1. Pi Hsi invited K'ung Fû-tsze to visit him. K'ung Fû-tsze was inclined to do so.
2. Tsze-lu said: Master, once I heard you say that one of noble character does not associate with those committing evil. Now, although Pi Hsi is holding the village of Chung-mau hostage, you consider meeting with him?
3. K'ung Fû-tsze said: Yes, I did say this. But it is also said: That which is hard enough, though ground with force, can never be worn thin. And that which is pure white, though seeped in a dark fluid, can never be made black.
4. Am I a bitter gourd! How can I be hung up, out of the way, and not be eaten?

Chapter VI: The term "Everywhere under Heaven" means everywhere on earth.

Chapter VII, Passage 1: Pi Hsi was an official under the chief of the Ch'ao family in the state of Tsin (in Honan province). He incited rebellion.

Passage 3: Through these two sayings, K'ung Fû-tsze sought to teach his disciples that one of character, such as he, with a strong foundation of personal integrity, will never be tainted by associating with one of dishonorable character.

Passage 4: K'ung Fû-tsze wants to meet with the individual committing the evil actions to try to help resolve the situation. He pleads that he does not want to be a mere valueless, bitter fruit. He longs to be of use in bringing peace to the region.

子曰由也女聞六言六蔽矣乎對曰未也居吾語女好仁而不好學

其蔽也愚好知而不好學其蔽也蕩好信而

不好學其蔽也賊好直而不好學其蔽也絞好

勇而不好學其蔽也亂好剛而不好學其蔽也狂

子曰小子何莫學夫詩詩可以興可以觀可以羣可以怨

邇之事父遠之事君多識鳥獸草木之名

CHAPTER VIII

1. K'ung Fû-tsze asked: Yû, have you heard of the *Six Cloudings of the Mind* that attach to the *Six Virtues*? Yû replied that he had not.
2. K'ung Fû-tsze asked him to sit down so that he might teach him.
3. The *Six Cloudings of the Mind* are:

Love of Benevolence, without virtue:
This clouds the mind with foolishness.
Love of Knowledge, without virtue:
This clouds the mind with scatterings.
Love of Sincerity, without virtue:
This clouds the mind with naivety.
Love of Straightforwardness, without virtue:
This clouds the mind with rudeness.
Love of Boldness, without virtue:
This clouds the mind with insolence.
Love of Determination, without virtue:
This clouds the mind with eccentricity.

CHAPTER IX

1. K'ung Fû-tsze said: My disciples, why do you not study the *Book of Odes*?
2. The odes elevate one's mind.
3. They promote introspection.
4. They teach the art of social intercourse.
5. They help one subdue one's feelings of resentment.
6. They teach one about one's duty to one's father inside the home, and about one's duty to one's prince outside the home.
7. Through them, one attains knowledge about nature: the birds, beasts, plants, and trees.

Chapter VIII: Without virtue, one's mind will be covered by a cloud. One without virtue will not be able to recognize truth as it really is. For example, if one is benevolent and does not possess virtue, one may help those who do not need help, just to curry personal favor, rather than helping those who are truly needy.

Chapter IX: K'ung Fû-tsze felt that the ancient *Chinese Classic*, the *Book of Odes* (the *Book of Poetry)*, helps one: think at a higher level; recognize one's own character; interact with others; mellow one's feelings; accept responsibility; and understand the world around oneself.

子謂伯魚曰女為周南召南矣乎人而不為周南召南其猶正牆面而立也與

子曰禮云云玉帛云乎哉樂云樂云鐘鼓云乎哉

子曰色厲而內荏譬諸小人其猶穿窬之盜也與

子曰鄉原德之賊也

子曰道聽而塗說德之棄也

子曰鄙夫可與事君也與哉其未得之也患得之既得之患失之苟患失之無所不至矣

CHAPTER X

K'ung Fû-tsze advised Po-yû to study the *Châu-nan* and the *Shâo-nan*. One who has not studied these, is like one who stands with one's face right up against a wall.

CHAPTER XI

K'ung Fû-tsze said: Some people say: "These are the rules of propriety, these are the rules of propriety." But I do not believe adornment of gems and silken robes make one proper. Some people say: "This is music, this is music." But I do not believe disordered sounds of bells and drums make one cultured.

CHAPTER XII

K'ung Fû-tsze said: One who puts on a stern face, while remaining cowardly inside, is unprincipled. Is such an individual not like a common thief who breaks into a home or climbs over a wall?

CHAPTER XIII

K'ung Fû-tsze said: One who cannot distinguish right from wrong can harm an entire village.

CHAPTER XIV

K'ung Fû-tsze said: One who walks along a road and immediately tells others what one has heard along the way, has lost one's virtue.

CHAPTER XV

1. K'ung Fû-tsze said: They are lowly creatures. How can one serve the prince in their company?
2. When they do not have an official position, they worry about attaining it. When they have one, they worry about losing it.
3. When worried about losing their position, they will stop at nothing to keep it.

Chapter X: The *Châu-nan* and the *Shâo-nan* are the first two books of the *Shih-ching* (the *Chinese Classic Book of Poetry*). K'ung Fû-tsze felt that one who has not studied these will have a shallow view of life.

Chapter XI: It is not the ritual that makes propriety. It is the mind set of those involved in the ceremony that make it.

Chapter XIV: One who cannot hold a secret and gossips has abandoned virtue.

Chapter XV: This refers to mercenary soldiers who kill for money, not principle.

子曰古者民有三疾今也或是之亡也古之狂也肆今之狂也蕩

古之矜也廉今之矜也忿戾古之愚也直今之愚也詐而已矣

子曰巧言令色鮮矣仁

子曰惡紫之奪朱也惡鄭聲之亂雅樂也

惡利口之覆邦家者

子曰予欲無言子貢曰子如不言則小子何述焉子曰

天何言哉四時行焉百物生焉天何言哉

孺悲欲見孔子孔子辭以疾將命者出戶取瑟而歌使之聞之

Chapter XVI

1. K'ung Fû-tsze said: The ancients had three failings. Present day people have the same three failings, but manifest them differently.
2. Among the ancients, those who were proud were careless. Presently, those who are proud are totally reckless.
Among the ancients, those who possessed stern dignity were reserved. Presently, those who are stern are quarrelsome.
Among the ancients, those who were simple were straightforward. Presently, those who are simple are manipulative.

Chapter XVII

K'ung Fû-tsze said: Fine words and a pretentious appearance are seldom associated with one possessing true virtue.

Chapter XVIII

K'ung Fû-tsze said: I loathe the way purple has taken the place of vermilion; the way the folk music of Yâ has been intermingled with the classical music of Chăng; and how sly speech has been used to destroy families and kingdoms.

Chapter XIX

1. K'ung Fû-tsze said he could do without speaking.
2. Tsze-kung said: If you never spoke, how could we, your disciples, learn from you and transmit your doctrines?
3. K'ung Fû-tsze said: Does Heaven speak? The four seasons proceed along their natural course without speaking, yet all things still flourish. Does Heaven say anything?

Chapter XX

Zû Pei wished to see K'ung Fû-tsze. K'ung Fû-tsze declined, stating he was ill. When the bearer of this message went out the door, he took his lute and began to sing so that Zû Pei might hear him.

Chapter XVI: K'ung Fû-tsze said that those traits that manifested as minor defects in ancient times, manifested as major vices during his time.

Chapter XVIII: Red was the orthodox color of the dynasty during the Spring and Autumn Periods. During K'ung Fû-tsze's era, the red was mixed with shades of black to create purple. K'ung Fû-tsze considered this sacrilegious.

Chapter XX: K'ung Fû-tsze refused to see Zû Pei because he was not respectful to his elders. The playing of the lute must have been a code message to Zû Pei.

宰我問三年之喪期已久矣君子三年不為禮必壞三年不
為樂樂必崩舊穀既沒新穀既升鑽燧改火期可已矣子曰
食夫稻衣夫錦於女安乎曰安女安則為之夫君子之
居喪食旨不甘聞樂不樂居處不安故不為也今女安則
為之宰我出子曰予之不仁也子生三年然後免於父母之
懷夫三年之喪天下之通喪也子也有三年之愛於其父母乎

子曰飽食終日無所用心難矣哉不有博奕者乎為之猶賢乎已

Chapter XXI

1. Tsâi Wo inquired about the three year mourning period after the death of one's parents. He thought one year should be long enough.

2. Tsâi Wo expressed concern: If people abstain from ritual for three years, the rituals will suffer. If people abstain from music for three years, the music will be forgotten.

3. Within a year, old grain is exhausted and new grain sprouts. Within a year, through fire-drilling, new fire is created. Why then, is one year not sufficient for mourning?

4. K'ung Fû-tsze inquired: If you, after one year or mourning, were to eat good rice and wear embroidered clothes, would you feel comfortable? Tsâi Wo replied: I would.

5. K'ung Fû-tsze said: If you would, then do so. One of virtue, however, would not enjoy the taste of pleasant food, nor derive pleasure from music, nor seek comfort in lodging, for the entire three-year period of mourning. Hence, such an individual would not indulge himself. But if you feel at ease doing so, then go ahead.

6. When Tsâi Wo left the room, K'ung Fû-tsze said: He lacks human feeling. A child does not leave its parent's arms for three years. A three year period of mourning is practiced to reciprocate one's gratitude for their sacrifice. I wonder if Yü (Tsâi Wo) ever enjoyed three years of love from his parents?

Chapter XXII

K'ung Fû-tsze said: It is difficult to deal with those who gorge themselves with food all the time and who are totally idle. Are there not games of dice and checkers? Even playing these games would be better than doing nothing at all.

Chapter XXI, passage 1: The period of mourning observed by sons after the death of their parent, or by princes after the death of their emperor, ranged from twenty-five months to three years, depending upon the region of the country.

Passage 3: Fire was created by drilling into wood. The wood used for this varied with the season.

Passage 4: Rice was a delicacy in K'ung Fû-tsze's era. Coarse food was to be eaten, and coarse clothes were to be worn during the period of mourning.

Passage 5: During the three year period of mourning after the death of one's parent, a son was to live in a thatched hut built for this purpose.

子路曰君子尚勇乎子曰君子義以為上君子有勇而無義

為亂小人有勇而無義為盜

子貢曰君子亦有惡乎子曰有惡惡稱人之惡者惡居下流

而訕上者惡勇而無禮者惡果敢而窒者曰賜也亦

有惡乎惡徼以為知者惡不孫以為勇者惡訐以為直者

子曰唯女子與小人難養也近之則不孫遠之則怨

子曰年四十而見惡焉其終也已

CHAPTER XXIII

Tsze-lû asked: Does one of character esteem courage? K'ung Fû-tsze said: One of character considers righteousness to be of greater importance. If one of high rank possesses courage, but not righteousness, such an individual will be inclined towards insubordination. If one of low status possesses courage, but not righteousness, such an individual will be inclined towards theft.

CHAPTER XXIV

1. Tsze-kung asked: Does one of character harbor any dislikes? K'ung Fû-tsze said: He does. He hates those who circulate the faults of others; those of low station who slander their superiors; those with courage who do not practice self-restraint; those who are bossy, and those who are narrow-minded.
2. K'ung Fû-tsze asked: And you Tsze-kung, do you harbor any hatreds? Tsze-kung replied: I hate those who pry into matters, and call their information wisdom; those who act as cowards, and call their actions brave; and those who betray secrets, and call it honesty.

CHAPTER XXV

K'ung Fû-tsze said: Of all people, women and subordinate men are the most difficult to understand. If you are familiar with them, they become presumptuous. If you maintain a reserve towards them, they become resentful.

CHAPTER XXVI

K'ung Fû-tsze said: If one is not likeable by age forty, one will not be likeable for the rest of one's life.

Chapter XXV: K'ung Fû-tsze was referring to concubines and maid servants when he used the term *women*. It was common to have concubines and maid servants during his era. He was referring to men servants and eunuchs when he used the term *subordinate men*.

Chapter XXVI: It was believed that by age forty, one's character was developed and that one who was to become a person of character was already on such a path by the age of forty.

微子　第十八

微子去之箕子為之奴比干諫而死孔子曰殷有三仁焉

柳下惠為士師三黜人曰子未可以去乎曰直道而事人焉往而不三黜枉道而事人何必去父母之邦

BOOK XVIII WEI TSZE
The Viscount of Wei

CHAPTER I

1. When the tyrant (Châu) took the throne: the viscount of Wei withdrew from the court; the viscount of Chî became a slave to the tyrant; and Pî-kan protested against him, losing his life while so doing.
2. K'ung Fû-tsze said: Each of these three men of the Yin dynasty were men of virtue.

CHAPTER II

Hûi of Liû-hsiâ, the chief criminal judge, was dismissed from office three times. Someone said to him: Is it not yet time for you to leave this region? Hûi replied: I want to serve people in an upright manner. I am not sure if there is any place I can go and not suffer dismissal thrice. I do not want to give up my values and serve people in a crooked manner. Therefore, I see no need for me to leave the country of my parents.

Book XVIII discusses specific individuals within Chinese history who lived virtuously. These individuals fulfilled their responsibilities to their sovereigns honorably. If it were not possible to do so, they retired from public life rather than compromise their principles.

Chapter I: The viscount of Wei, the viscount of Chî, and Pî-kan were three honorable individuals of the Yin dynasty. The chief of Wei was an older brother, by a concubine, of the tyrant of Châu, the last ruler of the Yin dynasty, 1154–1122 BCE. Pî-kan and the viscount of Chî were both uncles of the tyrant. Wei withdrew from court, rather than serve the tyrant. Chî had himself thrown into prison and feigned madness rather than serve the tyrant. Pî-kan persisted in trying to stop the tyrant. The tyrant put Pî-kan to death by tearing out his heart, saying: This is what the heart of a sage looks like.

Chapter II: Hûi of Liû-hsiâ worked under the minister of crime and had many people working under him. Although he was dismissed from office three times, he would not leave his country. He said that wherever he went, he would not give up his values, so he might as well risk the same fate in his own country.

齊景公待孔子曰若季氏則吾不能以季孟之間待之曰

吾老矣不能用也孔子行

齊人歸女樂季桓子受之三日不朝孔子行

楚狂接輿歌而過孔子曰鳳

兮鳳兮何德之衰往者不可諫

來者猶可追已而﹑﹑今之從政者殆而

孔子下欲與之言趨而辟之不得與之言

CHAPTER III

With due respect, Duke Ching of Ch'î said he could not pay K'ung Fû-tsze as he would pay the head of the Chî family. He said he would reimburse K'ung Fû-tsze at that level due him according to his family status, a status intermediate between the head of the Chî family and head of the Măng family. The duke also said: I am so old that I cannot even use K'ung Fû-tsze doctrines. Hearing this latter statement, K'ung Fû-tsze took his departure.

CHAPTER IV

The people of Ch'î sent the duke of Lû a present of female musicians. Chî Hwan received them. For three days, the duke did not hold court. K'ung Fû-tsze took his departure.

CHAPTER V

1. The madman of Ch'û, Chieh-yü, passed by K'ung Fû-tsze's carriage, singing and saying: O Făng! O Făng! How your virtue has degenerated! It is useless to bemoan the past, but the future may still be saved. Give up your vain pursuits. During these times, danger awaits those who engage in government.

2. K'ung Fû-tsze came down from his carriage hoping to speak with Chieh-yü. Chieh-yü rushed away, however, before he could do so.

Chapter III: In 517 BCE, K'ung Fû-tsze went to Ch'î. Duke Ching of Ch'î recognized K'ung Fû-tsze's wisdom and virtue and sought to employ him. The duke said he would pay him the sum appropriate for one whose status was midway between that of the Chî family and the Măng family. The Măng family was weaker then the Chî family. Such reimbursement was appropriate. It was better than the reimbursement the Lû family had given the Măng family. But when Duke Ching of Ch'î said he was too old to use K'ung Fû-tsze's teachings, K'ung Fû-tsze left. He wanted to secure a position where his doctrines would be of use.

Chapter IV: This chapter explains why K'ung Fû-tsze left public office in Lû. This was in the ninth year of the duke's reign. K'ung Fû-tsze was at the height of his career as minister of justice. Some felt he handed the responsibilities of a prime minister. Neighboring states began to fear his administration and worried that under his guidance, the state of Lû might gain sufficient wisdom to overthrow other states. To prevent this, the duke of Ch'î sent the duke of Lû a gift of fine horses and beautiful female musicians. Enamored with these gifts, the duke of Lû ignored K'ung Fû-tsze, his government, and his people. Forlorn and dejected, K'ung Fû-tsze left.

Chapter V: Chieh-yü was actually not a madman but a wise individual who feigned madness. He lived as a hermit to escape forced employment in a government he found corrupt. Chieh-yü used the term *făng* to compare K'ung Fû-tsze to the divine phoenix bird because of his moral accomplishments.

長沮桀溺耦而耕孔子過之使子路問津焉長沮曰夫執輿者

為誰子路曰為孔丘曰是魯孔丘與曰是也曰是知津矣問於

桀溺曰子為誰曰為仲由曰是魯孔丘之徒與對曰然

滔滔者天下皆是也而誰以易之且而與其從辟人之士也

豈若從辟世之士哉耰而不輟子路行以告夫子憮然曰

鳥獸不可與同群吾非斯人之徒與而誰與

天下有道丘不與易也

子路從而後遇丈人以杖荷蓧子路問曰子見夫子乎丈人曰四

體不勤五穀不分孰為夫子植其杖而芸子路拱而立止

CHAPTER VI

1. Ch'ang-tsü and Chieh-nî were working in the field when K'ung Fû-tsze passed them. He sent his disciple Tsze-lû to ask where the waters of the river were shallow enough to cross.

2. Ch'ang-tsü asked: Who is that holding the reins of the carriage? Tsze-lû said: It is K'ung Fû-tsze. Ch'ang-tsü questioned: But isn't K'ung Fû-tsze from Lû? The reply was: Yes. To which Ch'ang-tsü stated: Then he must know this river.

3. Tsze-lû asked Chieh-nî who he was. Chieh-nî replied that he was Chung Yû, a disciple of K'ung Fû-tsze of Lû. Then he said: Disorder has swelled up like a flood and spread over the entire empire. Who can change it? Follow us, withdraw from all this and from the entire world. After these words, Chieh-nî returned to covering up seeds and farming intently.

4. Tsze-lû went back, reporting these remarks to K'ung Fû-tsze. K'ung Fû-tsze sighed and said: One cannot live amongst the birds and beasts. They are not the same as us. If one does not associate with human beings, with whom can one associate? If only moral principles prevailed throughout the empire, there would be no need for me to continue my teaching.

CHAPTER VII

1. Tsze-lû, following K'ung Fû-tsze, fell behind. He met an old man carrying a bamboo basket on a pole across his shoulder. Tsze-lû asked if he had seen his Master. The old man replied: Your four limbs are not those of one who has toiled. I doubt you can even distinguish the five kinds of grain. Who is your Master? With this, the old man leaned on his staff, bent down, and continued to weed.

2. Tsze-lû stood there with his hands place respectfully across his breast.

3. The old man invited him to spend the night in his house. He cooked a fowl and some millet, and fed Tsze-lû well. He also introduced his two sons to Tsze-lû.

Chapter VI: Ch'ang-tsü and Chieh-nî were two Taoist recluses who chose to abandon the corruption of the empire, and live among nature. When Chieh-nî told Tsze-lû that he was Chung Yû, a disciple of K'ung Fû-tsze, this was not the truth.

K'ung Fû-tsze did not want to abandon the responsibility he felt towards society. Even though times were corrupt and difficult, he preferred to remain in society. He believed that this was the time his teachings were needed most.

子路止，殺雞為黍而食之，見其二子焉。明日，子路行以告。子曰：隱者也。使反見之。至則行矣。子路曰：不仕無義。長幼之節，不可廢也；君臣之義，如之何其廢之？欲潔其身，而亂大倫。君子之仕也，行其義也。道之不行，已知之矣。

逸民：伯夷、叔齊、虞仲、夷逸、朱張、柳下惠、少連。子曰：不降其志，不辱其身，伯夷、叔齊與！謂柳下惠、少連，降志辱身矣，言中倫，行中慮，其斯而已矣。謂虞仲、夷逸，隱居放言，身中清，廢中權。我則異於是，無可無不可。

4. The following day, Tsze-lû left the old man and returned to K'ung Fû-tsze. He told him all that had transpired. K'ung Fû-tsze said that the old man must have been a recluse. He sent Tsze-lû back to meet with him again. But when Tsze-lû returned to the site, the old man was gone.

5. Tsze-lû said: Not to take office is an abdication of responsibility. Just as the obligations between the aged and the young must not be abandoned, neither should those between the sovereign and the subject. If all people sought to remain so pure that they did not confront the tainted ills of society, all humanity would lapse into chaos. One of character must consider it one's moral responsibility to face responsibility and to do all one can to benefit the rest of humankind, even if such attempts seem hopeless.

CHAPTER VIII

1. Those who have left the world to live as recluses are Po-î, Shû-ch'î, Yü-chung, Î-yî, Chû-chang, Hûi of Liû-hsiâ, and Shâo-lien.

2. K'ung Fû-tsze said: Po-î and Shû-ch'î refused to compromise their principles or taint their characters.

3. Hûi of Liû-hsiâ and Shâo-lien, relaxed their principles and brought disgrace upon themselves. Nevertheless, they still tried to spread moral principles through their words and deeds.

4. Yü-chung and Î-yî went into seclusion, and gave up criticizing the government. Yet they were pure in their lives. Having been forced from their positions, they adapted well to their circumstances.

5. I am different from all of them. I have no desire either to advance in or to retreat from the world. I seek only to do what is right.

Chapter VII: The old man was a Taoist recluse who had abandoned society rather than become part of a corrupt government. In the final passage, Tsze-lû seeks to vindicate and explain the actions of his master, K'ung Fû-tsze. Although the old Taoist recluse was no longer visible, he may have been nearby.

Chapter VIII: Po-î and Shû-ch'î refused to take office in the Châu dynasty. They fled the world and starved to death. Hûi of Liû-hsiâ and Shâo-lien served in the court of Lû during a time of turmoil. Hûi of Liû-hsiâ was dismissed three times. Both Hûi of Liû-hsiâ and Shâo-lien, though not able to fulfill their goals, never abandoned their values.

大師摯適齊，亞飯干適楚，三飯繚適蔡，四飯缺適秦，鼓方叔入於河，播鼗武入於漢，少師陽、擊磬襄入於海。

周公謂魯公曰：君子不施其親，不使大臣怨乎不以，故舊無大故則不棄也，無求備於一人。

周有八士：伯達、伯适、仲突、仲忽、叔夜、叔夏、季隨、季騧。

CHAPTER IX

1. Chih, the grand music master, went to Ch'î.
2. Kan, bandmaster at the second meal, went to Ch'û. Liâo, bandmaster at the third meal, went to Ts'âi. Ch'üeh, bandmaster at the fourth meal, went to Ch'in.
3. Fang-shû, the drum master, went north of the Yellow river.
4. Wû, master of the hand drum, withdrew to the Han river.
5. Yang, assistant to the music master, and Hsiang, master of the musical stone, withdrew to an island in the sea.

CHAPTER X

The duke of Châu told his son, the duke of Lû: A virtuous prince will not forsake kinsmen, nor will he give faithful ministers cause for resentment. Barring significant cause, he will not dismiss longtime, trusted officers, nor will he seek perfection in anyone.

CHAPTER XI

There were eight officers in Châu: Po-tâ, Po-kwo, Chung-tû, Chung-hwû, Shû-yâ, Shû-hsiâ, Chî-sui, and Chî-kwa.

Chapter IX: This was during the time of Duke Âi, and after K'ung Fû-tsze had rectified the music of Lû. Various musicians played for the monarchy during different meals. The art of music had been decaying in the state of Lû. K'ung Fû-tsze reorganized it so that musicians would not have to lower their standards. The princes listened to music during their meals, and different musicians played at each meal. When the musicians retired, they went to live at different sites. K'ung Fû-tsze learned to play from Hsiang.

Chapter X: These were the instructions the duke of Châu gave his oldest son concerning virtuous government when he was about to leave the capital to become the first duke of Lû.

Chapter XI: These eight officers from the early period of the Châu dynasty were said to have been brothers. They were four sets of twins born to the same mother. All proved to be honorable and distinguished.

子張曰士見危致命見得思義祭思敬喪思哀其可已矣

子張曰執德不弘信道不篤焉能為有焉能為亡

子夏之門人問交於子張子張曰子夏云何對曰子夏曰可者與之其不可者

推之子張曰異乎吾所聞 君子尊賢而容眾嘉善而矜不能我

之大賢與於人何所不容我之不賢與人將拒我如之何其拒人也

BOOK XIX   TSZE-CHANG
Tsze-Chang

CHAPTER I

Tsze-chang said: A true scholar holding public office, if faced with danger, will sacrifice his or her life. This same individual, when presented with gain, will think of righteousness. When sacrificing, this individual will think of reverence. And when mourning, he or she will feel sincere grief. Such an individual is sincerely honorable.

CHAPTER II

Tsze-chang said: If one recognizes virtue, but does not cultivate it, and if one believes in righteousness, but does not hold firmly to it, how can such an individual be considered one of value?

CHAPTER III

The disciples of Tsze-hsiâ asked Tsze-chang for his thoughts concerning friendship. Tsze-chang turned the question around and asked the disciples what their teacher, Tsze-hsiâ, had taught them. Tsze-hsiâ's disciples replied: Tsze-hsiâ say that one should befriend those who can help one advance and avoid those who cannot. Tsze-chang replied that his perspective was quite different. He said: One of character esteems the wise, yet accepts all; praises the virtuous, yet sympathizes with the foolish. Then Tsze-chang said: If I were an individual of great virtue, who would I possibly reject? If I were an individual lacking virtue, who might reject me? What right does any individual have to reject another?

Book XIX: K'ung Fû-tsze, himself, does not enter into the dialogue in Book XIX. This book contains sayings uttered by several of K'ung Fû-tsze's most respected disciples. Yen Yüan was K'ung Fû-tsze's most honored disciple, Tsze-chang was the next most commonly referenced disciple, and Tsze-hsiâ was the third. The statements of the disciples generally reflect the teachings of K'ung Fû-tsze, but are not always exactly the same as his statements.

Chapter III: Tsze-hsiâ's statements about friendship apply to the young, those still developing their characters. The young would do well to associate with peers who can act as role models for them. Tsze-chang's teachings apply to one already developed in character who is able to discriminate the good from the bad in people's characters. Such individuals will still maintain their own values, even in the presence of those with lower values.

子夏曰雖小道必有可觀者焉致遠恐泥是以君子不為也

子夏曰日知其所亡月無忘其所能可謂好學也已矣

子夏曰博學而篤志切問而近思仁在其中矣

子夏曰百工居肆以成其事君子學以致其道

子夏曰小人之過也必文

子夏曰君子有三變望之儼然即之也溫聽其言也厲

CHAPTER IV
Tsze-hsiâ said that one can find value even in trivial activities. But
if such activities are carried too far, they may become engrossing.
Therefore, one of character will prefer not to engage in them.

CHAPTER V
Tsze-hsiâ said: One who evaluates the qualities one needs to cultivate on a daily basis, and retains the meaningful one has gained on a
monthly basis, will gradually attain wisdom.

CHAPTER VI
Tsze-hsiâ said: One must seek to cultivate oneself and must hold
firmly to one's values. One must be sincere in one's requests for
guidance, and should reflect upon all that others have taught. This is
the path to virtue.

CHAPTER VII
Tsze-hsiâ said: Artisans must live in their shops to excel in their
work. One of character must live in self-cultivation to attain perfect
virtue.

CHAPTER VIII
Tsze-hsiâ said: One without character will always gloss over one's
own faults.

CHAPTER IX
Tsze-hsiâ said: One cultivating character undergoes three changes:
When viewed from afar, such an individual appears stern; when
viewed while approaching, such an individual appears kind; when
heard speaking, such an individual sounds resolute and intelligent.

Chapter IV: The trivial activities alluded to are not the small activities involving
the necessities of daily living. They are those trivial activities people engage in to
squander leisure time.

Chapter VII: In ancient China, the homes and shops located in the various regions
of a town were designated for those within specific trades. The youth of each family grew up proficient in their specific trade, because they lived amidst individuals
skilled in that field. Similarly, one must live constantly immersed in one's own
moral values to cultivate them to the fullest.

子夏曰君子信而後勞其民未信則以為厲己也

未信則以為謗己也信而後諫

子夏曰大德不踰閑小德出入可也

子游曰子夏之門人小子

當洒掃應對進退則可矣抑末也本之則無如之何子夏

聞之曰噫言游過矣君子之道孰先傳焉孰後倦焉譬諸草

木區以別矣君子之道焉可誣也有始有卒者其惟聖人乎

CHAPTER X

Tsze-hsiâ said: One of character will seek to gain the confidence of people before placing responsibilities upon them. If such confidence is not gained, people will consider such responsibilities oppressive. One of character will seek to gain the confidence of the prince before giving him advice. If such confidence is not gained, the prince will consider such advice criticism.

CHAPTER XI

Tsze-hsiâ said: In upholding great virtues, one must never cross the boundary. In upholding minor virtues, one may hover just over the boundary.

CHAPTER XII

1. Tsze-yû said: The disciples and followers of Tsze-hsiâ are trained in sprinkling and sweeping the ground; in answering and responding to questions; and in entering and leaving a room. But these are only branches of learning. If these disciples do not know the essentials of character. How can they be considered educated?
2. Tsze-hsiâ heard this remark and said: Tsze-yû is mistaken. A wise teacher must not distinguish between subjects of primary and secondary importance so distinctly as to totally neglect some. The teacher must consider each disciple as a budding plant, each needing to be cultivated differently according to his or her natural tendencies. The teacher must not make a fool of any student and must cultivate each student's mind gradually and methodically, from beginning to end.

Chapter XI: The validity of this passage has been questioned because, in general, K'ung Fû-tsze taught that one should try not to cross the boundaries of virtue under any circumstances.

Chapter XII: These matters have to do with the respectful way to greet guests, to prepare for ceremonies, and to perform rituals. Tsze-yû was criticizing Tsze-hsiâ for teaching his disciples the physical details of performing rituals, but not the underlying philosophical concepts. Tsze-hsiâ, however, felt that he knew his students well and knew how each should be taught. He felt that each student must be taught the basics of life so that they might function as productive human beings, and only then should they be gradually guided to understand moral and philosophical principles.

子夏曰仕而優則學、而優則仕

子游曰喪致乎哀而止

子游曰吾友張也為難能也　然而未仁

曾子曰堂堂乎張也難與並為仁矣

曾子曰吾聞諸夫子人未有自致者也必也親喪乎

曾子曰吾聞諸夫子孟莊子之孝也其他可能也

其不改父之臣與父之政是難能也

CHAPTER XIII

Tsze-hsiâ said: After completing one's duties as an officer, one should devote oneself to learning. After completing one's duties as a student, one should devote oneself toward becoming a competent officer.

CHAPTER XIV

Tsze-hsiâ said: In mourning, grieve fully. Then stop!

CHAPTER XV

Tsze-hsiâ said: My friend Chang possesses skill in various fields. But he is not perfectly virtuous.

CHAPTER XVI

Philosopher Tsăng said: How righteous is the manner of Chang! It is difficult to practice virtue along with him.

CHAPTER XVII

The philosopher Tsăng said that he heard K'ung Fû-tsze say: Those who previously might never have expressed the lofty aspects of their characters, may do so when mourning their parents.

CHAPTER XVIII

Philosopher Tsăng said that he heard K'ung Fû-tsze say: In most respects, Măng Chwang's filial piety was comparable to that of others. But in his refusal to dismiss the ministers his father had placed in government prior to his death, his piety exceeded others.

Chapter XIII: During this era, children of nobility inherited their official titles and positions. They were not necessarily afforded formal education. Tsze-hsiâ believed that if they were not able to fulfill these responsibilities well without formal education, they should be brought to school to learn music, ritual, and values.

Chapter XIV: One must carry out mourning sincerely, but not so much as to endanger one's own health through excess grief and abstinence.

Chapter XVI: Philosopher Tsăng is ridiculing Chang, stating that he is aloof in his righteousness.

Chapter XVIII: Măng Chwang was head of the Măng family of Lû. After the death of his father, he did not replace any of the ministers in his father's government until the three year period of mourning had elapsed. This was out of respect to his father.

孟氏使陽膚為士師問於曾子曾子曰上失其道民散久矣

如得其情則哀矜而勿喜

子貢曰紂之不善不如是之甚也是以君子惡居下流天下之惡皆歸焉

子貢曰君子之過如日月之食焉過也人皆見之更也人皆仰之

衛公孫朝問於子貢曰仲尼焉學子貢曰文武之道未墜於地在人賢者識其大者不賢者識其小者莫不有文武之道焉夫子焉不學亦何常師之有

CHAPTER XIX

The head of the Măng family appointed Yang Fû as chief justice. Later, Yang Fû consulted the philosopher Tsăng. Tsăng advised him: Because the rulers have failed in their duties, the people have long been misguided. When you uncover the facts concerning such injustices, do not rejoice in your ability. Rather, grieve and feel pity that such acts were committed.

CHAPTER XX

Tsze-kung said: The wickedness of Châu was not nearly as bad as his reputation warranted. Knowing this, one of character will avoid leading a disreputable life, for one now knows that one will be charged with greater wickedness than one has actually committed.

CHAPTER XXI

Tsze-kung said: Mistakes of the virtuous are like eclipses of the sun and the moon. Everyone sees them. Yet everyone also gazes up in reverence when they are corrected.

CHAPTER XXII

1. Kung-sun Ch'âo of Wei, asked Tsze-kung: Where did K'ung Fû-tsze obtain his knowledge?
2. Tsze-kung replied: The doctrines of Wăn and Wû have not yet turned to dust. Although lesser individuals remember only mundane teachings, many worthy individuals remember theirs. So many know and revere King Wăn and King Wû for their honorable characters and lofty doctrines, where could a man like K'ung Fû-tsze have gone without having learned these?

Chapter XIX: One should not glory at the fall of a wayward individual, but should feel remorse concerning one's own failure to guide such an individual correctly.

Chapter XX: One's faults live long after one's death and remain associated with one's name. Châu was the last emperor (c. 1099–1066 BCE) of the Shang (Yin) dynasty. He was the most brutal tyrant in China's history. If ministers spoke up to him, he had them killed. After he was defeated in a revolution, he burned himself to death, thus ending the Shang dynasty.

Chapter XXI: All take notice when the virtuous succumb to faults. But all take greater notice when they correct these faults and rise up again.

Chapter XXII: Tsze-kung states that K'ung Fû-tsze obtained much of his wisdom from the teachings of King Wăn and King Wû. He stated that such teachings had not yet turned to dust (fallen to the ground and dissipated) and were still valued.

叔孫武叔語大夫於朝曰子貢賢於仲尼子服景伯以告子貢子貢曰譬之宮牆賜之牆也及肩窺見室家之好夫子之牆數仞不得其門而入不見宗廟之美百官之富得其門者寡矣夫子之云不亦宜乎

叔孫武叔毀仲尼子貢曰無以為也仲尼不可毀也他人之賢者丘陵也猶可踰也仲尼日月也無得而踰焉人雖欲自絕其何傷於日月乎多見其不知量也

CHAPTER XXIII

1. Shû-sun Wû-shû, a great officer of the court, was heard to say: Tsze-kung's wisdom is superior to that of K'ung Fû-tsze.

2. Tsze-fû Ching-po reported this to Tsze-kung. Tsze-kung said: If one compares learning to a wall, my wall only reaches to my shoulders. Therefore, others may easily peer over and observe the valuable architecture of the houses within it.

3. But the height of K'ung Fû-tsze's wisdom is comparable to a wall several fathoms high. If one cannot find the gate to enter, one can not even imagine the splendor of its ancestral temple and its many beautiful buildings.

4. Those who can find the gate are few. That this officer made such a remark is merely an indication of his limited vision. This is all one can expect of him.

CHAPTER XXIV

Shû-sun Wû-shû spoke critically of K'ung Fû-tsze. Tsze-kung said: It is wrong to do so. K'ung Fû-tsze is beyond criticism. The virtue of other individuals are mere hillocks and mounds that can be stepped over. The virtue of K'ung Fû-tsze is as the sun and moon. It can not be stepped over. Shû-sun Wû-shû's words reveal that he overestimates his own intelligence. It is of no harm either to the sun or the moon if one does not wish to soak in their light.

Chapter XXIII: Shû-sun Wû-shû was a minister of Lû. He belonged to one of the three noble houses that controlled the state of Lû. Tsze-kung was a prominent disciple of K'ung Fû-tsze who eventually became prime minister of both Lû and Wei. Tsze-fû Ching-po was another of K'ung Fû-tsze's disciples. Tsze-kung refutes the statement that his wisdom is superior to that of K'ung Fû-tsze. He says that one must question the intelligence of the individual making such a statement before accepting it.

陳子禽謂子貢曰子為恭也仲尼豈賢於子乎子貢曰君子一言以為知一言以為不知言不可不慎也夫子之不可及也猶天之不可階而升也夫子之得邦家者所謂立之斯立道之斯行綏之斯來動之斯和其生也榮其死也哀如之何其可及也

1. Ch'ăn Tsze-ch'in told Tsze-kung: You are too modest. Do you truly believe K'ung Fû-tsze to be superior to you?
2. Tsze-kung said: Through one word, one can be deemed wise. Through one word, one can be deemed foolish. One must be careful what one says.
3. Tsze-kung continued: The level of wisdom of K'ung Fû-tsze cannot be reached any more then Heaven can be reached by climbing the steps of a flight of stairs.
4. If K'ung Fû-tsze were head of state or leader of a great family: he would cultivate the populace, and they would develop character; he would guide the people, and they would find correct paths; he would imbue people with inner peace, and multiples would flock to him; he would inspire people, and they would function together harmoniously. K'ung Fû-tsze has been honored while alive, and will be honored when dead. How can I equal him?

Chapter XXV: Tsze-kung rebukes Ch'ăn Tsze-ch'in for even insinuating that he might consider him equal to K'ung Fû-tsze.

堯曰咨爾舜天之曆數在
爾躬允執其中四海困窮天祿
永終舜亦以命禹
曰予小子履敢用玄牡敢昭告于皇皇后帝有罪不敢赦帝
臣不蔽簡在帝心朕躬有罪無以萬方萬方有罪罪在朕躬

BOOK XX YÂO YÜEH
Yâo Said

CHAPTER I

1. Yâo proclaimed:
   Shun, the succession to the throne as declared by Heaven,
   now rests in you.
   Faithfully hold fast to the Due Mean.
   For if distress and want befall the people between these four seas,
   the blessings of Heaven will cease forever.

2. Shun used the same terms when passing the throne on to Yü.
3. T'ang uttered the following:
   I, humble son Lî,
   wish to sacrifice a black ox
   and proclaim to you, oh austere ruling God,
   that I will not cover up the deeds of evil people,
   and will not fail to reward loyal ministers
   for their deeds.
   I will consider all carefully within my conscience.
   If I, myself, commit any wrong-doings,
   let repercussions fall not on the people of my vast empire.
   If within my vast empire,
   others commit wrongdoings,
   let blame fall upon me.

Book XX is not related to any of the prior books. It contains sayings of two sovereigns, three kings, and K'ung Fû-tsze. It lends insight into the responsibilities of China's ancient monarchy and to the rulers' beliefs in their Heavenly ordained status. The region referred to as "the land between the four seas" is China.

Chapter I, passage 1: King Yâo was a legendary sage-king. He was greatly admired by K'ung Fû-tsze. He employed Shun as his minister because of his humanitarian character. After reigning seventy-three years, commencing 2357 BCE, Yâo abdicated the throne. He ceded the throne to Shun. Accession to the monarchy was perceived as having been predetermined by Heaven. Yâo beseeched Shun to rule with wisdom and moderation, lest the blessings of Heaven would cease. Shun remained king for thirty years. The philosophy of following the *Due Mean* refers to following a life path of moderation and avoidance of excesses.

Passage 2: Shun passed the throne on to his minister Yü. He did not pass it to his own son because he found him unworthy. Yü ruled honorably. He tamed the Yellow River by creating a system of dams and dikes.

279

周有大賚善人是富雖有周親不如仁人百姓有過在予一人

謹權量審法度修廢官四方之政行焉興滅國繼絕世舉

逸民天下之民歸心焉

所重民食喪祭寬則得眾敏則有功公則說

4. The duke of Châu pledged to confer great benefits upon his people, proclaiming:

I will reward the virtuous in particular.
Although I possess many close relatives,
these will not equal the number of virtuous men I will amass.
If one amongst them commits any wrong-doings,
I, alone, will bear that responsibility.
In ruling,
I will ensure accuracy of weights and measures,
I will study the statutes of the law,
I will reinstate dismissed officers,
I will bring virtuous government back to the kingdom,
I will rebuild states that have been destroyed,
I will re-establish broken family lines of succession,
I will summon back virtuous officers who left to be recluses.
Then, all under heaven will turn their hearts toward our nation.
I will keep my people as my main concern.
I will ensure they have food, tradition, and sacrifices.
I will be lenient, and win the masses.
I will be sincere, and win their trust.
I will be diligent, and secure success.
I will be just, and all will be content.

Passage 3: T'ang was the founder of the Shang dynasty. He was one of the sage kings admired by K'ung Fû-tsze. He recited this prayer from the *Shû-ching*, the *Book of History*, when he successfully overthrew the Hsiâ dynasty.

Emperors of ancient China perceived Heaven as their father, Earth as their mother, and each of themselves as a Son of Heaven.

Black bulls were used for sacrifice, but eventually the Yin dynasty replaced these with white bulls.

T'ang beseeched Heaven that if wrongs were committed within his empire, that retribution fall not upon his people, but upon him.

Passage 4: This was the duke of Châu's [King Wu's] pledge to the army and princes of various states who supported him when he went to war. He had ten competent ministers. Rather than conferring responsibilities upon undeserving relatives, he delegated responsibility to those individuals he deemed most capable. He ensured that there was honesty in business, i.e. that weights and measurements were standardized; that worthy states, families, and individuals that had been removed were reinstated; and that all people were treated with compassion and justice.

281

子張問於孔子曰何如斯可以從政矣

子曰尊五美屏四惡斯可以從政矣子張曰何謂五美

子曰君子惠而不費勞而不怨欲而不貪泰而不驕威而不猛

子張曰何謂惠而不費

子曰因民之所利而利之斯不亦惠而不費乎擇可勞而勞之又

誰怨欲仁而得仁又焉貪君子無眾寡無大小無敢慢斯不

亦泰而不驕乎君子正其衣冠尊其瞻視儼然人望而畏之

斯不亦威而不猛乎

1. Tsze-chang asked K'ung Fû-tsze: How should one in authority properly conduct government? K'ung Fû-tsze replied: Uphold the *Five Virtues* and banish the *Four Vices*. Then one's government will function properly. Tsze-chang asked: What are the *Five Virtues*? K'ung Fû-tsze replied:

A virtuous leader is charitable, yet not extravagant.
A virtuous leader designates labor, but does not overburden people.
A virtuous leader seeks enough to ensure stability, but not excess.
A virtuous leader maintains dignity, but is not proud.
A virtuous leader maintains self-respect, but is not fierce.

2. Tsze-chang asked: What is meant by being a leader who is charitable, yet not extravagant? K'ung Fû-tsze responded:

Such a leader ensures that all people secure
the greatest benefits possible from their efforts.
Would not such a leader be considered charitable,
yet not extravagant?
Such a leader permits people to chose their own livelihoods.
Would not such a leader be free of complaints?
Such a leader ensures that government has enough
to sustain itself, yet not more.
Would not such a leader be considered free of greed?
Such a leader confers respect upon all,
both in public and in private,
both the great and the small.
Would not such a leader be considered dignified,
yet not proud?
Such a leader handles all matters as if in cap and robe,
with serious gravity and respect.
Would not such a leader be shown reverence,
yet not be feared?

Chapter II: These are K'ung Fû-tsze's beliefs concerning the responsibilities of a ruler who was seeking to govern following the wisdom of the ancient sages and emperors. Such actions reflect the highest of noble principles.

子曰不知命無以為君子也

不知禮無以立也不知言無以知人也

子張曰何謂四惡子曰不

數而殺謂之虐不戒視成謂之暴

慢令致期謂之賊猶之與人也出納之吝謂之有司

3. Tsze-chang then asked, What are the *Four Vices*?
K'ung Fû-tsze replied that the *Four Vices* were:

Putting people to death for their actions
without having taught them right from wrong.
This is cruel.
Suddenly requiring people to fulfill a job,
without having told them how to accomplish it.
This is oppression.
Issuing orders without telling others it is urgent,
and then punish them if the job is not completed immediately.
This is meanness.
Being stingy in paying others.
This is selfishness.

CHAPTER III
1. K'ung Fû-tsze said: Without thinking deeply about the wishes of Heaven, can one be truly virtuous?
2. Without knowing and embodying the *Rules of Propriety*, can one establish one's character?
3. Without seeking understanding of the meaning behind words, can one truly understand the thoughts of others?

Chapter III, Passage 1: Both the ancient worthies and K'ung Fû-tsze believed that decrees of Heaven governed all matters, including: life and death; wealth and poverty; feast and famine; success and failure; difficulty and ease. K'ung Fû-tsze felt that one must think deeply about what Heaven truly wants, lest one might succumb to lower passions.

Passage 2: K'ung Fû-tsze felt that one must study the *Rules of Propriety* to guide one in cultivation of self-discipline.

Passage 3: K'ung Fû-tsze believed that one's words were the voice of one's heart. To understand others, one must pay careful attention to what others say. Only then will one attain understanding concerning the inderlying thoughts behind their words.

THE ANALECTS OF CONFUCIUS

BACKGROUND

CHINESE PHILOSOPHY PRIOR TO K'UNG FÛ-TSZE

K'ung Fû-tsze did not feel that he was the creator of the wisdom that he taught. He felt he was merely a common man transmitting wisdom from ancient times to present ones. He held tremendous respect for the wisdom of the ancients and for the *Chinese Classical* texts. Through studying the *Classics*, he learned of those values and lifestyles that both commoners and leaders might best follow to help create meaningful lives for themselves and for all society. Through his study of the *Classics,* he observed that throughout history, distinct patterns of events had occurred. He also noted that if certain patterns were followed, all would prosper.

Accordingly, for one seeking further insight into K'ung Fû-tsze's philosophy, a basic knowledge of the *Chinese Classical* texts is certainly valuable. These *Classics* are not considered holy books or works inspired by divine revelation. Rather, they are respected as the works of wise historians, poets, sages, and scholars of ancient China.

The first of the great *Chinese Classics* is the *Book of Historical Documents*, or the *Shû King*. It was begun c. 2,400 BCE, during the reign of Emperor Yâo, and was completed approximately 615–619 BCE, during the reign of King Hsiang. Although its initial chapters discuss events of prior eras, by 2,200 BCE, it primarily discussed those events occurring contemporaneously to its documentation of them.

The second of the great *Chinese Classics* is the *Book of Poetry*, or the *Shih King*. It contains over one thousand poems, of which approximately 305 poems are considered meaningful. Five of the poems were written during the Shang dynasty, 1766–1123 BCE, and the rest were written from 1123–586 BCE. The poems, or *Odes* shed light upon religious beliefs, manners, customs, and events that occurred during China's ancient past.

The third of the great *Chinese Classics* is the *Book of Changes*, or the *Yî Ching*. The *Yî Ching* is commonly referred to as the *I Ching* (*I* meaning change and *Ching* meaning classic). Hence, it is the *Chinese Classic Book* explaining the phenomena of *Change*. The *I Ching* is based upon the relationships of a series of lines arranged in threes (trigrams) and then in sixes (hexagrams). There are sixty-four hexagrams in total. Creation of the initial trigrams has been attributed to Fû-hsî (3,400 BCE), the founder of the Chinese nation. Unfortunately, much of the ancient knowledge Fû-hsî attached to the relationships of these trigrams has been lost.

The present day version of the *I Ching*, with its combinations of trigrams and hexagrams, has been attributed to China's great King Wăn (born 1,231 BCE). Although there is reason to believe that texts explaining the meanings of the hexagrams existed during the Hsiă and Shang dynasties, no such texts have been preserved.

It is said that during the time he was imprisioned by the tyrants who overthrew the Shang dynasty, King Wăn studied the *I Ching*. It was then that he deciphered the meaning of each hexagram. His son, the duke of Chou, studied the *I Ching* further and deciphered the meaning of each line of each hexagram.

Six hundred years later, K'ung Fû-tsze added the deeply philosophical meanings and analyses of each of these lines. These are the analyses that have come down to us today. K'ung Fû-tsze's philosophical interpretations are termed the *Wings* of the *I Ching*. They have become an integral part of the text. All of these initial and secondary analyses, together, constitute the present day *I Ching*, or what is commonly referred to as the *Book of Changes*.

From its inception, the *I Ching* has been used as a book of divination. In 213 BCE, when the tyrant of the Ch'in dynasty ordered the burning of all historical and scientific documents, copies of the *I Ching* were not burned. That was because most people only thought of the *I Ching* as a book of divination. They did not know that it was also a book of wisdom and deep philosophical concepts. This was fortunate, however. Because of this, the invaders did not order its burning and its wisdom has been preserved to the present day.

Teachings of the *I Ching* also include the wisdom of *Feng Shiu*, of the *Yin* and the *Yang*, and of the perpetual, infinite process of change. The wisdom of the *I Ching* teaches that in nature, there are no vacuums. When anything is changed or displaced, it is replaced by something else. The *I Ching* teaches that by studying the changes within the lines and figures of the hexagrams, one can gain insight the changes that occur within all external phenomena. The spacial and physical relationships of all cyclicly changing matter and energies in existence can be understood by one who has attained full understanding of the teachings of the *I Ching*.

The fourth of the great *Chinese Classics* is the *Lî Kî*, or the *Record of the Rites*. It is actually a compilation of three books, collectively termed *The Three Rituals*. These books describe the rituals of ancient China. The first book discusses the manner in which government officers should conduct themselves. This book was handed down from the Shang dynasty. The second book discusses the manner in which scholars and officers should conduct themselves. The third book, which is actually a collection of 214 smaller books handed down from the Han dynasty, discusses the rituals that should be followed by the populace in general.

The fifth of the great *Chinese Classics* is the *Khun Khiû*, or the *Spring and Autumn Chronicles*. It contains an overview of the events that occurred in K'ung Fû-tsze's home state of Lû over 242 years, from 722–481 BCE. Although much of the information compiled within it had been recorded prior to the time of K'ung Fû-tsze, the actual writing of it has been attributed to him.

In summary, the great *Classics of China* described above are referred to as the *Five Kings*. These are the ancient texts to which K'ung Fû-tsze refers when he states he received all of his wisdom from the writings of the ancients.

In addition, there are four other great Chinese classics, referred to as the *Four Shû*. They include works created by four great Chinese philosophers. They are the *Lun Yü* (the *Analects of Confucius*) by K'ung Fû-tsze; the *Works of Mencius* by Mencius (371–289 BCE); the *Tâ Hsio* (the *Great Learning*) attributed to K'ung Fû-tsze's disciple Tsăng Shăn; and the *Chung Yung* (the *Doctrine of the Mean*) attributed to K'ung Fû-tsze's grandson, K'ung Chî.

LIST: CHINESE CLASSICAL TEXTS

Five Kings
The Five Great Chinese Classical Works

The *Book of Historical Documents*, or the *Shû King*.
   Begun c. 2,400 BCE and completed 619–615 BCE

The *Book of Poetry*, or the *Shih King*
   1766–586 BCE

The *Book of Changes* (the *Yî Ching*), also known as the *I Ching*
   3,400–213 BCE

The *Lî Kî*, or the *Record of the Rites*
   One of three books the duke of Kâu used to describe the
   rituals of ancient China.

The *Ch'un-ch'iu*, or the *Spring and Autumn Chronicles*
   722–481 BCE Attributed to K'ung Fû-tsze

The *Four Shû*
The Later Works of Four Great Chinese Philosophers

The *Lun Yü* (*Analects of Confucius*)
   By K'ung Fû-tsze

The *Works of Mencius*
   By Mencius (371–289 BCE)

The *Tâ Hsio* (the *Great Learning*)
   Attributed to K'ung Fû-tsze's disciple Tsăng Shăn

The *Chung Yung* (the *Doctrine of the Mean*)
   Attributed to K'ung Fû-tsze's grandson, K'ung Chî.

THE ERA IN WHICH K'UNG FÛ-TSZE LIVED

In order to understand K'ung Fû-tsze's teachings, one must gain insight into the era in which he lived. One would also do well to attain an understanding of China's turbulent history. China's recorded history begins with the Shang dynasty (c. 1766–1122 BCE). Centered in China's northern plain, the Shang is the earliest dynasty from which there is sufficient archeological evidence to analyze its culture. Shang society was founded upon a highly organized agrarian economy. It had planned cities, irrigation techniques, painting and music, a monarchy, and an elaborate class system. Bronze was worked to create needles, sacrificial vessels, spears, and knives.

In 1122 BCE, people of the Châu civilization invaded the Shang civilization. They invaded from the lands south-west of the Shang empire and conquered the Shang. The Châu emperor divided the region into small vassal states. These vassal states became independent city-states. Over time, the Châu dynasty lost power, and many of the small city-states became increasingly more powerful. These states, however, tried to dominate one another. The result was that the people were constantly at war with one another.

Although the Châu dynasty controlled all of China, the history of the people of the eastern region of China has been divided chronologically into two periods: the Ch'un-ch'iu Period (722–481 BCE) and the Period of Contending States (480–221 BCE). The Ch'un-ch'iu Period derived its name from the historical text, the *Ch'un-ch'iu*, written by K'ung Fû-tsze. It records the history of its city-states from 722–481 BCE.

Although this was an era during which the rival city-states were at constant civil war with each other, each competing for bounty and power, the population still grew, commerce expanded, and the arts flourished. The smelting of iron was begun, and tools and weapons, previously made of wood and bronze, were now made of iron.

The conduct of both the individuals and of governments during this era was guided by *li*: proper conduct, propriety, ritual, and ceremonies. Reverence for *li* helped to maintain stability and safety both during times of peace and times of war. During the later years of the Ch'un-ch'iu Period, gradual decay in *li* occurred. The state of Châu formed alliances with its neighboring states and attempted to create some stability. The western state of Ch'in, however, was extremely aggressive. It began attacking all the states surrounding it. By 221 BCE, the leaders of the state of Ch'in had defeated all the other states. It was they who unified the lands into what has become present-day China.

Hence, the era in which K'ung Fû-tsze lived witnessed the decline of feudalism, the instability of constant civil wars, the violence of foreign invasions, and a tremendous amount of internal intrigue and treachery. Great states seized smaller neighboring states, civilizations were destroyed, and virtue was no longer respected.

K'ung Fû-tsze was deeply concerned about the general lack of virtue and the moral decay in the many states throughout which he traveled. In K'ung Fû-tsze's native state of Lû, the duke was more interested in dancing girls than in K'ung Fû-tsze's wisdom concerning the honorable running of government. In the state of Wei, the ruler was corrupt, his wife was incestuous, and the government was run by an evil minister. In the state of Sung, K'ung Fû-tsze was almost assassinated by a jealous nobleman. In the state of Ch'en, a small and weak state, the entire state was under daily threat of annexation by its larger southern neighbor, the state of Ch'u. In the state of Ch'en, the weak prince would not listen to K'ung Fû-tsze's moral philosophy. It was only in the state of Ts'ai, already under occupation by the state of Ch'u, that K'ung Fû-tsze finally found a virtuous ruler who valued his teachings.

By carefully studying the patterns of history, as well as the conduct of the existing rulers, K'ung Fû-tsze realized that if the leaders of a nation did not uphold the highest ethical standards in their own conduct, their subjects certainly would not either. Unethical conduct on the part of the leaders could not help but lead a nation into total moral decay, anarchy, and revolution. Therefore, K'ung Fû-tsze recognized that his teachings must not be directed solely towards the general public, but also towards their rulers.

LIST: DYNASTIES OF CHINA

Emperor Yao   (Legendary) 3rd millenium BCE
Emperor Shun (Legendary) 3rd millenium BCE

The Three Dynasties
Hsia Dynasty   c. 2200–1750 BCE
Shang (Yin) Dynasty   c. 1750–1110 BCE
Châu (Chou) Dynasty   c. 1110– 249 BCE
                 Spring & Autumn 722–481 BCE
                 Warring States   403–222 BCE
Ch'in Dynasty   c. 221–206 BCE
Han Dynasty`   206 BCE–220 CE
S & N Dynasties   420–489 CE
Sui Dynasty   581–618 CE
Tang Dynasty   618–907 CE
Five Dynasties   907–960 CE
                 Later Liang
                 Later T'ang
                 Later Chin
                 Later Han
                 Later Chou
Sung Dynasty   960–1279 CE
Yüan (Mongol)   1271–1368 CE
Ming Dynasty   1368–1644 CE
Ch'ing (Manchu)   1644–1912 CE
Republic   1912–1949 CE
People's Republic   1949–

[Adapted from: Chan, Wing-tsit, xv, and Huang, Chichung, 189–190].

K'UNG FÛ-TSZE'S LIFE
551–479 BCE

K'ung Fû-tsze was born in 551 BCE. His family was from the state of Lû in eastern China, in the southern portion of Shantung province. His ancestors had descended from a royal family of the state of Sung. His heritage can be traced back to the Shang dynasty, c. 1750–1110 BCE, the dynasty that preceded the Châu dynasty, c. 1110–249 BCE.

Well before K'ung Fû-tsze was born, his family lost its nobility. This fall from nobility occurred in the early eighth century BCE. One of K'ung Fû-tsze's ancestors had been charged with the safety of the young duke of Sung. The young duke was assassinated and the individual who had been assigned to safeguard him suddenly died. Because of this, the rest of the family was forced to flee from the state of Sung. They found a safe haven in the state of Lû.

Little is known of K'ung Fû-tsze's youth except that he was orphaned at an early age, he was poor, and he was fond of learning. The most reliable account of his life is a biography recorded in the *Shih Chi*, or the *Historical Records* of China, compiled during the Han dynasty, c. 86 BCE.

K'ung Fû-tsze's father, Shû-lîang Hêh, had apparently been a soldier. Although he married early in life, his first wife bore him only nine daughters and no sons. Simultaneous to this marriage, he kept a concubine. She bore him two sons, Măng-p'î and Po-nî. In those times, it was considered necessary that Shû-lîang Hêh have sons through marriage. Although advanced in years, over sixty years of age, he entered into a second marriage to have a legitimate son through marriage. He requested to be given a wife from the Yen family and was given their youngest daughter, Chăng-tsâi. Chăng-tsâi bore him K'ung Fû-tsze.

K'ung Fû-tsze's given name was actually K'ung Ch'iû. The title *Fû-tsze* was conferred upon him, as it had been conferred upon other ministers of the courts in ancient China, as a term equivalent to "Your Excellency." Later, his disciples addressed him as K'ung Fû-tsze out of respect for his having served as Minister of Justice in his native state of Lû. Over time *Fû-tsze* became the title by which people addressed all teachers and took on the meaning of *Master*. Hence, the term K'ung Fû-tsze actually means *Master K'ung*. The Westernized term *Confucius* was first used in 1687 by four Roman Catholic missionaries living in China, it being their phonetic transliteration of the word K'ung Fû-tsze.

When K'ung Fû-tsze was three years of age, his father died. After this, his family lived in abject poverty. His mother died when she was quite young and K'ung Fû-tsze in his early teens. He was forced to seek employment in menial positions. He found employment as a granary clerk and an animal husbandry supervisor. At the age of fifteen, he began to cultivate an interest in studies. He sought out teachers who had studied the ways of King Wen and King Wu, two well-respected historical figures considered sage-kings, or sage rulers, in ancient China.

Little is known of K'ung Fû-tsze's marriage except that he married at age nineteen and his wife was from the state of Sung. The following year, she bore them a son, Lî, and the year after that, a daughter. When Lî was born, the duke of Lû gave K'ung Fû-tsze a gift of a carp, a species of fish. Hence, K'ung Fû-tsze named his son Lî (carp). The fact that the monarchy gave K'ung Fû-tsze a gift reveals that he was respected by the royalty of Lû. An inscription on an ancient grave reveals that K'ung Fû-tsze and his wife also had another daughter, but she apparently died when very young.

K'ung Fû-tsze outlived all of his children. His son died three years before he did. As regards the other members of the family, K'ung Fû-tsze had two half-brothers, Mǎng-p'î and Po-nî, through the concubine of his father. Although his brother Po-nî was older than he, K'ung Fû-tsze acted as head of the family, possibly because Po-nî was crippled.

By the age of twenty-six, K'ung Fû-tsze had gained respect throughout his community as a scholar. He was being consulted about rituals and statecraft. By age thirty, he was well versed in the classics. He started a school to educate children of the poor. In 517 BCE, when the duke of Lû was defeated in battle and forced to flee to the state of Chou (Châu), K'ung Fû-tsze followed suite. K'ung Fû-tsze remained in Chou until that region became politically unstable. Then he returned to the state of Lû. He devoted himself to teaching school and editing classical works of Chinese literature. His school flourished and students from distant states came to receive his teachings.

In 501 BCE, the duke of Lû appointed K'ung Fû-tsze magistrate. He then elevated him to the position of Minister of Public works, and then to the position of Minister of Justice. With K'ung Fû-tsze heading these important cabinets, the state of Lû progressed remarkably well. Rulers of the neighboring state of Ch'i, however, became jealous. They sought to disrupt the stability of the Lû government. To do so they sent a troop of singing girls and teams of show horses to distract the ministers. They succeeded. The duke of Lû and his ministers indulged themselves many days with the singing girls, and began to totally disregard the rules of performing official state sacrifice to Heaven.

Because of this, in 497 BCE, K'ung Fû-tsze left his official position. He began fourteen years of wandering in search of an honorable and wise prince who might employ him in a government founded on virtuous principles. His disciples followed him. The search was fruitless. K'ung Fû-tsze met with princes of numerous states, but none recognized the value of his teachings.

The first state he entered was Wei. The reigning prince was more interested in military conquests and in women than in K'ung Fû-tsze's theory of humane government. Many years later, however, several of K'ung Fû-tsze's disciples were given important positions in the royal court of the state of Wei. Because of this, during his later years, K'ung Fû-tsze found the state of Wei a safe place to which he might return. He did so often, between his journeys to other states.

The next state K'ung Fû-tsze planned to enter was Chen. On the way there, his disciples and he were attacked by a band of people who mistook K'ung Fû-tsze for a brutal tyrant. He finally reached Chen, but the minister there only engaged him in a minor position. He held this position for three years. Then the state of Chen was invaded by the state of Wu. K'ung Fû-tsze and his disciples were forced to flee again. This time they entered the state of Ch'u.

The king of Ch'u sincerely wished to give K'ung Fû-tsze a position in his royal court. He escorted K'ung Fû-tsze and his disciples to Ch'u. The king's plans, however, were thwarted by the prime-minister.

K'ung Fû-tsze and his disciples left the state of Ch'u for the state of Sung. The minister of Sung, however, tried to kill K'ung Fû-tsze. He uprooted a tree under which K'ung Fû-tsze and his disciples were performing rituals. K'ung Fû-tsze was able to survive the assault by disguising himself and fleeing.

In 492 BCE, the prime minister of Lû had become very ill. He urged his son, Kang-zi, to call K'ung Fû-tsze back. The prime minister wanted K'ung Fû-tsze to be his son's guide and teacher when he became prime minister. The son, however, chose one of K'ung Fû-tsze's disciples to fill this position instead.

By 484 BCE, K'ung Fû-tsze was sixty-seven years of age. He missed Lû, the land he considered home. The new prime minister of Lû, Kang-zi, aided by several of K'ung Fû-tsze's disciples had defeated invading forces. At the request of these disciples, K'ung Fû-tsze returned to Lû. This was the eleventh year of duke Ai's reign. Duke Ai and prime minister Kang-zi consulted K'ung Fû-tsze often. K'ung Fû-tsze spent most of these later years studying, analyzing, and teaching the wisdom of classic Chinese literature. K'ung Fû-tsze said that if he had fifty years left to live, he would like to spend all of them studying the *I Ching*.

Three years later, when a minister of Chou assassinated one of the lords of the state of Lû. K'ung Fû-tsze recommended retribution. The duke did not follow his recommendations. K'ung Fû-tsze felt that the value of his years of accumulated wisdom were no longer appreciated. He gradually retired from giving advice.

During the final years of his life, K'ung Fû-tsze was alone and saddened. Many of those acquaintances and disciples to whom he had grown close had passed on. In 485 BCE, the year before his return to Lû, his wife died. Two years after his return to Lû, in 482 BCE, his son, Lî, died. The following year, 481 BCE, his favorite disciple, Yen Hûi, died. The following year, the most faithful of his disciples, Tsze-yû, lost his life amidst a civil unrest in the state of Wei. Saddened by grief, K'ung Fû-tsze passed on. The year was 479 BCE. K'ung Fû-tsze was seventy-two years of age.

MAP: CHINA DURING KUNG- FÛ-TSZE'S TIME

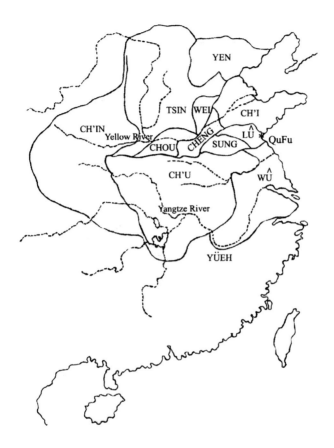

Map of China during the Ch'un-Ch'iu Period, 722–481 BCE,
divided into its many city-states.

* QuFu= Birthplace of K'ung Fû-tsze, 551 BCE.

[Adapted from: *Atlas of the World's Religions*, Ninian Smart, p. 70. *Atlas of China*,
Chiao-min Hsieh Map IV-2. *The Analects: Confucius*, David Hinton, *iv*].

301

THE PHILOSOPHY OF K'UNG FÛ-TSZE

K'ung Fû-tsze was a man of integrity, wisdom, and concern for others. His teachings laid the foundation upon which the Chinese civilization has endured for over 2,500 years. K'ung Fûtsze did not teach transcendent phenomenon or of life after death. He taught about the ability of each human being to change himself or herself. He was a practical, straightforward, honest man. He believed that if each person did his or her best to be good, decent, honest, fair, and moral, then all humanity would benefit. He encouraged people to stand up for what they believed was right, to respect others, and to be the best person they could.

He did not seek to be great or famous, he lived by no illusions. He merely sought, and devoted all his energies, to being good, decent, and honorable. He encouraged others to value and strengthen their own moral characters, and to focus on that which was within the scope of human control. When asked about God, he simply answered that he did not yet know men, so how could he know God?

K'ung Fû-tsze was a man with inner strength and conviction. He recognized that one striving to live one's entire life honorably, must first develop a strong sense of right and wrong. Essentially, one must develop character. One must anticipate and accept the ridicule of those with lower values, and one must not judge them. Instead of judging others, one must look within oneself and first judge one's own faults. K'ung Fû-tsze taught that one cannot change others, one can only change oneself.

Chinese philosophy has evolved founded upon the teachings of two men: K'ung Fû-tsze and Lao Tzu. Their respective teachings are the *Confucian Analects* and the *Tao Te Ching*. Both of these works tell of a noble ideal termed "The Way." The Way refers to two "Ways:"
- The "Way Things Are"
  The way of the perpetual flow of existence.
- The "Way of Humanity."
  The way humankind functions within this perpetual flow of existence. The way it can sustain itself.

K'ung Fû-tsze recognized that human beings cannot change the flow of creation, but that human beings can certainly affect the way they act towards their fellow human beings. It was this "way" that K'ung Fû-tsze sought to teach. He taught that to live adhering to the "way," one must act with concern, truthfulness, kindness, respectfulness, and sincerity towards all others.

K'ung Fû-tsze did not spout forth flowery, poetic messages. His was not an act. His teachings were straight, direct, and honest. He did not want people to love him. He just wanted people to respect his teachings, respect themselves, respect others, and do what was right.

K'ung Fû-tsze directed his teachings towards both those in positions of leadership and those within the general populace. His theory of ethics was intertwined with his theory of government. He believed that the chaos of his day was the result of a lack of foundational values. He believed that if a government was corrupt, there would be no impetus for the populace to act honorably. Such a society would subsist at an "each man for himself" mentality. K'ung Fû-tsze observed that respect and concern for others must flow from the top down. Therefore, he passionately sought to encourage leaders to uphold righteousness as their guiding principle.

K'ung Fû-tsze also believed that not all the responsibilities for the functioning of a stable, honorable society belonged to the leadership. He felt that each and every individual in a society, from the highest to the lowest, must live up to his or her own responsibility and show appropriate respect to those above and below him or her in society. Without such mutual respect amongst all, society would lapse into anarchy. This concept is referred to as the *Rectification of Names* (or positions).

The term *Rectification of Names* means that each person must recognize and accept his or her place and responsibility in a society. A child should act as a child, showing respect to parents. The same individual, in his or her role as a parent, should act as a parent, offering guidance to children. That same individual, in his or her role as a worker, should act as a worker, showing respect to leaders. The same individual, in his or her role as a leader, should act as a leader, offering direction to workers. Essentially, each individual must recognize and accept his or her position in relation to others, and live up to that position to the best of his or her abilities.

K'ung Fû-tsze recognized that the stability of a society must be well grounded even at the tiniest level of its foundation. If individual family members follow virtuous principles, a family will function harmoniously. If all families function respectfully and harmoniously, that society will function well. The benefits of a well-functioning, stable society will then revert back and benefit each and every family and individual in that society. Thusly a cycle of self-cultivation evolves.

K'ung Fû-tsze believed that each individual possesses the ability to modify and improve his or her own character. He also recognized that for a society to function for the betterment of all, each individual must live up to his or her highest level of virtue. It is important to remember when reading K'ung Fû-tsze's teachings, that so many of his teachings have been incorporated into both Eastern and Western cultures, that nowadays they may be taken for granted. They were not standard values, however, 2,500 years ago, during the time K'ung Fû-tsze lived and taught. Even K'ung Fû-tsze's teaching, "Do not do to others, what you do not want done to yourself," was a new concept. It was not incorporated into European values until 500 years later.

On initially looking at K'ung Fû-tsze's teachings, one might think he was merely an ethicist or a righteous snob. Nothing could be further from the truth. K'ung Fû-tsze was a dreamer, an idealist, a man of wisdom, a man of integrity, and a man of compassion. His greatest concern was for the elderly, the destitute, the orphans, and the children. He wanted all to be treated compassionately. He sincerely wanted rulers to treat subjects with humane concern and dignity. Nevertheless, he was realistic. He recognized that to do so, society must attain, and sustain, the highest moral and ethical standards possible.

K'ung Fû-tsze observed that one must begin to instill values into the earliest seedlings of a society, the children. If young people are taught to follow the guidance of their elders, they will not make incorrect choices that will harm their futures. He also observed that if the younger and older members of a family functioned harmoniously, the entire family will benefit. He applied the same concept of familial respect and concern for one's elders to the functioning of the government. If governmental officials follow the precepts laid down by the honorable founders of their state, all will live in sufficiency and safety. If they abandon such traditions and follow individualistic goal, disharmony is sure to follow.

The following are just a few of the foundational principles set forth by K'ung Fû-tsze's in the *Analects of Confucius*:

- Do not do to others what you do not want done to yourself
- Regard righteousness above all
- Be sincere
- Be fair and just
- Treat all others with respect
- Maintain values at all times: a moment's surrender to temptation may lead to a lifetime of suffering
- Be honest
- Seek harmony
- Respect tradition
- Cultivate patience
- Be consistent and constant
- Fulfill responsibilities
- Do not seek extremes, for all that reaches an extreme will reverse itself and revert to the opposite extreme
- Live in simplicity
- Be loyal
- Value knowledge
- Refine your character
- Value integrity
- Carefully consider what is correct and what is not
- Admit mistakes
- Be modest and humble
- Treat others with concern, compassion, and tenderness

K'ung Fû-tsze lived for the advancement of humanity and truth. His sole mission was to guide others to do what was right, honorable, and fair. His teachings were neither spiritual nor dreamy. They were the teachings of a real, direct, honest, ethical, and sincere man, the humble teacher and sage of 2,500 years ago, K'ung Fû-tsze of Lû.

THE CONFUCIAN ANALECTS

The *Analects of Confucius*, or the *Lun Yü*, is considered the principal source of K'ung Fû-tsze's teachings. By analyzing many of the events discussed in the *Confucian Analects*, historians have been able to determine that they were not actually written by the immediate disciples of K'ung Fû-tsze. Rather, they were probably written by the disciples of these disciples, most likely during the fourth century BCE.

The term *Analects* means "selections." The *Confucian Analects* represent a collection of various discourses and dialogues between K'ung Fû-tsze and others, predominantly between himself and his disciples. The *Analects* is divided into twenty divisions termed 'books.' These books, however, are actually chapters within the *Analects*. There is no progression or continuation of plot between the different books. Concepts within earlier books are just as profound as concepts within later ones. And later books do not necessarily relate to concepts found within initial books. One book, Book XIX, does not contain any statements directly uttered by K'ung Fû-tsze. It contains the teachings of his immediate disciples.

There are twenty books within the *Analects*. Initially, scholars during the time of the Han dynasty discovered two versions of the *Analects*. One was found in K'ung Fû-tsze's native state of Lû, and the other in the adjacent state of Ch'î. The version from the state of Lû contained twenty chapters and the version from the state of Ch'î, twenty-two chapters.

In 150 BCE, a third copy of the *Analects* was discovered. It was found plastered within the walls of the ancient house where K'ung Fû-tsze had lived. The discovery occurred when the son of Emperor Ching, the ruler of Lû, ordered the remaining walls of the house in which the K'ung family had lived for generations to be torn down. One might wonder what a manuscript was doing plastered within a wall. This manuscript, and several others, had been placed within the framework of these walls and plastered over to hide them.

These books were undoubtedly hidden in this manner in 213 BCE to protect them. In 213 BCE, the rulers of the Ch'in dynasty issued an edit for all books within the entire empire to be burned. At that time, the descendents of K'ung Fû-tsze hid copies of several important texts, including the *Analects*, in their walls. This copy of the *Analects* discovered within the walls of the K'ung family home became known as the '*old Lun Yü.*'

During the first century BCE, a prince of Ân-ch'ang, named Chang Yû, (died 4 BCE), undertook an analysis comparing the versions of the *Analects*. He compared those found within the state of Lû to those found within the state of Ch'î. His analysis was twenty books long. Chang Yû came to the conclusion that the Lû version was the more accurate.

Centuries later, during the Han dynasty reign of Emperor Hsien (190–220), one of China's greatest scholars, Chăng Hsüan, undertook an extensive analysis of all three versions of the *Analects*: the Lû version, the Ch'î version, and the *old Lun Yü* version. He found the actual philosophical differences between them to be minimal. It was at this time that the canon of what was to become considered the accurate *Analects* was finalized.

Throughout China's history, numerous Chinese scholars have written commentaries on the *Analects*. The first Europeans to recognize the wisdom of the *Analects* and to translate it into Western languages were Catholic missionary priests. Two priests living in different regions of China, Father de Mailla and Father Amiot, undertook a methodical endeavor to translate and interpret the *Analects*. In Paris, 1687, they published a Latin translation of three Chinese classics called *Confucius Sinarum Philosophus* (*The Chinese Philosopher Confucius*). Unfortunately, however, only portions of these translations remain.

The translation of the *Analects* that has become the most respected translation within the Western world has been the 1863 translation of James Legge. In 1839, James Legge went to Malacca, China, as a Protestant missionary. He translated many ancient works and created a Chinese-English dictionary that explained what the Chinese characters probably meant at the time they were written, two thousand five hundred years prior.

The *Confucian Analects* is the foundation upon which Chinese philosophy has been grounded for the last 2,500 years. Its teachings are deep, sincere, and wise. All peoples of the world would do well to avail themselves of its teachings.

THE PRINCIPAL DISCIPLES OF K'UNG FÛ-TSZE

It has been said that K'ung Fû-tsze had a following of over three thousand disciples. Of these, seventy-seven were recognized as scholars of ability who genuinely understood his teachings. They are referred to as the seventy-seven worthies. Several, of whom more is known than merely their name and age, and who have been mentioned within the *Analects*, are described below. Both their formal and informal names are included.

According to Chinese tradition, people were often referred to by different names: their family name, given name, styled name, and respectful name. Even K'ung Fû-tsze was referred to by his family name, K'ung; his given name, Ch'iû; and his respectful name, Fû-tsze, meaning minister or teacher. The following list of disciples, and the names by which they were sometimes referred, may help to clarify some of these variations in terminology.

Within English versions of the *Analects*, the names of people, places, and dynasties are often spelled differently. That is because they are written as they sound phonetically, and are transliterated from Chinese characters to Roman type letters. There are two systems of Chinese to English transliteration: the Wade-Giles and the Hanyu Pinyin system. Wade-Giles has been the main system of transliteration for most of the 20th century. The Hanyu Pinyin system began to replace it in 1979 and has the advantage of not requiring accent marks. Both systems are often used interchangeably. The Wade Giles system is used in this text because it is the system that has been most commonly used in transliterations of China's ancient text.

THE DISCIPLES

• Yen Hûi—(Tsze-yüan, Yen Yüan, or Hûi):
Yen Hûi was K'ung Fû-tsze's favorite disciple. He was known for his peaceful wisdom. A native of Lû, he became a disciple when quite young. He was thirty years younger than K'ung Fû-tsze. After Yen Hûi joined K'ung Fû-tsze, the other disciples grew closer to him. Yen Hûi's hair turned white when he was only twenty-nine and he died at age thirty-two. K'ung Fû-tsze wept at his death, and both the emperor and he offered sacrifices for Yen Hûi.

309

• Yû Zo—(Tsze-zo):
A native of Lû, he was a prominent disciple often referred to as philosopher Yû. He was recognized among the other disciples for his excellent memory and his fondness of the study of antiquity. Because he is quoted so often within the *Analects*, it is believed that several of his disciples helped to compile it.

• Min Sun—(Tsze-ch'ien):
A native of Lû, it is said that when he first came to K'ung Fû-tsze, he had a starved look. It is uncertain how many years younger than K'ung Fû-tsze he was. He had been torn between the glitter and abundance of the world, and the philosophical teachings of K'ung Fû-tsze. He chose to follow K'ung Fû-tsze. He was distinguished for his filial piety and purity of character.

• Zan Kăng—(Po-niû):
A native of Lû, he was seven years younger than K'ung Fû-tsze. After K'ung Fû-tsze became minister of justice, he appointed Po-niû to the government position he had previously held.

• Zan Yung—(Chung-kung):
He was from the same clan as Po-niû and was twenty-nine years younger than K'ung Fû-tsze. Although he came from a family that was not well respected and his father had many faults, K'ung Fû-tsze did not hold these against Zan Yung.

• Zan Ch'iû—(Tsze-yû):
He was related to the prior two disciples and was twenty-nine years younger then K'ung Fû-tsze. He was versatile, respectful, kind, and fond of learning. It was due to his influence that K'ung Fû-tsze finally returned to Lû.

• Pû Shang—(Tsze-hsiâ):
He was from Wei and was forty-five years younger than K'ung Fû-tsze. A scholar, he read extensively. He lived to a great age. In 406 BCE, he gave copies of the *Chinese Classic Books* to prince Wăn of Wei. When his son died, he wept himself blind.

• Chung Yû—(Tsze-lû and Chî-lû):
From the P'ien region of Lû, he was nine years younger than K'ung Fû-tsze. He told K'ung Fû-tsze that his favorite possession was his sword, and learning was useless to him. Then K'ung Fû-tsze taught him that if he fine-tuned his sword, it would penetrate deeper. Chung Yû became a loyal disciple. After he joined K'ung Fû-tsze's group of disciples, no one would say a bad word about K'ung Fû-tsze. When Tsze-lû became chief lawyer of P'û, he commanded others to receive K'ung Fû-tsze.

• Twan-mû Ts'ze—(Tsze-kung):
A native of Wei, he was thirty-two years younger than K'ung Fû-tsze. He possessed a naturally quick mind. Among the disciples, he was one of the most well spoken. Tsze-kung praised K'ung Fû-tsze's wisdom, saying he thirsted for it. He said that to hide such wisdom, was to hide wealth. K'ung Fû-tsze said that once Tsze-kung joined him, other scholars came from far and wide to converse with him. Tsze-kung was present at K'ung Fû-tsze's death, and mourned him for six years.

• Yen Yen—(Tsze-yû):
A native of Wû, he was forty-five years younger than K'ung Fû-tsze. He was known for his literary skill. When made head of Wû-ch'ăng, he transformed the region with music and tradition.

• Tsâi Yü—(Tsze-wo):
A native of Lû, his age is not known. Although he was a man of principle, his quick tongue and temper were his weakness.

• Tsăng Shăn—(Tsze-yü):
A native of south Wû-ch'ăng, he was forty-six years younger than K'ung Fû-tsze. At the age of sixteen, his father sent him to learn under the sage. His name is the second in frequency, after Yen Hûi, mentioned in the Confucian school. It was said that there was no subject he had not studied. He was respectful, virtuous, and self-disciplined. He was noted for his filial piety and for being a voluminous writer. It is said that under the guidance of K'ung Fû-tsze he wrote the *Classic of Filial Piety.*

311

• Chwan-sun Shih—(Tsze-chang):
A native of Ch'ǎn, he was forty-eight years younger than K'ung Fû-tsze. He was recognized for his lack of pride and for his humbleness concerning his noble station.

• Tan-t'âi Mieh-ming—(Tsze-yü):
A native of Wû-ch'ǎng, he was either thirty-nine or forty-nine years younger than K'ung Fû-tsze. K'ung Fû-tsze admits that when he first met Tsze-yü, he did not think highly of him because of his unattractive appearance. After completing his studies, Tszu-yü traveled as far as the Yang-tsze River. He amassed three hundred disciples who sought his wisdom. When K'ung Fû-tsze heard of this, he admitted that he had misjudged Tszu-yü because of his appearance.

• Fû Pû-ch'î—(Tsze-tsien):
A native of Lû, he was at least thirty years younger than K'ung Fû-tsze. He became distinguished as a writer and as a man who treated others with respect.

• Kung-yê Ch'ang—(Tsze-ch'ang):
From either Lû or Ch'û, he became K'ung Fû-tsze's son-in-law.

• Yüan Hsien—(Tsze-sze):
A native of Sung, he was thirty-six years younger than K'ung Fû-tsze. He was known for his pure character and his honesty. He was also respected for his contentment in a life of poverty. After K'ung Fû-tsze died, he went to live in obscurity in Wei.

• Nan-kung Kwo—(Tsze-yung):
When fire broke out in the palace of duke Âi, others ran to save the treasury. Nan-kung Kwo worked to save the library. Preservation of a copy of the *Châu Lî* has been attributed to him.

• Kung-hsî Âi—(Chî-ts'ze):
A native of either Lû or Ch'î, he was commended by K'ung Fû-tsze for refusing to take office under corrupt families that wanted to overthrow the prince. He chose a life of severe poverty rather than sacrifice his principles.

BIBLIOGRAPHY

Chan, Wing-tsit, trans. and comp. *A Source Book of Chinese Philosophy*. Princeton, NJ: Princeton University Press, 1963.

Clayre, Alasdair. *The Heart of the Dragon*. Boston: Dragonbook ApS., 1984.

Fingarette, Herbert. *Confucius—The Secular as Sacred*. NY: Harper & Row, 1972.

Fitzgerald, C. P., *The Horizon History of China*. NY: American Heritage Publ., 1969.

Fung, Yu-lan. *A Short History of Chinese Philosophy*. Edited by Derk Bodde. NY: The Free Press, 1948.

Giles, Lionel, trans. *The Analects of Confucius*. Shanghai: Limited Editions Club, 1933.

Hibbert, Christopher. *The Emperors of China*. London: Stonehenge Press, 1981.

Hinton, David, trans. *The Analects, Confucius*. NY: Counterpoint, 1998.

Hsieh, Chiao-min. *Atlas of China*. NY: McGraw-Hill, 1973.

Huang, Chichung, trans. *The Analects of Confucius*. NY: Oxford University Press, 1997.

Kim, Yong Choon. *Oriental Thought: An Introduction to the Philosophical and Religious Thought of Asia*. Totowa, NJ: Littlefield, Adams & Co, 1973.

Lau, D.C. trans. *Confucius: The Analects*. London: Penguin Books, 1997.

Legge, James. *Confucius: Confucian Analects, the Great Learning, and the Doctrine of the Mean*. NY: Dover Press, 1971. Unabridged republication of the second revised edition published by the Clarendon Press, Oxford, 1893 as Vol. I of *The Chinese Classics*.

———. *Chinese-English Four Books Commentary*. Shanghai: Sang Wu Publisher, 1914.

———. *The Ch'un Ts'ew with The Tso Chuen*. Vol. 5 of *The Chinese Classics*: Hong Kong, 1872.

———. *The She King*. Vol. 4 of *The Chinese Classics*: Hong Kong, 1871.

———. *The Shoo King*. Vol. 3 of *The Chinese Classics*: Hong Kong, 1865.

Morton, W. Scott. *China: Its History and Culture*. 3rd ed. NY: McGraw-Hill, 1995.

Schwartz, Benjamin I. *The World of Thought in Ancient China*. Cambridge: Harvard University Press, 1985.

Shaughnessy, Edward L., ed. *China: Empire and Civilization*. Oxford, England: Oxford University Press, 2000.

Smart, Ninian, ed. *Atlas of the World's Religions*. NY: Oxford University Press, 1999.

Waley, Arthur, trans. *The Analects of Confucius*. NY: Random House, 1938.

Wilhelm, Richard. *The I Ching: The Book of Changes*. Princeton, NJ: Princeton University Press, 1967.

Wu, Yi. *Chinese Philosophical Terms*. San Bruno, CA: Great Learning Publishing Company, 1990.

———. *I Ching: The Book of Changes and Virtues*. San Bruno, CA: Great Learning Publishing Company, 1998.

Wu-Chi, Liu. *Confucius: His Life and Time*. NY: Philosophical Library, 1955.

Yutang, Lin, ed. and trans. *The Wisdom of Confucius*. NY: Random House, 1938.

Printed in the United States
77132LV00001B/19-66